国际铁人三项联盟
竞赛规则

ITU Competition Rules

中 国 铁 人 三 项 运 动 协 会 / 审 定

北京体育大学出版社

策划编辑：董英双
责任编辑：吴　珂
审稿编辑：董英双
责任校对：凯　瑞

图书在版编目（CIP）数据

国际铁人三项联盟竞赛规则 / 中国铁人三项运动协会审定. -- 北京 : 北京体育大学出版社, 2018.6
ISBN 978-7-5644-2938-6

Ⅰ. ①国… Ⅱ. ①中… Ⅲ. ①铁人三项全能运动—竞赛规则—世界 Ⅳ. ①G888.14

中国版本图书馆CIP数据核字(2018)第128285号

国际铁人三项联盟竞赛规则　　中国铁人三项运动协会 审定

出　　版：北京体育大学出版社
地　　址：北京市海淀区信息路48号
邮　　编：100084
邮 购 部：北京体育大学出版社读者服务部 010-62989432
发 行 部：010-62989320
网　　址：http://cbs.bsu.edu.cn
印　　刷：北京艾普海德印刷有限公司
开　　本：787 × 1092毫米　1/16
成品尺寸：170 × 240毫米
印　　张：17.25

2018年7月第1版第1次印刷

定　价：60.00元

前　言

《国际铁人三项联盟竞赛规则》由中国铁人三项运动协会依照 2017 年 12 月国际铁人三项联盟（ITU）执委会批准发布的《ITU Competition Rules》组织翻译编订。

《国际铁人三项联盟竞赛规则》的翻译编订力求忠实于原文。由于规则文本体量庞大，翻译和审校工作可能存在疏漏之处，如在理解和执行过程中出现争议，以国际铁联官方语言英文版为准。欢迎广大读者提出意见和建议，以便我们今后修订和完善。

参加此版本规则翻译与审校工作的有王炳、王志强、阮志洋、杨飞、怀宁宁、郑辉等（姓名按照笔画排序）。北京体育大学出版社对本书的出版、发行给予了大力支持和帮助，在此一并致谢。

中国铁人三项运动协会

2018 年 3 月

ITU Competition Rules

Approved by the ITU Executive Board, in December 2017

The ITU Competition Rules is the master source document, found on ITU's website at www.triathlon.org. The web based document acts as the official (authorised) reference document and is maintained based on authorised amendments in accordance with recommendations by the ITU Technical Committee and accepted by the ITU Executive Board.

Contact

International Triathlon Union (ITU)
Maison du Sport International
Av. de Rhodanie 54
Lausanne CH -1007, Switzerland
Tel +41 21 614 60 30
Fax +41 21 614 60 39
Email: ituhdq@triathlon.org
For general information about ITU visit www.triathlon.org

国际铁人三项联盟竞赛规则

2017 年 12 月经国际铁联执委会批准

国际铁联竞赛规则是最重要的基础文件，可在国际铁联官方网站（www.triathlon.org）上查阅。该文件作为官方参考文件，由国际铁联技术委员会提出修订意见，经国际铁联执委会批准后生效。

联系方式：

国际铁人三项联盟（ITU）
地址：　Maison du Sport International
　　　　Av. de Rhodanie 54
　　　　Lausanne CH -1007, Switzerland
电话：　+41 21 614 60 30
传真：　+41 21 614 60 39
电邮：　ituhdq@triathlon.org
更多关于国际铁联的信息可查阅 www.triathlon.org

TABLE OF CONTENTS

目 录

ITU

国际铁人三项联盟
竞赛规则

ITU Competition Rules

1.INTRODUCTION

1.1. Purpose:

a.) The International Triathlon Union (ITU) is the sole governing body, responsible for the Competition Rules for Triathlon, Duathlon and its other related multisports. The complete list of sports under the jurisdiction of ITU is included as Appendix A and Appendix J;

b.) The ITU Technical Committee (ITU TC) will ensure technical aspects of ITU competitions are of the highest quality;

c.) The ITU Competition Rules specify the conduct and behaviour of athletes during ITU competitions. Where the ITU Competition Rules do not specify, the rules of International Swimming Federation (FINA), International Cycling Union (UCI), International Association of Athletics Federations (IAAF), International Ski Federation (FIS), IPC Swimming, IPC Athletics and IPC Nordic Skiing will apply in their specific segments, unless ITU Technical Committee decides otherwise;

d.) The ITU Event Organisers' Manual (EOM) and its related documents set safety and logistical standards for host National Federations (NFs) and for the Local Organising Committees (LOCs);

e.) The ITU Technical Officials' Certification Programme sets the standards for certifying ITU Technical Officials;

f.) It will be clearly indicated when a rule applies to a specific competition.

1.2. Intention:

a.) The ITU Competition Rules are intended to:

(i) Create an atmosphere of sportsmanship, equality, and fair play;

(ii) Provide safety and protection;

(iii) Emphasise ingenuity and skill without unduly limiting the athlete's freedom of action;

(iv) Penalise athletes who gain an unfair advantage.

b.) Definitions of all terms used in the ITU Competition Rules are provided in Appendix D. Any difficulty in the interpretation or application of the ITU Competition Rules should be referred to the ITU Technical Committee.

1.3. Language and Communication:

a.) The official language of ITU Events is English:

(i) National Federations are responsible for providing translation services from/to English for their own athletes;

(ii) Local Organising Committees will communicate at least in English, even if another language is used in parallel.

1.4. Modifications:

a.) The ITU Competition Rules will be adapted for other modern multisport competitions, which fall within ITU's jurisdiction;

1. 绪 论

1.1 宗 旨

a）国际铁人三项联盟（译者注：以下简称“国际铁联”）是铁人三项、骑跑两项以及其他相关分项的唯一管理机构，并负责为其制定相关的竞赛规则。国际铁联管辖的所有运动项目见附件 A 和附件 J。

b）国际铁联技术委员会（ITU-TC）将确保国际铁联举办的比赛在技术方面达到最高质量标准。

c）国际铁联竞赛规则具体规定了在国际铁联比赛中运动员应遵守的行为规范。国际铁联竞赛规则中未明确说明的情况，如国际铁联技术委员会未另行做出决定，将分别参照国际游泳联合会（FINA）、国际自行车联盟（UCI）、国际田径联合会（IAAF）、国际滑雪联合会（FIS）、国际残奥委员会（IPC）游泳项目、田径项目和越野滑雪项目的规则。

d）国际铁联比赛操作手册（EOM）为举办比赛的会员协会（NFs）和比赛当地组委会（LOCs）制定了安全保卫和后勤保障等工作的标准。

e）国际铁联技术官员（ITO）认证管理办法为国际铁联技术官员的认证设定标准。

f）部分仅仅适用于特定比赛的规则，将在文中予以说明。

1.2 目 的

a）国际铁联制定本竞赛规则的目的是：

（1）创造一种公平、公正并体现良好体育道德的竞赛环境。

（2）提供安全和保护措施。

（3）强调独创性和技巧性，不过分限制运动员自由发挥的空间。

（4）对非法获利的运动员给予处罚。

b）附件 D 提供了本规则中使用的所有名词的定义和解释。在解释或执行规则的过程中遇到任何困难应立即向国际铁联技术委员会提出。

1.3 语言及交流

a）国际铁联比赛的官方语言是英语：

（1）会员协会有责任按照要求为其所属运动员提供英文翻译服务。

（2）无论是否同时使用其他语言，比赛当地组委会至少要能够使用英语进行交流。

1.4 规则的调整

a）在规则适用过程中，对于国际铁联管理权限范围内的其他分项的比赛，本规则可进行相应调整。

b.) An athlete must not be permitted an advantage not intended by a rule, or to conduct him/herself in a dangerous way. To implement this, every infringement related in the ITU Competition Rules has a sanction attached. Technical Officials base their judgments on whether an advantage, not intended by the Rules, has been gained;

c.) ITU Competition Rules will be applicable to international competitions hosted by National Federations affiliated with ITU.

1.5. Exceptions:

a.) The ITU Competition Rules will be applicable to all events sanctioned by ITU and are to be implemented by the appointed Technical Delegate as appropriate. Where the ITU Competition Rules conflict with the laws of the jurisdiction in which the event is to be held, the ITU Competition Rules will override the laws of the jurisdiction to the extent of the inconsistency. Athletes must be notified of the implications of these laws as early as possible and not later than prior to the start of the event;

b.) Exceptions for special circumstances in a particular event may only be gained from ITU with prior approval. A request for an exception to the ITU Competition Rules must be made in writing 30 days prior to the event to the ITU Technical Committee through by assigned Technical Delegate;

c.) Exceptions for special circumstances in a particular athlete may only be gained from ITU with prior approval. A request for an exception to the ITU Competition Rules must be made in writing 30 days prior to the event to the ITU Technical Committee by the assigned Technical Delegate from the National Federation to whom the application has been submitted or is being submitted;

d.) The ITU Techical Committee may consult with other ITU committees, commissions or appropriate parties;

e.) For any rule exceptions related to events sanctioned by ITU, but not run within the competition system of ITU or any of the Continental Confederations, a permanent panel will be created with one representative from each of the three parties: ITU Technical Committee, ITU Staff, Event Rights Holder. The final proposal from the panel will go to the ITU Technical Committee for endorsement.

1.6. Specific Regulations:

a.) A Technical Delegate may approve the addition of specific regulations for a particular competition, provided that:

(i) Each additional specific regulation does not conflict with another ITU Competition Rules;

(ii) Each additional specific regulation is made available in written form and is announced at the athletes' briefing; and

(iii) Each additional specific regulation and the reasons for its inclusion are advised to the ITU Technical Committee one week before the day on which the event is to be conducted. The ITU Technical Committee may invalidate the incorporation of an additional specific regulation only on the authority of the ITU Executive Board.

b）运动员不可以在规则说明的范围之外获利或者实施危险的行为。为保证此条款的顺利实施，本规则对于各种犯规情况的处罚办法进行了说明。技术官员根据其判断来决定运动员是否在规则说明的范围之外获利。

c）国际铁联竞赛规则适用于由国际铁联会员协会举办的国际比赛。

1.5 例外情况

a）国际铁联竞赛规则适用于所有国际铁联批准的比赛，并由其任命的技术代表加以执行。在国际铁联竞赛规则与比赛举办地的法律发生冲突的情况下，国际铁联竞赛规则在冲突的部分有效（译者注：此处可理解为，为顺利举办国际铁联比赛而需在某一特定条件下实施法律通常不允许的行为，当地法律应给予必要的授权），运动员应尽早地获知相关法律条文的含义，最晚不得迟于比赛开始前。

b）特定赛事的例外情况必须事先得到国际铁联的批准，特殊规则的申请应在赛前30天以书面的形式由任命的技术代表提交给国际铁联技术委员会。

c）特定运动员的例外情况必须事先得到国际铁联的批准。特殊规则的申请应由任命的技术代表在国家会员协会申请的基础上，于赛前30天以书面的形式提交给国际铁联技术委员会。

d）国际铁联技术委员会可以咨询或与国际铁联其他委员会，或与相关团体与组织协商。

e）受国际铁联管辖但在国际铁联或洲际联盟竞赛系统之外的比赛，其例外规则须由分别来自国际铁联技术委员会、国际铁联工作人员、赛事举办方的代表各1名组成的专门委员会确定，该委员会的最终提议须提交至国际铁联技术委员会认可。

1.6 特别规则

a）技术代表可以批准某一特定比赛执行特别规则，前提是：

（1） 每一条增加的特别规则不与国际铁联其他规则发生冲突。

（2） 每一条增加的特别规则都在赛前以书面形式通知参赛人员并在运动员技术会上宣布。

（3） 每一条增加的特别规则以及增加的原因都在赛前一周通知国际铁联技术委员会。国际铁联技术委员会只可通过国际铁联执委会使得某条增加的特别规则失效。

1.7. Intellectual Property:

a.) ITU Events are the exclusive property of ITU, which owns all rights associated including, without limitation, the rights to organise, exploit, broadcast and reproduce ITU Events. These rights include any type of digital media, whether that be photographic or video in nature, captured from within the boundaries of the field of play, regardless of ownership of the capturing device. All the personal data from the athlete entered into any ITU event and the data produced from the event, including the results are exclusive property of ITU.

1.8. Unauthorised Exceptions or Additions:

a.) The unauthorised exception to, or addition of, a competition rule will prevent an event from being sanctioned and will invalidate a sanction, which has already been granted to an event. This could result in legal complications, particularly in the case of accidents during the event and in subsequent requests for approval from National Federations and/or municipal authorities to use roads and waterways. Insurance authorities have also warned that claims made under such circumstances may be considered invalid.

1.9. Rule Updates:

a.) The ITU Competition Rules may be changed from time to time by the ITU Technical Committee at its discretion, with the approval of the ITU Executive Board. Any rule change(s) shall be advised in writing to affiliated National Federations at least 30 days before it/they is/are to take effect unless the ITU Executive Board decides otherwise. Updated ITU Competition Rules will be posted on the ITU website (www.triathlon.org).

2. CONDUCT OF ATHLETES

2.1. General Conduct:

a.) Triathlon and ITU's other related multisports involve many athletes. Competition tactics are part of the interaction between athletes. Athletes will:

(i) Practice good sportsmanship at all times;
(ii) Be responsible for their own safety and the safety of others;
(iii) Know, understand and follow the ITU Competition Rules, available from their National Federations and on www.triathlon.org;
(iv) Obey traffic regulations and instructions from race officials;
(v) Treat other athletes, race officials, volunteers, and spectators with respect and courtesy;
(vi) Avoid the use of abusive language;
(vii) Inform a Technical Official after withdrawing from the competition. Failing to do this may result in a suspension;
(viii) Compete without receiving assistance other than from event personnel and race officials;

1.7 产权声明

a）国际铁联举办的所有赛事版权均属国际铁联独有，其权利包括但不限于赛事组织、开发、传播和复制。其版权包括在赛场内拍摄的任何形式的数字媒体，无论图片还是视频，也不论拍摄设备归谁所有。所有国际铁联赛事参赛运动员个人数据以及比赛所产生的数据，包括比赛结果均由国际铁联独有。

1.8 未经授权的例外情况或特别规则

a）未经授权的例外情况或特别规则的增加将会导致比赛得不到批准，或者已经得到批准的比赛失去举办权。这种情况会导致法律纠纷，尤其是在比赛中发生事故后向会员协会和 / 或市政当局申请使用道路和航道的情况下。保险部门也声明这些情况下的索赔可能被认定为无效。

1.9 规则的更新

a）国际铁联技术委员会根据其判断，可经国际铁联执委会批准适时对竞赛规则进行修订。所有修订的部分应至少在生效前 30 天书面通知各会员协会，除非国际铁联执委会另有决定。更新的规则将在国际铁联网站上（www.triathlon.org）公布。

2. 运动员行为

2.1 总 则

a）全世界有众多运动员从事铁人三项及国际铁联管辖的其他分项。比赛的战术、策略是运动员之间相互竞争的一个方面，运动员应做到：

（1） 始终奉行和遵守良好的体育道德风尚。

（2） 对自己和他人的安全负责任。

（3） 知道、理解并遵守国际铁联竞赛规则（可从其会员协会或国际铁联官方网站 www.triathlon.org 获取）。

（4） 遵守交通规则，听从技术官员的指导。

（5） 对待其他运动员、技术官员、志愿者和观众要尊重而有礼貌。

（6） 不使用不文明语言。

（7） 退出比赛后应通知技术官员。如运动员未能通知技术官员，可导致停赛。

（8） 比赛中不得向赛事工作人员和技术官员以外的其他人员寻求帮助。

(ix) Avoid using ambush marketing;
(x) Avoid displaying any kind of demonstration of political, religious or racial propaganda;
(xi) Not dispose of rubbish or equipment around the course except at clearly identified places, such as aid stations or rubbish disposal points. All items must be kept with the athlete and returned to their transition spot;
(xii) Not attempt to gain an unfair advantage from any external vehicle or object;
(xiii) Follow the prescribed course;
(xiv) Not use any device that will distract the athlete from paying full attention to their surroundings:
- Athletes may not use communication devices of any type, including but not limited to cell phones, smart watches, and two-way radios, in any distractive manner during the competition. A "distractive manner" includes but is not limited to making and receiving phone calls, sending and receiving text messages, playing music, using social media, and taking photographs. Using a communication device in a distractive manner during the competition will result in disqualification;
- Cameras, phone cameras, and video cameras are prohibited unless permission is given by the ITU or the license holder of the event. If such permission is given, it is the athlete's responsibility to notify the Head Referee of such permission prior to the start of the competition. Athletes seen with an unauthorized camera, phone camera, or video camera will be disqualified.

2.2. Outside assistance:

a.) The assistance provided by event personnel or Technical Officials is allowed but is limited to providing drinks, nutrition, mechanical and medical assistance, upon the approval of the Technical Delegate or Head Referee. Athletes competing in the same competition may assist each other with incidental items such as, but not restricted to, nutrition and drinks after an aid station, pumps, tubular tyres, inner tubes and puncture repair kits;

b.) Athletes may not provide any item of equipment to an athlete competing in the same competition which results in the donor athlete being unable to continue with their own competition. This includes but is not restricted to complete bicycle, frame, wheels and helmet. The penalty for this will be disqualification of both athletes.

c.) An athlete cannot physically assist the forward progress of another athlete on any part of the course. This will result in both athletes being disqualified.

2.3. Drug Abuse:

a.) Athletes and guides will follow the ITU Anti-Doping Rules;

（9） 避免隐性营销行为。

（10）不得进行任何形式的政治、宗教和种族宣传。

（11）不得将垃圾或者比赛装备丢弃于赛道附近，饮水站和垃圾丢弃点等指定区域除外。运动员须保存好所有参赛装备和物品并放回转换区自己的位置上。

（12）不允许试图借助任何外部车辆或物体获得不公平利益。

（13）按规定路线行进。

（14）不得使用任何可能使运动员注意力不能专注于赛事环境的装置：

- 比赛期间运动员不得以任何“分散注意力的方式”使用通讯设备，包括但不限于手机、智能手表和收发两用无线电设备。“分散注意力的方式”包括但不限于：接打手机、接收或发送信息、播放音乐、使用社交媒体和拍照。比赛期间如果以分散注意力的方式使用通讯设备，将导致被取消参赛资格。
- 未经国际铁联或赛事组委会的允许，禁止使用照相机、手机摄像和摄影机。如果得到许可，运动员有责任在比赛开始前告知裁判长。如若运动员未经许可使用照相机、手机摄像或摄影机，将被取消参赛资格。

2.2 外界援助

a）在技术代表和裁判长的许可下，赛事工作人员和技术官员可以向运动员提供援助，但是仅限于提供饮品、营养品、器械和医疗服务。参加同场比赛的运动员可以互相提供附带器材物品，如营养品、饮料（在饮水站之后）、气筒、管胎、内胎和补胎设备。

b）运动员不能向同场竞技的运动员提供可能导致自身无法完成比赛的器材物品，包括但不限于比赛自行车、车架、车轮和头盔。否则，两名运动员都将被取消比赛资格。

c）比赛进程中运动员不得向其他运动员提供身体上的帮助以加快其比赛进程，否则，两名运动员都将被取消比赛资格。

2.3 使用兴奋剂

a）运动员和引导员应遵守国际铁联关于反兴奋剂的规则和规定。

b.) All athletes and guides are responsible for familiarising themselves with the ITU Anti-Doping Rules including medical and doping control tests, testing obligations, rights, responsibilities and procedures, penalties and appeal processes, and prohibited substances and methods;

c.) ITU has implemented the ITU Anti-Doping Rules and abides by rules set by the World Anti-Doping Agency (WADA) Code.

2.4. Health:

a.) Triathlons and ITU's other related multisports are strenuous. To be able to compete, athletes should be in excellent physical condition. Their health and welfare is of paramount importance. By starting in a competition, the athletes declare they are in good health and are in appropriate physical condition to complete the competition;

b.) Time limits for the swim leg, bike leg and overall finish time may be established for each competition by the ITU Technical Delegate. These limits must be published in the pre-event registration material;

c.) ITU encourages all the athletes to undergo a periodic health evaluation (PHE) and to undergo a pre-participation evaluation (PPE) prior to engaging in competitive sport. An annual PPE is mandatory for all athletes competing in Youth, Junior, U23, Elite and Paratriathlon events from January 1st, 2018 in any ITU event as outlined in Appendix J. More information about PPE can be found in Appendix Q.

2.5. Eligibility:

a.) All athletes must be in good standing with their National Federations. To ensure this, for ITU and Continental Confederation events, all the entries must be done by the National Federations, not by the athletes themselves;

b.) Athletes under suspension are not allowed to compete in any ITU event, in any competition sanctioned by ITU members, or in any competition held under the ITU Rules;

c.) An athlete's age is determined by their age on December 31st in the year of competition;

d.) Athletes aged 15 to 17 years old are eligible to compete in the Youth category;

e.) Athletes aged 16 to 19 years old are eligible to compete in the Junior category;

f.) Athletes aged 18 to 23 years old are eligible to compete in the U23 category;

g.) All Pro/Elite athletes must be registered on the ITU online system by their respective National Federation in the category they are competing in. They cannot compete in the same calendar year as an Age Group athlete in the same multisport as outlined in Appendix J. Athletes competing in the World Triathlon Series will be automatically tagged as an Elite/Pro in the system.

h.) The different qualification criteria can be found in the ITU Qualification Criteria and published in www.triathlon.org;

b）所有运动员和引导员都有义务熟悉国际铁联关于反兴奋剂的规则和规定，包括医学和兴奋剂检测、接受检测的义务、权利、责任和检测程序、处罚、申诉程序和违禁物质清单。

c）国际铁联目前已采用世界反兴奋剂组织（WADA）的反兴奋剂规则。

2.4 身体条件

a）铁人三项和国际铁联管辖的其他分项是高强度的运动项目。要参加此类运动项目的比赛，运动员必须要具备良好的身体条件。运动员的健康和利益至关重要。在参赛的同时，运动员即声明其健康状况和身体条件良好，可以完成比赛。

b）每次比赛的游泳赛段、自行车赛段及全程的关门时间将由技术代表（TD）决定。这些关门时间须印制在赛前相关的报名资料内。

c）国际铁联鼓励所有的运动员进行周期性健康评估（PHE）并在比赛前进行赛前健康评估（PPE）。从 2018 年 1 月 1 日起，参加附录 J 所述国际铁联赛事的所有的少年组、青年组、23 岁以下组、优秀组和伤残组运动员必须进行年度赛前健康评估才能参赛。更多信息请查阅附录 Q。

2.5 参赛资格

a）所有参赛运动员必须与其所属会员协会保持良好的关系。国际铁联和洲际联盟所有比赛的报名，由会员协会执行，而不可由运动员本人进行。

b）被停赛的运动员不允许参加国际铁联任何比赛，或国际铁联会员协会批准的任何比赛，或任何在国际铁联规则之下举行的比赛。

c）运动员年龄以参加比赛当年 12 月 31 日时的年龄计算。

d）运动员年龄在 15 至 17 岁之间，有资格参加少年组比赛。

e）运动员年龄在 16 至 19 岁之间，有资格参加青年组比赛。

f）运动员年龄在 18 至 23 岁之间，有资格参加 23 岁以下组比赛。

g）所有职业 / 优秀运动员必须根据其在各自国家协会参加的比赛组别，在国际铁联网上系统进行注册。不能以分龄组运动员身份参加在同年举办的附录 J 中所述相同的多项目运动。参加世界铁人三项系列赛的运动员，系统将自动标记其为优秀 / 职业运动员。

h）国际铁联发布了不同赛事的参赛资格标准，见 www.triathlon.org.

i.) Specific qualification criteria affecting Major Games and Recognised Games are published in www.triathlon.org;
j.) Specific qualification criteria affecting events sanctioned by ITU, but not part of the ITU events structure, are published in the respective website of such events;
k.) Athletes may not compete within 36 hours in more than one triathlon or multisport event (see Appendix I) when one event is of standard distance or longer. Exceptions will be for the team relay events at the defined super-sprint distances (see 16.1.a.), PTVI1, PTVI2 and PTVI3 guides and aquathlon;
l.) Age limits: Athletes must be a minimum age to compete in any event, as outlined in Appendix A. Continental Confederations may add other age limits for Continental Championships, for youth and younger categories with super-sprint events. The age limits as outlined in Appendix A cannot be modified;
m.) An athlete who competes in a category different from his/her age, in a distance in which it is not allowed, or before the 36 hour period, will be disqualified from the events he/she took part in. Any awards, prizes and points will be removed;
n.) An athlete who undergoes sexual reassignment and wishes to participate in any competition must meet all the current conditions and criteria established by the International Olympic Committee (IOC) and WADA prior to doing so. The request to participate in any competition further to said sexual reassignment must be made expressly by the athlete to the ITU Medical and Anti-Doping Committee at least 30 days prior to event in which he or she wishes to compete. The ITU Medical and Anti-Doping Committee shall determine whether or not the current IOC and WADA criteria have been met and provide the athlete a written and reasoned decision to that effect. Any such decision on eligibility may be appealed as a Level 3 appeal (see section 13.);
o.) Where the eligibility of a female athlete is questioned due to possible hyperandrogenism and a formal written request has been made to do so, the ITU Medical and Anti-Doping Committee and other experts shall evaluate the suspected case of female hyperandrogenism. In so doing, the ITU Medical and Anti-Doping Committee shall respect and apply the current IOC Regulations on Female Hyperandrogenism which are in effect at the time of the request. The ITU Medical and Anti-Doping Committee will then notify the athlete in question of its determination by way of a written and reasoned decision. Any such decision on eligibility may be appealed as a Level 3 appeal (see section 13.);
p.) Athletes who are competing under ITU flag will be entered in the competition by the National Federation the athlete is moving to. They will compete with the same rights than any other athlete in terms of awards, prizes and points.

i）大型赛事和特许赛事的特别参赛资格标准公布于 www.triathlon.org.

j）不在国际铁联赛事体系内、但和国际铁联赛事相关的特殊资格标准，公布在其赛事各自的网站。

k）如其中一场是标准距离或更长距离比赛，则运动员不允许在 36 小时之内参加两场或两场以上铁人三项或多项运动赛事（见附件 I）的比赛。只有特定的超短距离的接力组比赛（见第 16.1.a 条）、PTVI1、PTVI2 、PTVI3 引导员和游跑两项可例外。

l）年龄限制：参赛运动员的年龄必须符合附件 A 中的最低年龄限制。洲际联合会可为洲际锦标赛制定其他年龄限制规则，如超短距离的少年组和更低年龄组。附件 A 中的年龄限制规则不可更改。

m）运动员参加非本人所属年龄段、非规则允许的比赛距离或者 36 小时之内的第二场比赛，将被取消比赛资格或成绩，其所获奖品、奖金和积分将予以取消。

n）拟参加任何国际铁联赛事的变性运动员，必须符合国际奥委会和国际反兴奋剂机构（WADA）的现行的要求与标准。变性运动员必须于任何相关赛事举办前 30 天，向国际铁联医学委员会和反兴奋剂委员会明确提出申请，国际铁联医学和反兴奋剂委员会将决定其是否符合国际奥委会（IOC）和国际反兴奋剂机构（WADA）的标准，并为运动员提供书面的、理据充分的决定书。所有对参赛资格决定的申诉可用第三级申诉的方式进行申诉（见第 13 章）。

o）如果女性运动员由于可能的雄性激素过多症导致参赛资格受到质疑，且运动员提出正式的书面申请时，国际铁联医学委员会和反兴奋剂委员会和其他专家将根据国际奥委会现行的有关女性运动员雄性激素过多症相关规定对嫌疑案例进行评估，并提供书面的、理据充分的参赛资格决定书。所有对参赛资格决定的申诉可用第三级申诉的方式进行申诉（见第 13 章）。

p）运动员代表国际铁联参加比赛须由其即将加入的国家协会为其报名。其在比赛的奖品、奖金和积分等方面享受与其他运动员同等的权利。

2.6. Insurance:

a.) All athletes competing in an event must have personal insurance coverage guaranteed by their National Federation. This insurance will cover:

(i) Any accident occurring before, during and after any competition;

(ii) Any sickness that an athlete could suffer during a trip to a competition or event;

(iii) Liability caused by an athlete during the competition.

b.) The athlete's National Federation guarantees the existence of this insurance by entering an athlete in an event. Local Organising Committees or National Federations organising an event cannot force the athletes to pay for a competition day fee for insurance purposes.

2.7. Registration:

a.) Entry:

(i) National Federations will register their athletes for ITU Events following their National Federation qualification system or other ITU approved qualification system;

(ii) All athletes qualify to any ITU Event as outlined in Appendix J by the eligibility rules outlined in 2.5 and by the qualification criteria outlined in Appendices E;

(iii) Prior to competing in ITU Triathlon World Championships, ITU Triathlon World Cups, ITU World Triathlon Series events, ITU World Paratriathlon Series, ITU Paratriathlon World Cups and ITU Multisport World Championships, Elite, U23, Junior athletes and Paratriathletes must sign the ITU Athletes' Agreement, which states that any dispute arising from the ITU Rules that cannot be settled by its existing appeal procedure, shall be settled finally by the Court of Arbitration for Sport (CAS) to the exclusion of recourse to ordinary courts. Once signed, the ITU Athletes' Agreement is valid until the end of the competition year it has been signed in. The Athletes' Agreement is published on www.triathlon.org;

(iv) National Federations are responsible for entering their athletes and coaches for all ITU Events using the ITU online system on www.triathlon.org;

(v) All Paratriathletes, PTVI1, PTVI2 and PTVI3 Guides, Age Group, Youth, Junior and U23 athletes must provide picture ID at registration/packet pick-up prior to competition.

b.) Pre-Race Briefings:

(i) Coaches' Meeting: If a coaches' meeting is scheduled, it will take place one hour before the Athletes' Briefing. The Technical Delegate will conduct the Coaches' Meeting. The agenda will include the announcement of the Competition Jury and all the technical details of the event as well as specific information for coaches. Coaches' accreditations will be distributed at this meeting, or if the Coaches' Meeting is not scheduled, accreditations will be distributed at the end of the Elite/U23/Junior/Youth Athletes' Briefing;

2.6 保 险

a）国家会员协会必须保证参赛运动员投保足够的保险。保险应覆盖：

（1） 任何铁人三项比赛之前、期间、之后发生的意外事故。

（2） 运动员奔赴比赛路途之中可能遇到的疾病。

（3） 比赛期间由某运动员引起的责任。

b）运动员所在会员协会为运动员报名时，应保证参赛运动员均办理保险。承办比赛的当地组委会或会员协会不可出于保险目的强制性向参赛运动员收取费用。

2.7 报名和报到

a）报 名

（1） 运动员参加国际铁联的比赛，应通过其所属的会员协会按照其会员协会的资格系统或其他国际铁联批准的资格系统报名。

（2） 所有符合规则 2.5 参赛资格和附件 E 参赛资格标准的运动员可以报名参加附件 J 中的国际铁联赛事。

（3） 在参加国际铁联世界杯赛、世界铁人三项系列赛、国际残疾人比赛、分项世界锦标赛之前，优秀组、23 岁以下组、青年组和残疾人组的运动员必须签署国际铁联运动员参赛协议，该协议声明由于国际铁联（ITU）规则和规定引起的任何争议，如果无法通过现有申诉程序得到解决，则由瑞士洛桑的国际体育仲裁法庭（CAS）做出最终判决，而不得向普通民事法庭提出诉讼。国际铁联运动员参赛协议签署后，有效期至比赛当年年底。运动员参赛协议公布于 www.triathlon.org。

（4） 各会员协会负责通过国际铁联网站 www.triathlon.org 上的在线报名系统为其参赛运动员和教练员报名。

（5） 所有伤残运动员、PTVI1、PTVI2 和 PTVI3 引导员、分龄组、少年组、青年组和 23 岁以下组运动员必须在赛前报到和领取参赛包时提供带有照片的身份证明。

b）赛前技术会

（1） 教练员会议：如果安排教练员会议，则教练员会议应在运动员技术会之前一小时举行。会议由技术代表主持。会议议程包括比赛仲裁委员会的公告、所有的技术细节以及为教练员特别提供的信息。教练员的证件将在此会议上发放。若没有安排教练员会议，则教练员证件将在优秀组、23 岁以下组、青年组、少年组运动员技术会结束时发放。

(ii) Age Group Team Managers' and Coaches' Briefing: At World Championships and at Continental Championships (if applicable), the Technical Delegate will conduct the Age Group Team Managers' and Coaches' briefing. Only Age Group Team Managers and Coaches registered on www.triathlon.org are allowed to attend. The agenda of this briefing will include the announcement of the Competition Jury and all the necessary information for the event. A separate briefing will be conducted for Paratriathlon (outlined in 17.5);

(iii) Paratriathlon Coaches' Meeting: If a Paratriathlon Coaches' Meeting is scheduled, it will take place before the Paratriathlon Briefing. The Technical Delegate will conduct it and the agenda will include the announcement of the Competition Jury and all technical details of the event as well as the specific information on paratriathlon procedures. Coaches' accreditations will be distributed at this meeting, or if the Team Managers' Meeting is not scheduled, accreditations will be distributed at the end of the Paratriathletes' Briefing;

(iv) Elite/U23/Junior/Youth/Paratriathletes Briefings: At all ITU Events, the Technical Delegate will conduct the Athletes' Briefing. Elite/U23/Junior/Youth athletes and Paratriathletes including their Handlers/Guides must be in attendance. Coaches may also attend the briefing. The following penalties apply to athletes who miss the briefing:

- Athletes/Paratriathletes including their Handlers/Guides not attending the briefing, without informing the Technical Delegate about their absence, will be removed from the start list;
- Athletes/ Paratriathletes including their Handlers/Guides entering the briefing hall after the briefing has started and athletes not attending the briefing, but who have informed the Technical Delegate about their absence, will have a delayed start. The delay will be according to the time penalty applicable for the specific distance (see 3.3.f.)(ii)) ;
- For the World Triathlon Series, ITU Triathlon World Cup events, World Paratriathlon Series or ITU Paratriathlon World Cup events, if an athlete misses more than two briefings in a calendar year, they will be removed from the start list for the third missed briefing and each missed briefing thereafter, even if they informed the Technical Delegate in advance.

(v) Athletes/Paratriathletes with their Handlers/Guides must register prior to entering the briefing venue;

（2） 分龄组领队和教练员技术会：在国际铁联世锦赛中，将召开分龄组领队和教练员技术会，会议由技术代表主持。会议只允许在国际铁联网站 www.triathlon.org 注册的分龄组领队和教练员参加。会议内容包括比赛中仲裁委员会的公告以及所有相关的必要信息。此外，将为伤残组别召开单独的会议（见 17.5）。

（3） 伤残组教练员会：如果召开伤残组教练员会，那么该会议将在伤残组技术会前一天举行。会议由技术代表主持，会议内容包括仲裁委员会的公告及所有比赛相关的必要信息，也包含伤残运动员比赛应注意的特殊事项。教练员的证件将在此会议上发放，如果没有安排领队会，教练员证件将在伤残运动员技术会之后发放。

（4） 优秀组、U23 组、青年组、少年组、伤残组运动员技术会：所有的国际铁联比赛中，将召开优秀组运动员技术会，会议由技术代表主持。优秀组、U23 组、青年组、少年组运动员和伤残组运动员包括其助理 / 引导员必须参加。优秀组教练员也可以参加。不参加技术会的运动员将受到以下处罚：

- 未出席技术会并未向技术代表请假的运动员、伤残运动员包括其助理 / 引导员，将从出发名单除名。
- 迟到或未出席技术会，但向技术代表请假的运动员、伤残运动员包括其助理 / 引导员，比赛中将延迟出发。延迟时间将会根据适用于其比赛距离的时间处罚规则进行 [见 3.3.f ）（2）]。
- 参加世界铁人三项系列赛、世界杯赛、世界伤残人铁人三项系列赛、世界杯赛的运动员，如果在同一年内缺席技术会超过两次，则从第三次缺席技术会开始，无论其是否事先报告了技术代表，将被从出发名单上除名。

（5） 运动员、伤残运动员包括其助理 / 引导员进入技术会会议室前须签到。

(vi) For ITU World Triathlon Series and ITU Triathlon World Cup events, there is one single Athletes' Briefing for female and male elite athletes. This briefing will be held at 18:00 local time two (2) days prior to the first elite competition day. For all other ITU Events or for other athlete categories (U23, Junior, Youth), the briefing will take place at 18:00 either one (1) or two (2) days before the first competition day of the related event and category. Alteration to this time should be announced on the ITU website 45 days in advance.

(viii) The pre-race briefings are not open to media.

c.) Packet Pick-Up:

(i) All ITU Events - Age Group:

- All athletes must pick up their own race packet at the official competition registration area during a designated time. Packet pick-up will be opened on two (2) separate days, starting from 3 days prior to their competition. The hours shall be from 09:00 to 19:00. If a National Federation is unable to make the designated registration time, they must request a different time at least 14 days in advance, in writing to ITU;
- The race packets will contain a minimum of: five (5) official race numbers (one (1) for body, one (1) for bicycle and three (3) for helmet) and four (4) safety pins, numbered swim cap, timing chip, accreditation pass, athletes' guide, tickets for all of the social functions. Local Organising Committee gifts may be distributed at the same time.

(ii) All ITU Events - Elite, U23, Junior, Youth and Paratriathlon competitions:

- All athletes will pick up their own race packet at Registration following the Athletes' Briefing;
- The race packet will include: three (3) helmet numbers, one (1) bike number, body decals for both arms and both legs, accreditation pass, athletes' guide, tickets for all of the social functions. Local Organising Committee gifts may be distributed at the same time.

d.) Check-in:

(i) Age Group competitions with more than 700 athletes entered will schedule the Check-in the day before the competition. Age Group events with fewer athletes, and Elite, U23, Junior, Youth and Paratriathlon will have the bike check on same day;

(ii) Technical Officials will conduct the check-in at the athletes' lounge or at the transition area and will include the following:

- Distribution of the swim caps and timing chips (except for the Age Group events);

（6） 国际铁联世界铁人三项系列赛及世界杯比赛中，男子、女子优秀组运动员的赛前技术会一同召开，会议时间为第一场优秀组比赛前第二天的下午 18:00 点（当地时间）。所有国际铁联其他所有比赛或其他组别运动员（U23、青年组和少年组）的技术会应在与之相关的比赛第一比赛日的前一天或两天的下午 18:00 点（当地时间）举行，如技术会在其他时间召开则应提前 45 天在国际铁联网站上公布。

（7） 赛前技术会不向媒体开放。

c）领取参赛包

（1） 国际铁联所有比赛——分龄组

- 所有运动员必须在规定时间内，在比赛正式报到处领取参赛包。领取参赛包的时间应从比赛前第 3 天开始，安排 2 天，每天的领取时间应为 09:00 至 19:00。如果某个会员协会无法在规定的时间内领取参赛包，则必须提前 14 天以书面形式向国际铁联申请为其安排其他时间。
- 参赛包中至少包含以下物品：5 块官方比赛号码（1 块号码布、1 块自行车号码、3 块头盔号码），4 个安全别针带有比赛号码的游泳帽，计时芯片，证件运动员指南，参加比赛相关活动的门票。当地组委会提供的礼物也可以一并提供。

（2） 所有国际铁联比赛——优秀组、23 岁以下组、青年组、少年组和伤残组

- 所有运动员在赛前技术会后领取参赛包。
- 参赛包中包含以下物品：3 块头盔号码，1 块自行车号码，4 套纹身号码，证件运动员指南，参加比赛相关活动的门票。当地组委会提供的礼物也可以一并提供。

d）检 录

（1） 当分龄组的运动员人数超过 700 人时，应在赛前一天提前安排检录。分龄组运动员较少时，以及优秀组、23 岁以下组、青年组、少年组和伤残组的自行车检查可以安排在本组比赛当天。

（2） 比赛当天，技术官员将在运动员准备区或转换区进行检录，包括：

- 发放游泳帽和计时芯片（分龄组比赛除外）。

- Control of the athletes' uniform, which must comply with the ITU Guidelines Regarding Authorised Identification published on www.triathlon.org. Each uniform should be photographed. If an athlete needs to replace the uniform, this process has to be done again;
- The bike check is regulated under section 5.3;
- Distribution of the race packets to the athletes who missed the briefing.

2.8. Uniform:

a.) All athletes competing in ITU Events are required to wear their uniform conforming to the ITU Guidelines Regarding Authorised Identification;

b.) The ITU Guidelines Regarding Authorised Identification set the space limitation on the athletes uniforms to include commercial logos;

c.) Athletes must follow the following rules with respect to wearing uniforms:

(i) Athletes must wear the uniform during the entire competition and award ceremony. Long sleeves and long pants are allowed for the award ceremony;

(ii) The uniform must cover the whole torso in the front. The back may be uncovered from the waist up;

(iii) Arms may be covered in middle and long distance events, except during the swim, when wetsuits are forbidden. Arms must not be covered on standard distance and shorter events, except in extreme weather conditions. The decision rests with Technical Delegate in consultation with the Medical Delegate (if applicable) to allow or make mandatory long sleeves.

(iv) Wetsuits, when authorised, may cover the arms but not the hands.

(v) Athletes are allowed to wear uniforms with sleeves extending from the shoulder up to but not covering the elbow except super-sprint, sprint and standard distance triathlon.

(vi) Paratriathletes competing in PTWC1 and PTWC2 class are allowed to wear uniforms with sleeves extending from the shoulder up to but not covering the elbow;

(vii) Covering the legs below the knees is not allowed in the swim segment when the use of wetsuits is forbidden;

(viii) A one-piece uniform is preferred. If a two-piece uniform is used, both pieces must overlap and no torso must be visible during the entire competition, except middle and long distance events where the midriff is allowed to be exposed;

(ix) If the suit has a zipper it must be located at the back and will not be longer than 40 cm. This rule does not apply for middle and long distance events;

(x) The uniform must be worn over both shoulders for the duration of the competition;

- 检查运动员比赛服，比赛服必须遵循《国际铁联（比赛服）授权认证指南》（见 www.triathlon.org），并应为每件比赛服照相，如果运动员需要更换比赛服，那么此过程需重新进行。
- 自行车检查的有关规定见 5.3。
- 为所有未参加技术会的运动员发放参赛包。

2.8 比赛服

a）所有参加国际铁联比赛的运动员均需身着各自会员协会的比赛服，且须符合《国际铁联（比赛服）授权认证指南》。

b）《国际铁联（比赛服）授权认证指南》规定了包括商标在内的各种标志的空间限制。比赛服上不允许出现任何有关政治、宗教和种族的宣传内容。

c）关于比赛服，运动员须遵守以下规则：

（1）在整个比赛和颁奖仪式中，运动员必须身着比赛服。颁奖仪式可以着长袖长裤。

（2）比赛服必须覆盖正面整个躯干，背部从腰部以上可以裸露。

（3）除禁止着防寒泳衣的游泳赛段之外，在中、长距离比赛中胳膊允许覆盖。除极端天气情况，在标准距离和短距离比赛中，胳膊不得覆盖。技术代表在与医务代表（如有）协商的基础上，可以允许或强制要求运动员着长袖。

（4）在允许使用防寒泳衣的情况下，可以覆盖手臂但不能覆盖手部。

（5）国际铁联赛事中（除超短、短距离和标准距离比赛），允许运动员比赛服的袖子延长至肘，但不能覆盖肘关节。

（6）国际铁联赛事中，允许参加伤残 PTWC1 和 PTWC2 级比赛的运动员比赛服的袖子延长至肘，但不能覆盖肘关节。

（7）如果比赛中禁止使用防寒泳衣，那么在游泳赛段膝盖以下部位不允许覆盖。

（8）建议使用连体式比赛服，如果使用分体式比赛服，则上、下两部分之间不得有空隙，也就是说两部分应重叠。除在中、长距离比赛中上腹部可以不覆盖的情况之外，运动员在整个比赛过程中都必须覆盖躯干。

（9）比赛服如果有拉链，应置于背后，最长不超过 40 厘米（中、长距离比赛项目除外）。

（10）在整个比赛过程中，比赛服不得离肩。

(xi) Elite, U23, Junior, Youth and Paratriathlon athletes must wear the same uniform from the start to the finish in standard distance or shorter events;
(xii) Rain jackets are allowed for middle and long distance events or when the Technical Delegate authorises it. Rain jackets must be the same design and colour as the uniform or transparent;
(xiii) Failure to comply with the ITU Competition Rules related to the uniform may result in an athlete having to wear a triathlon suit supplied by ITU. Alternatively, Technical Officials may request the athlete use a permanent marker or other means to eradicate logos on the uniform that do not comply with the Competition Rules. If during the competition or the award ceremony, an athlete wears a uniform with logos that do not comply with the Competition Rules (including the ITU Guidelines Regarding Authorised Identification), he/she will be disqualified.

d.) For reasons of religion, athletes are allowed to have the body totally covered (except the face) provided that:
(i) The uniform material is approved by FINA (applicable only for the non-wetsuit swim);
(ii) The uniform will not interfere with the bicycle mechanisms;
(iii) Extra identification elements are to be worn over the uniform, following the Technical Delegate's instructions.

2.9. Race numbers:

a.) Elite, U23, Junior and Youth athletes will not wear official race numbers.
b.) When, due to the competition schedule Age Groups are mixed with other athletes the Technical Delegate can decide on making the use of the official race numbers mandatory for all the athletes;
c.) Official race numbers:
(i) Mandatory for all in the Winter Triathlon events;
(ii) Age Group:
- May be worn for the wetsuit swim segment, but forbidden in a non wetsuit swim segment;
- Mandatory for the run segment;
- Must be visible on the front during the run segment.

d.) The use of the official race number in Paratriathlon is regulated in section 17;
e.) Body marking:
(i) Elite, U23, Junior, Youth and Paratriathlon:
- The Local Organising Committee or ITU will provide body marking decals, which the athletes must apply prior to the event;
- Body markings are to be applied to each arm and leg, unless instructed otherwise by the ITU Technical Delegate at the briefing;

（11）标准距离或短距离比赛中，优秀组、23 岁以下组、青年组和少年组运动员在整个比赛中必须穿着同一件比赛服。

（12）中、长距离比赛或技术代表同意的情况下，可以穿着雨衣。雨衣必须与比赛服的样式和颜色相同，或者是透明的。

（13）如果比赛服不符合国际铁联规则（包括比赛服规则）要求，运动员必须穿国际铁联提供的比赛服，或者技术官员可以要求运动员使用永久性标志物或其他方法以消除比赛服上不符合比赛规则规定的标志。如果运动员在比赛或颁奖仪式中穿着的比赛服标志不符合国际铁联的规则（包括《国际铁联（比赛服）授权认证指南》），将被取消资格。

d）出于宗教的原因，只要符合以下规定，允许运动员将除脸部以外的其他部位完全覆盖：

（1） 比赛服材料必须得到国际泳联的认可（仅适用于不使用防寒泳衣的游泳比赛中）

（2） 所穿服装不能影响自行车的正常运行。

（3） 根据技术代表的指示，在比赛服上使用身份识别元素。

2.9 比赛号码

a）优秀组、23 岁以下组、少年组和青年组运动员不必佩戴比赛号码布。

b）当分龄组比赛和其他组别运动员混合比赛时，技术代表有权强制规定所有运动员佩戴比赛号码布。

c）官方号码布

（1） 在所有冬季铁人三项比赛中必须使用。

（2） 分龄组

- 允许使用防寒泳衣的游泳赛段可使用，不允许使用防寒泳衣时禁用。
- 跑步赛段必须使用。
- 号码布须清晰可见，跑步赛段时置于体前。

d）关于伤残运动员比赛号码布的使用规定在第 17 章详细说明。

e）纹身号码

（1） 优秀组、23 岁以下组、少年组、青年组和伤残组

- 当地组委会或国际铁联将为优秀组运动员提供纹身号码贴纸，运动员们须在赛前将纹身标记转印至身体上。
- 如国际铁联技术代表未在技术会上做特别说明，纹身号码应转印至每一手臂和腿部。

- Body markings and/or decals using multiple digits will have numbers appearing one above the other, not side by side;

(ii) Age Group:

- The Local Organising Committee will provide body marking or body marking decals, who will apply them prior to the event;
- Body markings are to be applied to each arm, unless instructed otherwise by the ITU Technical Delegate at the briefing;
- Body markings and/or decals using multiple digits will have numbers appearing one above the other, not side by side;
- One calf of each athlete – if not covered - may be marked with the category and gender of the athletes (For example, the number M25 would appear on a male athlete in the 25 – 29 age category or F25 should appear on a female athlete in the same category).

2.10. Assignment of race numbers:

a.) General:

(i) Athletes' race numbers are assigned based on previous results in similar events, by using the most related rankings;

(ii) The Elite men's and women's events will be numbered starting with number 1, except in middle and long distance events;

(iii) Number 13 will be not used.

b.) Specific events numbering criteria:

(i) World Triathlon Series (WTS) and Grand Final:

- First criteria: WTS Ranking;
- Second criteria: ITU World Ranking;
- Third criteria: random.

(ii) Triathlon U23 World Championships:

- First criteria: WTS Ranking;
- Second criteria: ITU World Ranking;
- Third criteria: random.

(iii) Junior - Any event:

- First criteria: ITU World Ranking;
- Second criteria: Applicable Continental Junior Rankings (For example ETU, CAMTRI, etc.);
- Third criteria: random.

(iv) Triathlon World Cup events:

- First criteria: ITU World Ranking;
- Second criteria: random.

- 两位数和两位数以上的号码，必须按垂直方向排列，而非水平方向。

（2） 分龄组

- 当地组委会将在赛前提供身体标记服务或纹身号码贴纸。
- 除非国际铁联技术代表未在技术会上特别说明，纹身号码应书写或转印至两臂。
- 身体标记或纹身号码贴纸如有两个或两个以上数字，必须按垂直方向排列，而非水平方向。
- 如果未覆盖，运动员其中一只小腿上必须标记其所属的分组和性别（例如，号码 M25 应使用于男子 25 至 29 岁分龄组运动员，号码 F25 应使用于女子 25 至 29 岁分龄组运动员）。

2.10 比赛号码的分配

a）通用原则

（1） 运动员的比赛号码将根据以往参加同类别比赛的排名或积分分配。

（2） 男子、女子优秀组的比赛号码将分别从 1 号开始编号，中、长距离比赛除外。

（3） 不使用 13 号。

b）各项赛事比赛号码分配

（1） 世界铁人三项系列赛和总决赛

- 第一依据：当前的世界铁人三项系列赛排名。
- 第二依据：国际铁联世界排名。
- 第三依据：随机。

（2） U23 铁人三项世锦赛

- 第一依据：当前的世界铁人三项系列赛排名。
- 第二依据：国际铁联世界排名。
- 第三依据：随机。

（3） 青年组——所有赛事

- 第一依据：国际铁联世界排名。
- 第二依据：可以应用的洲际青年组排名（ETU、CAMTRI 等）。
- 第三依据：随机。

（4） 铁人三项世界杯赛

- 第一依据：国际铁联世界排名。
- 第二依据：随机。

(v) Triathlon Continental Cup events:
  - First criteria: ITU World Ranking;
  - Second criteria: random.

(vi) Triathlon Elite Continental Championships:
  - First criteria: Top 10 classification of the related Continental Championships in the previous year;
  - Second criteria: ITU World Ranking;
  - Third criteria: random.

(vii) Triathlon U23 Continental Championships:
  - First criteria: ITU World Ranking;
  - Second criteria: random.

(viii) Multisport – Any Elite event:
  - First criteria: ITU Related Rankings;
  - Second criteria: random.

(ix) Age Group - Any event:
  - First criteria: Age Group by Age Group;
  - Second criteria: Grouped by nations in alphabetical order starting by the host nation.

(x) Paratriathlon; any event:
  - First criteria: Athlete Medal Event in this order PTWC Women, PTWC Men, PTS2 Women, PTS2 Men, PTS3 Women, PTS3 Men, PTS4 Women, PTS4 Men, PTS5 Women, PTS5 Men, PTVI Women, PTVI Men;
  - Second criteria: Paratriathlon Ranking;
  - Third criteria: random.

(xi) Team Relay- Any event:
  - First criteria: One team per nation;
  - Second criteria: Same team event the preceding year;
  - Third criteria: random.

c.) Numbering of the final of events with a qualifying round format is regulated in sections 20.5 and 21.4.

2.11. Timing and Results:

a.) A competition will be won by the athlete who has the shortest time from the start signal to the moment when the athlete finishes the competition as defined in 6.2 a), 17.14 f) and 18.10, except if the event is conducted under the "rolling start system" as defined in 4.8.

（5） 铁人三项洲际杯赛

- 第一依据：国际铁联世界排名。
- 第二依据：随机。

（6） 铁人三项洲际锦标赛优秀组

- 第一依据：前一年度相关洲际锦标赛前 10 名。
- 第二依据：国际铁联世界排名。
- 第三依据：随机。

（7） 铁人三项洲际锦标赛 U23 组

- 第一依据：国际铁联世界排名。
- 第二依据：随机。

（8） 其他分项赛事——任何优秀组赛事

- 第一依据：国际铁联相关排名。
- 第二依据：随机。

（9） 分龄组——所有赛事

- 第一依据：年龄段。
- 第二依据：按照国家代码次序分组编号，东道主居首。

（10） 伤残组——所有赛事

- 第一依据：运动员的奖牌赛事按以下组别顺序：PTWC 女子，PTWC 男子，PTS2 女子，PTS2 男子，PTS3 女子，PTS3 男子，PTS4 女子，PTS4 男子，PTS5 女子，PTS5 男子，PTVI 女子，PTVI 男子。
- 第二依据：伤残运动员排名。
- 第三依据：随机。

（11） 团体接力——所有赛事

- 第一依据：每个国家（地区）一个队。
- 第二依据：前一年该赛事的成绩。
- 第三依据：随机。

c）如果设有资格赛和决赛，决赛的号码分配办法见 20.5 和 21.4。

2.11 计时和成绩

a）除非比赛采用 4.8 中界定的“滚动出发系统”，根据规则 6.2 a）、17.14f）和 18.10 的说明，从出发信号发出直至完成比赛用时最短的运动员赢得比赛。

b.) The official results will list the athletes according to their finish time and in accordance with the Olympic Results and Information Service (ORIS) standards, a sample of the results format is included in Appendix L. In the event that two athletes tie for a place, and their performances cannot be separated, they will be awarded the same rank, and the next athlete to finish behind them will occupy the same rank plus two places, with the subsequent athletes ranked in order of finishing. Time splits to be included are:
  (i) Swim or first segment;
  (ii) Transition 1;
  (iii) Bike or second segment;
  (iv) Transition 2;
  (v) Run or third segment;
  (vi) Overall finish time.

c.) Results will include the following Invalid Results Markers (IRM) and listed in this order:
  (i) athletes who do not finish the competition (DNF),
  (ii) any lapped athletes or athletes stopped by the last biker – first runner scenario (LAP),
  (iii) not classified participants or not making the cut-off time in any segment (NC),
  (iv) Non-eligible Paratriathletes (NE),
  (v) those who are disqualified (DSQ)
  (vi) and athletes or teams which did not start (DNS):
  (vii) If more than one athlete is marked DNF or LAP, those who completed the most laps should be listed first; if several athletes are marked DNF or LAP on the same lap, athletes should be listed according to their times at the previous timing point with the fastest first, or by ascending start number if no times were recorded up to the point at which they retired;
  (viii) If more than one participant is included in the same IRM group (different than DNF or LAP), they should be listed within the same group according to ascending start number;
  (ix) For DSQ athletes, the final results should not be displayed.

d.) Additional information will be displayed either at the header or the footer of the results:
  (i) Swim distance and number of laps;
  (ii) Bike distance and number of laps;
  (iii) Run distance and number of laps;
  (iv) Air temperature;
  (v) Water temperature;

b）正式成绩将根据运动员们的完成时间排列，正式成绩册的制作须符合 ORIS（译者注：Olympic Results and Information System，奥林匹克成绩处理和信息系统）标准。详细的格式请参考附件 L。如出现两名运动员并列且无法区分胜负，他们将被授予相同的名次，排在他们之后的一名运动员名次应增加 2 位，随后的运动员正常排名即可。分段成绩包括：

（1） 游泳比赛时间或第一赛段时间。

（2） 第一换项时间。

（3） 自行车比赛时间或第二赛段时间。

（4） 第二换项时间。

（5） 跑步比赛时间或第三赛段时间。

（6） 总时间。

c）成绩册应包括以下无效成绩标记（IRM），并按以下顺序列出：

（1） 没有完成比赛的运动员（DNF）。

（2） 被套圈的运动员或被“最后的自行车运动员 —— 第一个跑步运动员”情形终止比赛的运动员（LAP）。

（3） 未分级或在任何赛段被关门的运动员（NC）。

（4） 无资格伤残组运动员（NE）。

（5） 被取消比赛资格运动员（DSQ）。

（6） 未出发运动员或队（DNS）。

（7） 如果被标记 DNF 或 LAP 的运动员多于一人，则完成圈数较多的列前；如果被标记 DNF 或 LAP 的几名运动员完成圈数相同，则根据上个计时点的成绩，较好者列前；如果运动员退出时尚无任何计时成绩，则根据出发号码以升序排列。

（8） 如果不止一名运动员被标记同一种无效成绩标记（不同于 DNF 或 LAP），则同组运动员根据出发号码以升序排列。

（9） 被标记 DSQ 的运动员，最终成绩不予显示。

d）成绩册页眉或页角处应注明以下信息：

（1） 游泳的距离与圈数。

（2） 自行车的距离与圈数。

（3） 跑步的距离与圈数。

（4） 气温。

（5） 水温。

(vi) Wetsuit swim/No wetsuit swim;
(vii) Name and country of the Technical Delegate;
(viii) Name and country of the Head Referee;
(ix) Name and country of the members of the Competition Jury.

e.) For relay events, the rules above are applicable and the total time per athlete will be shown;
   (i) Results will be official once the Head Referee signs them. Incomplete results can be declared official at any time. The Head Referee will use all the resources available to decide the final position of every athlete. The information from technology will be used to assist in the decision making process. The Head Referee may decide, based on the available evidence, that a competition is tied if there is no way of defining which athlete crossed the line first. Results of tied athletes will be sorted according to race numbers. However, athletes who finish in a contrived tie situation, where no effort to separate their finish times has been made will be DSQ;
   (ii) Paratriathletes changing sport class after classification assessment before the event will be moved to the new sport class. Non-eligible Paratriathletes will be removed from the start list;

f.) Paratriathletes changing sport class after observation during competition will be moved to a new sport class. Non-eligible Paratriathletes will be displayed as NE.

g.) Official results may be modified by the following bodies, without adding or removing time of a penalty:
   (i) Head Referee up to 48 hours after the completion of the event;
   (ii) Competition Jury;
   (iii) ITU Technical Delegate as the result of a protest concerning timing and results;
   (iv) ITU Appeal Panel from the time of the medal ceremony till five days after the event;
   (v) ITU Technical Committee as the result of a results review process;
   (vi) ITU Technical Committee as the result of a change of a paratriathlon sport class process;
   (vii) ITU Arbitration Tribunal as the result of a level 2 appeal;
   (viii) Anti-Doping Hearing Panel;
   (ix) CAS as result of a level 3 appeal.

2.12. Exceptional conditions:

a.) The following list highlights some of the exceptional situations that may happen. Different scenarios from those indicated may arise, which need to be solved by the Technical Delegate following the same principles:
   (i) Before the competition:
   - A triathlon may be modified to a duathlon, aquathlon, or even in a 2 segments competition: swim-run, bike-run or run-bike, by the equivalent distance. Time trial starts are allowed. The preferred option will be a duathlon with the shorter run first;

（6） 是否着防寒泳衣。

（7） 技术代表姓名和国籍。

（8） 裁判长的姓名和国籍。

（9） 比赛仲裁委员会的姓名和国籍。

e）上述规则同样适用于接力比赛，并且应显示每名运动员的总时间。

（1） 由裁判长签名的成绩即成为正式成绩。非正式成绩可在任何时候被宣布为正式成绩。裁判长应使用包括科技手段在内的全部可能的资源去判断每位运动员的最终比赛名次。如果两名运动员同时抵达终点，裁判长可根据各种证据和自己的判断有权判定名次并列。并列运动员的成绩将根据比赛号码排序。但是，如果运动员故意造成人为的并列，将被取消比赛成绩（DSQ）。

（2） 经赛前分级评价改变参赛等级的伤残组运动员，将被移至新的分级组别参赛。未获资格的伤残运动员将从出发名单移除。

f）经比赛观察确认，可改变参赛分级的伤残组运动员将被移至新的分级组别。未获资格的伤残运动员标记为"NE"。

g）正式成绩可由以下人员或组织修改，但不得增加或消除处罚时间：

（1） 裁判长（比赛结束后 48 小时之内）。

（2） 仲裁委员会。

（3） 国际铁联技术代表基于对计时与成绩抗议的结果。

（4） 国际铁联申诉委员会自颁奖仪式后五天内。

（5） 国际铁联技术委员会基于对成绩审核的结果。

（6） 国际铁联技术委员会基于伤残组运动员分级更改的结果。

（7） 国际铁联仲裁法庭基于二级申诉的结果。

（8） 反兴奋剂听证委员会。

（9） 国际体育仲裁法庭基于三级申诉的结果。

2.12 例外情况

a）下文指出一些可能发生的例外情况。出现这些情况时技术代表需根据以下原则解决：

（1） 赛 前

- 铁人三项比赛可以调整为骑跑两项、游跑两项或距离相同但非连续完成的两段比赛：游泳—跑步、自行车—跑步或跑步—自行车。允许采用计时赛的出发方式。建议优先调整为以短距离跑为首段的骑跑两项。

- A duathlon may be modified to two segments: bike-run or run-bike. Time trial starts are allowed;
- The Technical Delegate may take other decisions if the above options are not possible to set up.

(ii) Modification of the competition once started:

- Any segment, but only one, may be shortened during the competition. The Technical Delegate and Technical Officials will take all reasonable actions to ensure the fairness of the event and the safety of the athletes. Otherwise, the competition will be stopped.

(iii) Modification of the third segment by shortening it:

- The athletes will stop the competition no later than the completion of the lap. Those who completed more than the 50% of the last segment will be considered as finishers and will be ranked according to the position in the preceding lap. All of the others, or if the competition is stopped before that moment, will not be considered in the results;
- In the case that all the athletes are stopped before the 50% of the third segment the competition will be restarted, if possible.

3. PENALTIES

3.1. General Rules:

a.) Failure to comply with the ITU Competition Rules may result in an athlete being verbally warned, issued with a time penalty, disqualified, suspended, or expelled;

b.) The nature of the rule violation will determine the subsequent penalty;

c.) A suspension or an expulsion will occur for very serious violations of either the ITU Competition Rules or the ITU Anti-Doping Rules;

d.) Reasons for penalty: An athlete may be issued a verbal warning, punished with a time penalty, or disqualified for failing to abide by the ITU Competition Rules.

e.) Infringements and penalties are listed in Appendix K;

f.) The Technical Officials are allowed to determine penalties, even if the infringement is not listed, if the Technical Official deems an unfair advantage has been gained, or if a dangerous situation has been created intentionally.

3.2. Warning:

a.) The purpose of a warning is to alert an athlete about a possible rule violation and to promote a "proactive" attitude on the part of Technical Officials. Also a Technical Official can determine a warning to an athlete to correct a minor infringement

- 骑跑两项可以调整为两段：自行车—跑步或跑步—自行车。允许采用计时赛的出发方式。
- 如果上述选择无法实现，技术代表可以做出其他选择。

（2） 比赛开始后的调整

- 比赛中任何段落都可以缩短，但只能缩短一段。技术代表和技术官员需采取一切必要的措施保证比赛的公平和运动员的安全。否则，停止比赛。

（3） 通过缩短距离对第三赛段进行调整

- 应在运动员跑完各圈前停止比赛。完成最后赛段 50% 的运动员将被视为完成比赛，并根据前一圈的位置确定名次。比赛停止时完成的比赛距离不足 50% 所有的其他运动员，将被认定为未完成比赛。
- 当停止比赛时所有运动员均未完成第三赛段的 50%，如可能，比赛将重新开始。

3. 犯规及处罚

3.1 总 则

a） 运动员违反国际铁联竞赛规则将受到口头警告、时间处罚、取消比赛资格、停赛或者禁赛的处罚。

b） 运动员的犯规性质将决定处罚方式。

c） 运动员严重违反竞赛规则或国际铁联反兴奋剂规则，将受到停赛和禁赛处罚。

d） 处罚的理由：运动员犯规将受到口头警告、时间处罚或取消比赛资格的处罚。

e） 具体的犯规行为及处罚方式见附件 K。

f） 即使某项具体的犯规行为未列入附件 K，如果技术官员认为运动员非法获利或故意制造了危险的状况，则技术官员有权实施处罚。

3.2 口头警告

a） 警告的目的是为了提醒运动员可能会出现犯规行为，以及促使技术官员形成更具“前瞻性”的执裁态度。警告也可以用于纠正运动员的轻微犯规。

b.) A warning may be given when:
 (i) An athlete violates a rule unintentionally;
 (ii) A Technical Official believes a violation is about to occur;
 (iii) No advantage has been gained.
c.) Giving a warning: The Technical Official will blow their whistle, the athlete will be stopped if necessary, asked to modify their behavior, and be allowed to continue the competition immediately afterwards.

3.3. Time Penalty:

a.) It is not necessary for a Technical Official to give a warning prior to issuing a more serious penalty;
b.) A time penalty is an appropriate penalty for infringements, which do not warrant a disqualification;
c.) Time penalties will be served in a designated penalty box, in the transition area or on spot;
d.) Technical Officials will decide when an athlete needs to be penalized with a time penalty;
e.) There are two type of infringements penalized with time penalties:
 (i) Drafting infringements as defined in 5.5;
 (ii) Other infringements. See appendix K for list.
f.) Time penalties vary depending on the type of infringement:
 (i) Drafting infringements:
  - 5 minutes in long distance events;
  - 5 minutes in middle distance events;
  - 2 minutes in standard distance events;
  - 1 minute in sprint and shorter events.
 (ii) Other infringements:
  - 1 minute in long distance events;
  - 30 seconds in middle distance events;
  - 15 seconds in standard distance events;
  - 10 seconds in sprint distance and shorter events.
g.) Penalty notification: The Technical Official will determine the time penalty, and notify the athlete as soon as it is safe to do so:
 (i) Drafting infringements:
  - Sounding a whistle, showing a blue card, calling in English the athlete's number and saying "Drafting penalty, you have to stop at the next penalty box". The Technical Official has to ensure the athlete received the penalty notification.
 (ii) Other infringements:
  - Start and swim infringements: Athletes will serve this penalty in transition 1 before touching any equipment. A Technical Official will be positioned by the athletes transition spot, who will sound a whistle, show a yellow card and time the penalty;

b）出现以下情况给予口头警告：

（1） 运动员无意中犯规。

（2） 技术官员认为犯规行为将要发生。

（3） 运动员没有通过犯规获利。

c）给予口头警告：技术官员将以吹口哨的形式警告，必要时可以命令运动员停止比赛，改正行为后再继续比赛。

3.3 时间处罚

a）在对运动员做出更严厉的判罚之前，技术官员无须先给予警告。

b）时间处罚适用于未导致取消比赛资格处罚的犯规行为。

c）时间处罚将在规定的处罚区、转换区或犯规现场进行。

d）技术官员决定一个运动员是否需要进行时间处罚。

e）两种类型的犯规行为适用于时间处罚：

（1） 5.5 中界定的尾随行为。

（2） 附录 K 中的其他犯规行为。

f）犯规类型不同处罚也不同：

（1） 尾随犯规

- 长距离比赛 5 分钟。
- 中距离比赛 5 分钟。
- 标准距离比赛 2 分钟。
- 短距离比赛 1 分钟。

（2） 其他犯规行为

- 长距离比赛 1 分钟。
- 中距离比赛 30 秒。
- 标准距离比赛 15 秒。
- 短距离比赛 10 秒。

g）处罚通知：由技术官员决定是否进行时间处罚，并在确保安全的情况下通知运动员：

（1） 尾随犯规

- 吹口哨，出示蓝牌，呼叫运动员的号码（用英语），同时说“尾随处罚，你必须在下一个处罚区停下”。当执技术官员必须确认运动员收到处罚提醒。

（2） 其他犯规

- 出发*（全部）*和游泳赛段*（仅分龄组）*：运动员将在第一换项接触其装备前接受处罚。技术官员将在运动员号位，吹哨、出示黄牌，再进行时间处罚。

- Bike segment infringements: Sounding a whistle, showing a yellow card, calling in English the athlete's number and saying "Time penalty, you have to stop at the next penalty box" or "Time penalty, you have to stop at the run penalty box". The Technical Official has to ensure the athlete receives the penalty notification (See table below);
- Infringements in transitions and run segment: Athletes may be notified about penalties by sounding a whistle, showing a yellow card, calling in English the athlete's number and saying "Time penalty, you have to stop" or by displaying the athlete's number on a panel posted at the penalty box. It is the athlete's responsibility to check this board (See table below).
- Athletes who are given a time penalty have the option to decide whether to stop at the penalty box and serve the penalty or continue to the finish. Not stopping will result in disqualification on crossing the finish line. The athlete may then appeal the penalty. Evidence will only be made available if an appeal is filed.

3.4. Applicable penalties for the different categories:

	Elite Draft Legal	Elite Draft-illegal Elite Paratriathlon	Age Group
Start	T1	T1	T1
Swim	Run penalty box	Run penalty box	T1
Transition 1	Run penalty box	Run penalty box	Warning at T1
Bike	Run penalty box	Bike penalty box	Bike Penalty box
Transition 2	Run penalty box	Run penalty box	Warning at T2
Run	Run penalty box	Run penalty box	Warning/Time Penalty on the spot

Notes: All the refences to Elite includes Elite, U23, Junior and Youth athletes. In Winter Triathlon run penalty box is replaced with ski penalty box. In Duathlon and Aquathlon events run penalty box means 2nd run penalty box.

3.5. Procedure while serving a time penalty:

a.) The Technical Official applying the time penalty is not required to give a reason for the penalty;

b.) When given a blue or yellow card, the athlete will follow the instructions of the Technical Official;

c.) Time penalty in Transition 1 (for any infringements up to this point):

(i) The Technical Official will hold a yellow card as the penalised athlete arrives at his/her position. The athlete will be ordered to stop in his/her transition space without touching any of their equipment, the Technical Official will start the timing. If the athlete touches or removes any of their equipment the Technical Official will ask the athlete to stop touching the equipment and the time will be paused. Once the athlete complies the count will continue;

- 自行车赛段：吹口哨，出示黄牌，呼叫运动员的号码（用英语），同时说“时间处罚，你必须在下一个处罚区停下”或“时间处罚，你必须在跑步处罚区停下”。当执技术官员必须确认运动员收到处罚提醒（见下表）。
- 转换区和跑步赛段：吹口哨，出示黄牌通知运动员，呼叫运动员的号码（用英语），同时说“时间处罚，你必须停下”或在处罚区外的公告牌上公布运动员的号码。注意公告牌是运动员的责任（见下表）。
- 接到时间处罚的运动员可以选择在处罚区停下接受处罚或继续比赛至结束。后者将导致到达终点时被取消资格。运动员可向仲裁委员会提出申诉。只有申诉被提交，证据才会被公布。

3.4 不同类别项目处罚的应用

	可尾随优秀组	**不可尾随的优秀组 伤残人优秀组**	**分龄组**
出发	T1	T1	T1
游泳	跑步处罚区	跑步处罚区	T1
第一换项	跑步处罚区	跑步处罚区	在 T1 警告
自行车	跑步处罚区	自行车处罚区	自行车处罚区
第二换项	跑步处罚区	跑步处罚区	在 T2 警告
跑步	跑步处罚区	跑步处罚区	警告 / 现场时间处罚

备注：优秀组包括所有优秀组、23 岁以下组、少年和青年运动员。在冬季铁人三项比赛中，滑雪处罚区替代跑步处罚区。骑跑两项和游跑两项中的跑步处罚区是指第二个跑步处罚区。

3.5 时间处罚的程序

a）技术官员在施行时间处罚时，不需要给出处罚理由。

b）当运动员被技术官员出示蓝牌或黄牌后，应听从技术官员的指示。

c）第 1 换项时的时间处罚（适用于*出发及分龄组*在此之前的犯规行为）：

（1） 技术官员将手持黄牌，在犯规运动员的自行车位置上等待，运动员抵达后，技术官员要求其停止比赛，并不得接触任何比赛装备后，技术官员开始计时。如果运动员接触或移动任何比赛装备，将停止计时，直至其停止接触装备再继续计时。

(ii) When the penalty time has been completed, the Technical Official will say "Go" and the athlete can continue with the competition.

d.) Time penalty at the Bike Penalty Box:

(i) The penalised athlete's race numbers are not displayed in a bike penalty box. It is the athlete's responsibility to report to the next penalty box on the course after receiving notification;

(ii) The penalised athlete will enter the penalty box, dismount the bike and inform the Technical Official of their race number the number of penalties to serve and the colour of card(s) received. The time penalty starts when the athlete complies with all above and ends when the Technical Official says "Go", at which time the athlete may continue with the competition. If the athlete leaves the area, the Technical Official will ask the athlete to return and the time will be paused. Once the athlete complies the count will continue;

(iii) While in the bike penalty box, athletes can consume only the food and/or water that is on the athlete's bike or person;

(iv) Athletes are prohibited from using the restroom while serving a penalty in the bike penalty box. The time of penalty will be paused while using the restroom;

(v) Making adjustments to equipment or performing any type of bike maintenance while serving a penalty in the bike penalty box is prohibited.

e.) Time penalty at the Run Penalty Box:

(i) The penalised athletes' race numbers are clearly displayed on a board at the penalty box;

(ii) The penalised athlete will proceed into the penalty box and inform the Technical Official of their race number and number of penalties to serve. The time penalty starts when the athlete complies with all above and ends when the Technical Official says "Go", at which time the athlete may continue with the competition. If the athlete leaves the area, the Technical Official will ask the athlete to return and the time will be paused. Once the athlete complies the count will continue;

(iii) The penalised athlete's number will be removed from the board once the penalty is served;

(iv) A penalised athlete may serve their penalty on any lap of the run;

(v) For relay events, the penalty may be served by any member of the team, who has not yet completed their portion of the event;

(vi) Penalties must be posted on the board before the athlete completes the first half of the run. Postings after this time are invalid.

3.6. Disqualification:

a.) General:

(i) A disqualification is a penalty appropriate for severe rule violations, such as but not limited to, repeated bike draft infringements, and/or dangerous or unsportsmanlike conduct;

（2） 处罚时间结束后，技术官员说“GO”（“走”），运动员方可继续比赛。

d）自行车处罚区的时间处罚：

（1） 自行车处罚区不张贴被处罚的运动员号码。接到通知的运动员有义务自行到下一个处罚区报到。

（2） 犯规运动员将进入下一个处罚区，下车并告知技术官员自己的比赛号码和收到的处罚牌的颜色。处罚时间从运动员完成上述程序开始计算，当技术官员说“GO”（“走”）处罚时间结束，运动员方可继续比赛。如果运动员离开处罚区，技术官员须要求其返回并暂停计时，直至其执行要求再开始计时。

（3） 在自行车处罚区，运动员仅可用运动员自己或自行车上的食物或 / 和水。

（4） 在自行车处罚区接受处罚时，运动员禁止使用洗手间。使用洗手间时，时间处罚的计时将被暂停。

（5） 在自行车处罚区接受处罚时，禁止调试设备或进行任何形式的自行车维护。

e）跑步处罚区的时间处罚：

（1） 犯规运动员的号码将在处罚区前的公告牌上清楚地张贴。

（2） 犯规运动员进入处罚区，并通知相关技术官员自己的号码和处罚次数。处罚时间从运动员进入处罚区开始计算，当技术官员说“GO”（“走”）处罚时间结束，运动员方可继续比赛。如果运动员离开处罚区，技术官员须要求其返回并暂停计时，直至其执行要求再开始计时。

（3） 已接受处罚的运动员的号码将从公告牌上删除。

（4） 犯规运动员可在跑步赛段的任何一圈接受处罚。

（5） 在接力比赛中，队中任何未完成自身赛段的运动员均可代表本队接受处罚。

（6） 犯规处罚通知必须在运动员完成跑步比赛前半程之前公布在公告牌上，之后公布的无效。

3.6 取消比赛资格

a）概 述

（1） 取消比赛资格是对运动员严重犯规行为，例如（但不仅限于）反复尾随犯规或危险的、违反体育道德行为的处罚。

b.) Assessment:

(i) If time and conditions permit, a Technical Official will assess a disqualification by:

- Sounding a whistle;
- Showing a red card;
- Calling (in English) the athlete's number and saying "Disqualified";
- For safety reasons, a Technical Official may have to delay issuing a disqualification.

(ii) Athletes will be informed about the penalties by displaying the athlete's number on the white board posted at the post finish area;

(iii) The athlete and or the National Federation needs to be contacted and informed of the disqualification if this is after the athlete has finished and the penalty has not been posted on the board. The athlete or National Federation must respond within 5 days to the Technical Delegate if they wish to appeal.

c.) Procedure after Disqualification:

(i) An athlete may finish the competition if a Technical Official issues a disqualification.

3.7. Suspension:

a.) General:

(i) A suspension is a penalty appropriate for a fraudulent or a very severe rule violation, such as but not limited to repeated dangerous or unsportsmanlike conduct;

(ii) A suspended athlete will not take part in ITU competitions or competitions sanctioned by National Federations affiliated with ITU during a suspension period.

b.) Assessment:

(i) The Head Referee will submit a report to the ITU Arbitration Tribunal including all the details of the action, and the reasons to recommend the athlete for suspension. This report will be submitted to the ITU Secretary General within one week of the competition. The ITU Secretary General will inform the affected National Federations.

c.) Suspensions will be assessed by the ITU Arbitration Tribunal for periods of three (3) months to four (4) years, depending on the violation;

d.) Suspensions based on contriving the ITU Anti-Doping Rules: If the suspension is an Anti-Doping Rule Violation, the athlete will not be able to compete in any other sport whose federation is recognised by ITU, IOC or GAIFS and vice versa.

e.) Reasons for Suspension:

(i) A list of infringements, which may result in a suspension, is described in Appendix K.

b）判 罚

（1） 如果时间与条件允许，技术官员将按照以下程序给予取消比赛资格的处罚：

- 吹口哨或喇叭。
- 出示红牌。
- 呼叫运动员的号码（用英语），同时说“Disqualified”（“取消比赛资格”）。
- 出于安全原因，技术官员可推迟处罚。

（2） 另一种处罚方式是，犯规运动员的比赛号码将被张贴在终点后的白板上。

（3） 若运动员已经完赛并且处罚未公布在公告板上，需要联系和通知运动员或国家协会该运动员被判取消比赛资格。运动员或国家协会必须在 5 天内回应技术代表是否有意申诉。

c）判罚取消比赛资格后的处理程序

（1） 运动员被判罚取消比赛资格后，也可以继续完成比赛。

3.7 停 赛

a）概 述

（1） 停赛适用于欺骗行为、十分严重的犯规行为，例如反复的危险动作或违反体育道德行为等。

（2） 在停赛期间，运动员不得参加国际铁联比赛或者国际铁联会员协会批准的比赛。

b）判 罚

（1） 裁判长将向国际铁联仲裁法庭提交包括所有犯规细节及建议停赛原因的的报告。这份报告应在赛后一周内提交至国际铁联秘书长。将由国际铁联秘书长通知运动员所属的协会会员。

c）停赛决定由国际铁联仲裁法庭签发，根据犯规行为的性质，停赛期可从 3 个月至 4 年。

d）因违反国际铁联反兴奋剂规则而停赛：如果停赛是因为使用违禁药物，运动员将不能参加任何其他被国际铁联、国际奥委会、国际体育单项联合会总会认可的国际体育组织所管辖项目的赛事，反之亦然。

e）判罚停赛理由

（1） 可导致判罚停赛的情况见附件 K。

f.) Disciplinary Notice:
  (i) When an athlete is suspended, the ITU will notify the concerned National Federation, in writing, within 30 days;
  (ii) All suspensions will be announced in the ITU newsletter and communicated to the IOC and respective parties.

3.8. Expulsion:

a.) General:
  (i) Athletes who have been expelled will not participate in ITU competitions or competitions sanctioned by National Federations affiliated with ITU for life.

b.) Reasons for Expulsion:
  (i) An athlete will be expelled for life for repeated rule violations that incur suspension as the penalty;
  (ii) Expulsion due to an Anti-Doping Rule Violation: If the expulsion is for an Anti-Doping Rule Violation, the athlete will not be able to compete in any other sport whose federation is recognised by ITU, IOC or SportAccord and vice versa.

c.) Disciplinary Notice:
  (i) When an athlete is expelled, the ITU will notify the concerned National Federation, in writing, within 30 days;
  (ii) Expulsions will be announced in the ITU newsletter and communicated to the IOC and the respective parties.

3.9. Right of Appeal:

a.) Athletes punished with a penalty have the right to appeal with the exception of a drafting violation.

3.10. Reinstatement:

a.) After suspension, an athlete must apply to the ITU Arbitration Tribunal for reinstatement.

4. SWIMMING

4.1. General Rules:

a.) Athletes may use any stroke to propel themselves through the water. They may also tread water or float. Athletes are allowed to push off the ground at the beginning and the end of every swim lap;

b.) Athletes must follow the prescribed swim course;

c.) Athletes may stand on the bottom or rest by holding an inanimate object, such as a buoy or stationary boat;

d.) In an emergency, an athlete should raise an arm overhead and call for assistance. Once official assistance is rendered, the athlete must retire from the competition;

e.) Athletes may sportingly maintain their own space in the water:
  (i) Where athletes make accidental contact in the swim and then immediately afterwards move apart no penalty will be incurred;

f）处罚的通知

（1）运动员被停赛，国际铁联在 30 天之内以书面形式通知其所属会员协会。

（2）所有被停赛的运动员将通过国际铁联简报公布，同时报国际奥委会和相关团体。

3.8 终身禁赛

a）概 述

（1）被终身禁赛的运动员终身不得参加国际铁联比赛或者国际铁联会员协会批准的比赛。

b）判罚终身禁赛的理由

（1）反复地被判罚停赛的犯规行为。

（2）因违反国际铁联反兴奋剂规则而终身禁赛：如果终身禁赛是因为使用违禁药物，运动员将不能参加任何其他被国际铁联、国际奥委会、国际体育单项联合会总会认可的国际体育组织所管辖项目的赛事，反之亦然。

c）处罚的通知

（1）如果一名运动员被停禁赛，则国际铁联将在 30 天内以书面方式通知其所属会员协会。

（2）所有被禁赛的运动员将通过国际铁联简报公布，同时报国际奥委会和相关团体。

3.9 申诉权

a）被指控犯规的运动员有申诉的权利，尾随犯规除外。

3.10 复 赛

a）停赛期满后，运动员必须向国际铁联仲裁法庭提出恢复参赛的申请。

4. 游 泳

4.1 总 则

a）运动员可以使用任何泳姿进行比赛，也可以踩水或漂浮。在游泳比赛每圈开始和结束时可蹬地前进。

b）运动员必须按照规定的比赛路线前进。

c）运动员可以站立在水底或抓住静止物体休息，如浮漂或静止的船只。

d）遇紧急情况，运动员应高举单臂求救。一经正式救助，运动员必须退出比赛。

e）运动员可在水中维持个人运动空间：

（1）运动员在水中发生意外接触随后立即分离，可免受处罚。

(ii) Where athletes make contact in the swim, and an athlete continues to impede the progress of the other athlete without moving apart, this action will result in a time penalty;

(iii) Where athletes deliberately target another athlete to impede their progress, gain unfair advantage and potentially cause harm will result in disqualification and may be reported to ITU Arbitration Tribunal for potential suspension or expulsion.

f.) Rules about water quality are outlined in section 10.

4.2. Wetsuit Use:

a.) Wetsuit use is governed by the following tables:

Elite, U23, Junior and Youth athletes:

Swim Length	Forbidden	Mandatory*
Up to 1500m	20 °C and above	15.9 °C and below
1501m and longer	22 °C and above	15.9 °C and below

* when mandatory, the wetsuit must cover at least the torso

Age Group athletes:

Swim Length	Forbidden	Mandatory*
Up to 1500m	22 °C and above	15.9 °C and below
1501m and longer	24.6 °C and above	15.9°C and below

* when mandatory, the wetsuit must cover at least the torso

4.3. Maximum stay in water:

Swim Length	Elite, U23, Junior and Youth	Age Group
Up to 300m	10 min.	20 min.
301m to 750m - below 31°C	20 min.	30 min.
301m to 750m - 31°C and above	20 min.	20 min.
751m to 1500m	30 min.	1h 10 min.
1501m to 3000m	1h 15 min.	1h 40 min.
3001m to 4000m	1h 45 min.	2h 15 min.

（2） 运动员在水中发生接触，其中一名运动员不离开反而继续阻碍另一运动员的路线时，给予时间处罚。

（3） 运动员故意阻碍其他运动员的路线、获得不公平的优先权、有意对其他运动员造成伤害时，将取消其比赛资格，或上报国际铁联仲裁法庭判以停赛或终身禁赛。

f）水质的规定见第 10 章。

4.2 防寒泳衣的使用

a）防寒泳衣的使用将根据以下表格操作：

优秀组、23 岁以下组、青年组和少年组运动员：

游泳比赛距离	下列温度以上禁止使用	下列温度以下必须使用
1500 米及以下	20℃及以上	15.9℃及以下
1501 米及以上	22℃及以上	15.9℃及以下

* 必须着防寒泳衣时，防寒泳衣必须至少覆盖躯干。

分龄组运动员：

游泳比赛距离	下列温度以上禁止使用	下列温度以下必须使用
1500 米及以下	22℃及以上	15.9℃及以下
1501 米及以上	24.6℃及以上	15.9℃及以下

* 必须着防寒泳衣时，防寒泳衣必须至少覆盖躯干。

4.3 在水中停留的最大时间

游泳比赛距离	优秀组 /23 岁以下组 / 青年组 / 少年组运动员	分龄组运动员
300 米及以下	10 分钟	20 分钟
301~750 米，31℃以下	20 分钟	30 分钟
301~750 米，31℃以上	20 分钟	20 分钟
751~1500 米	30 分钟	1 小时 10 分钟
1501~3000 米	1 小时 15 分钟	1 小时 40 分钟
3001~4000 米	1 小时 45 分钟	2 小时 15 分钟

4.4. Modifications:

a.) The swim distance can be shortened or even cancelled according to this table:

Original swim distance	Temperature of water						
	Above 32.0 °C	31.9°C-31.0 °C	30.9 °C – 15.0 °C	14.9 °C – 14.0 °C	13.9 °C – 13.0 °C	12.9 °C – 12.0 °C	Below 12.0 °C
Up to 750m	Cancel	750m	750m	750m	750m	750m	Cancel
1000m	Cancel	750m	1000m	1000m	1000m	750m	Cancel
1500m	Cancel	750m	1500m	1500m	1500m	750m	Cancel
1900m	Cancel	750m	1900m	1900m	1500m	750m	Cancel
2000m	Cancel	750m	2000m	2000m	1500m	750m	Cancel
2500m	Cancel	750m	2500m	2500m	1500m	750m	Cancel
3000m	Cancel	750m	3000m	3000m	1500m	750m	Cancel
3800m	Cancel	750m	3800m	3000m	1500m	750m	Cancel
4000m	Cancel	750m	4000m	3000m	1500m	750m	Cancel

*** Note**: *The temperatures above are not always the water temperature used in the final decision. If the water temperature is lower than 22°C and the air temperature is lower than 15°, then the adjusted value is to decrease the measured water temperature according to the next chart.*

(*)		Air temperature (All values in °C)										
		15	14	13	12	11	10	9	8	7	6	5
Water Temperature (All values in °C)	22	18.5	18.0	17.5	17.0	16.5	16.0	15.5	15.0	14.5	14.0	Cancel
	21	18.0	17.5	17.0	16.5	16.0	15.5	15.0	14.5	14.0	13.5	Cancel
	20	17.5	17.0	16.5	16.0	15.5	15.0	14.5	14.0	13.5	13.0	Cancel
	19	17.0	16.5	16.0	15.5	15.0	14.5	14.0	13.5	13.0	12.5	Cancel
	18	16.5	16.0	15.5	15.0	14.5	14.0	13.5	13.0	12.5	12.0	Cancel
	17	16.0	15.5	15.0	14.5	14.0	13.5	13.0	12.5	12.0	Cancel	Cancel
	16	15.5	15.0	14.5	14.0	13.5	13.0	12.5	12.0	Cancel	Cancel	Cancel
	15	15.0	14.5	14.0	13.5	13.0	12.5	12.0	Cancel	Cancel	Cancel	Cancel
	14	14.0	14.0	13.5	13.0	12.5	12.0	Cancel	Cancel	Cancel	Cancel	Cancel
	13	13.0	13.0	13.0	12.5	12.0	Cancel	Cancel	Cancel	Cancel	Cancel	Cancel

b.) If other weather conditions dictate, i.e., high winds, heavy rain, changing temperature, current, etc. the Technical Delegate in consultation with the Medical Delegate (if applicable) may adapt limits of the swim length or adopt provisions about the use of wetsuits. The final decision will be made one hour before the start and will be clearly communicated to the athletes by the Technical Delegate;

4.4 调 整

a）根据下表，游泳比赛可缩短距离甚至取消：

原游泳比赛距离	水温（°C）						
	32.0 以上	31.0~31.9	15.0~30.9	14.0~14.9	13.0~13.9	12.0~12.9	12.0 以下
750 米	取消	750 米	750 米	750 米	750 米	750 米	取消
1000 米	取消	750 米	1000 米	1000 米	1000 米	750 米	取消
1500 米	取消	750 米	1500 米	1500 米	1500 米	750 米	取消
1900 米	取消	750 米	1900 米	1900 米	1500 米	750 米	取消
2000 米	取消	750 米	2000 米	2000 米	1500 米	750 米	取消
2500 米	取消	750 米	2500 米	2500 米	1500 米	750 米	取消
3000 米	取消	750 米	3000 米	3000 米	1500 米	750 米	取消
3800 米	取消	750 米	3800 米	3800 米	1500 米	750 米	取消
4000 米	取消	750 米	4000 米	3000 米	1500 米	750 米	取消

注：上述水温指标可因气温状况不同而进行调整。如果水温低于 22 摄氏度且气温低于 15 摄氏度，则测量所得的水温数据应根据下表进行调整：

单位（°C）		气温										
		15	14	13	12	11	10	9	8	7	6	5
水温	22	18.5	18.0	17.5	17.0	16.5	16.0	15.5	15.0	14.5	14.0	取消
	21	18.0	17.5	17.0	16.5	16.0	15.5	15.0	14.5	14.0	13.5	取消
	20	17.5	17.0	16.5	16.0	15.5	15.0	14.5	14.0	13.5	13.0	取消
	19	17.0	16.5	16.0	15.5	15.0	14.5	14.0	13.5	13.0	12.5	取消
	18	16.5	16.0	15.5	15.0	14.5	14.0	13.5	13.0	12.5	12.0	取消
	17	16.0	15.5	15.0	14.5	14.0	13.5	13.0	12.5	12.0	取消	取消
	16	15.5	15.0	14.5	14.0	13.5	13.0	12.5	12.0	取消	取消	取消
	15	15.0	14.5	14.0	13.5	13.0	12.5	12.0	取消	取消	取消	取消
	14	14.0	14.0	13.5	13.0	12.5	12.0	取消	取消	取消	取消	取消
	13	13.0	13.0	13.0	12.5	12.0	取消	取消	取消	取消	取消	取消

b）如果受其他天气条件影响，如：强风、暴雨、温度变化及涌流变化等，国际铁联技术代表和医务代表可调整游泳比赛距离或规定使用防寒泳衣。最终决定由技术代表于比赛开始前 1 小时做出并向参赛运动员宣布。

c.) For aquathlon events (normally run-swim-run), the LOC should plan for a swim-run where the water temperature is expected to be below 22 °C. Where a run-swim-run aquathlon has been planned, but on competition day the water temperature is below 22 °C, the format will change to swim-run;

d.) Water temperature must be taken one hour prior to the start of the event on competition day. It must be taken at the middle of the course and in two other areas on the swim course, at a depth of 60 cm. The lowest measured temperature will be considered as the official water temperature.

4.5. Starting Position Selection: (Elite/U23/Junior/Youth athletes):

a.) Prior to the start of competition, athletes are lined up in the order of their start numbers, unless their positions have been reallocated after the Athletes' Briefing for a delayed start;

b.) The athletes go directly to their selected numbered position upon entering the pontoon and stay in that position behind the pre-start line until the start procedure. A selected position cannot be changed by any athlete during the Starting Position Selection process. An athlete cannot occupy more than one start position;

c.) Start Line Technical Officials note each athlete's race number and the starting position selected;

d.) Starting Position Selection ends when every athlete is in a starting position.

4.6. Start Procedure: (Elite/U23/Junior/Youth Athletes):

a.) After all athletes are in position (confirmed and noted by the Start Line Technical Officials) "On your marks!" is announced and the athletes step forward to the start line (without stepping on it);

b.) Any time after the announcement, the start signal will be given by blasting a horn. Athletes will move straight ahead towards the first buoy until they will reach the water.

c.) Technical Officials involved in the start procedure are:

(i) Two Start Technical Officials are standing next to each other in the middle of the start area behind the athletes:

- The first Start Technical Official is responsible for announcing "On your marks";
- The second Start Technical Official is responsible for giving the start signal.

(ii) Two False Start Technical Officials stand on both sides of the start area to have a clear view of the start:

- An air horn is used to provide a false start signal (several short horn blasts);
- A photo/video camera is used to identify early starters.

d.) False Start: In case of a false start (several athletes move forward before the start horn) the athletes must come back to their previously selected position. This will be controlled by the Start Line Technical Officials and the start procedure will begin again;

c）在游跑两项比赛中（通常为跑步—游泳—跑步），如果预期水温低于 22 摄氏度，当地组委会应该准备游泳—跑步的方案。如果跑步—游泳—跑步的方案已经设计好，但比赛日水温低于 22 摄氏度，比赛形式将改为游泳—跑步。

d）水温测量：水温测量必须在比赛当天比赛开始前一小时进行，在比赛路线的中央和另外两个位置、60 厘米水深处进行测量，取所测得的最低水温作为官方水温。

4.5 出发位置的选取（优秀组、U23 组、青年组和少年组）

a）比赛开始前，运动员按照比赛号码的顺序列队，除非运动员的出发排位在运动员技术会后被推迟出发。

b）运动员登上出发台后直接站到自己选取的出发位置上，并且一直保持在预出发线后，直至出发程序启动。运动员选取出发位置后不可更改。每名运动员不可占用两个或两个以上的出发位置。

c）出发技术官员负责记录每名运动员的比赛号码和所选取的出发位置。

d）所有运动员就位后，出发位置选取结束。

4.6 出发程序（优秀组、U23 组、青年组和少年组）

a）所有运动员就位后（出发线技术官员确认并记录后），发出口令“On your marks”（各就位），运动员上前一步至出发线（不能踩线）。

b）出发口令发出后，出发信号可在任意时刻发出，一般为喇叭声，听到出发信号后，运动员在入水前必须径直向第一浮漂移动。

c）技术官员参与出发程序：

（1） 2 名出发技术官员并肩站在运动员身后的出发区中间：

- 第一出发技术官员负责发出“On your marks”的口令。
- 第二出发技术官员负责发出出发信号。

（2） 2 名出发犯规技术官员站在出发区两侧，可以清晰地看到整个出发情况：

- 配备一个汽笛用于在出发犯规的情况下发出信号（连续几声短汽笛响）。
- 配备照相机或摄像机用于拍摄出发犯规情况。

d）出发犯规：在多名运动员抢跳（跑）的情况下，运动员必须回到先前选择的出发位置。出发线技术官员负责控制运动员，出发程序重新启动。

e.) Valid Start with Early Starters: In the case of an early start of a few athletes, the competition can continue, the False Start Technical Officials can decide that the start is valid. The early starters will receive a time penalty in Transition 1. In case of relay events, the time penalty has to be served by the first athlete of the team;

f.) The same procedure will apply for the start of any other multisport event starting with running with adaptations from swim start to run start.

4.7. Start procedure (Age Group/Paratriathlon athletes):

a.) Athletes are grouped at the pre start areas according to the assigned start wave;

b.) Athletes will be called to the start area and they will occupy the start positions according to the TOs instructions;

c.) After all athletes are in position "On your marks!" is announced;

d.) Any time after the announcement, the start signal will be given by blasting a horn. Athletes will move forward;

e.) False Start: In case of a false start (several athletes move forward before the start horn) the athletes must come back to their previously selected position. This will be controlled by the Start Line Technical Officials and the start procedure will begin again;

f.) Valid Start with Early Starters: In the case of an early start of a few athletes, the competition can continue, the False Start Technical Officials can decide that the start is valid. The early starters will receive a time penalty in Transition 1, according to the distance of the competition;

g.) The same procedure will apply for the start of any other multisport event starting with running with adaptations from swim start to run start;

h.) Athletes starting in any wave before the one that the athlete is assigned to, will be disqualified;

i.) Athletes who are late to the assigned wave will need the approval of the Start Technical Official. The athlete start time will be the start time of the assigned wave.

4.8. Start procedure (Interval Start System):

a.) Athletes are responsible for being at the start line on time;

b.) A video camera shall be used to record the entire start;

c.) The Start Technical Officials are responsible for synchronizing their own and the Timekeepers' watches;

d.) Start Technical Officials must provide all athletes with the opportunity to start at their correct times. An assistant responsible for recording the details for any violations at the start must be placed near the starter. The athletes' actual start time must be noted with both electric and hand timing, in case the Competition Jury decides his/her late start was due to force majeure;

e.) Athletes will be called to the start area and will occupy the start positions according to the TOs' instructions;

e）个别犯规但出发有效的情况：个别几名运动员抢跳（跑）的情况下，比赛可继续进行，出发犯规技术官员可认定出发有效。抢跳（跑）的运动员将在第一换项时接受时间处罚。在接力比赛中，上述时间处罚必须由队中第一名比赛运动员接受。

f）其他分项比赛也可在此程序基础上进行适当调整后运用于比赛出发。

4.7 出发程序（分龄组 / 伤残组运动员）

a）运动员根据出发时间表在出发准备区集结。

b）运动员将被召集到出发区域，根据技术官员的指示选取出发位置。

c）所有运动员就位后，发出口令"On your marks!"（各就位）。

d）口令发出后，出发信号可在任意时刻发出，一般为喇叭声，运动员听到出发信号后出发。

e）出发犯规：在出现出发犯规，多名运动员抢跳（跑）的情况下，运动员必须回到先前选择的出发位置。出发线技术官员负责控制运动员，出发程序重新启动。

f）个别犯规但出发有效的情况：个别几名运动员抢跳（跑）的情况下，比赛可继续进行，出发犯规技术官员可认定出发有效。抢跳（跑）的运动员将在第一换项时接受时间处罚，处罚时间根据比赛距离确定。

g）其他分项比赛也可在此程序基础上进行适当调整后运用于跑步出发。

h）运动员在其应出发时间前的任何组提前出发，将被取消资格。

i）运动员没有按照该组出发时间推后出发，须得到出发技术官员的批准。运动员的出发时间按照原定出发时间计算。

4.8 出发程序（间隔出发系统）

a）运动员有责任按时到达出发线。

b）应使用摄像机全程录制整个出发过程。

c）出发技术官员有责任保证出发时间与计时人员的时间同步。

d）出发技术官员必须保证所有运动员在正确的时间出发。发令员须配备出发助理以记录出发过程中的任何犯规行为。为了便于仲裁委员会确定运动员晚出发是否是由于不可抗力造成的，运动员的确定出发时间必须由手计时和电计时同时记录。

e）根据技术官员的指令，运动员将被召集到出发区域和指定的出发位置。

f.) Ten minutes before their start time, all the athletes should be ready at the start area;
g.) Five minutes before their start time, athletes will be asked to take their position at the start area;
h.) One minute before their start time, athletes will be asked to enter the water, or approach the start line;
i.) When all athletes are in position, the "start procedure " will be initiated. "On your marks!" will be announced;
j.) The start signal (horn blast) will be sounded at the exact start time of the wave;
k.) An athlete who is an "early starter" in a "valid start" will not be recalled to the start line;
l.) The early starters will receive a time penalty in Transition 1;
m.) An athlete who starts any time before the beginning of the "start procedure" or who starts in a wave they are not assigned to, will be disqualified;
n.) Athletes who are late to their assigned wave must get approval of the Start TO to start;
o.) The athlete start time will be the start time of the assigned wave, and no adjustment to his/her start time can be made.

4.9. Start Procedure (Rolling Start System)

a.) This start system is appropriate for long distance events with mass participation. It may be used in draft-illegal events, even if they are not long distance, or where the start conditions do not permit a wide space offering the athletes a safe start to the swim.
b.) This system is only applicable to Age Group competitions.
c.) There will not be a mass start.
d.) The Start Technical Official can interrupt the start procedure at any time.
e.) The Start Technical Official will determine the start time of any athlete in case of incidents at the start.
f.) If one athlete has two or more start times recorded, the first one will be the valid start time
g.) Athletes starting in any wave before the one that the athlete is assigned to, will be disqualified;
h.) Athletes who are late to the assigned wave will need the approval of the Start Technical Official. The athlete start time will be the start time of the first athlete in the assigned wave.

4.10. Equipment:

a.) Swim cap:
  (i) All athletes must wear the official event swim cap during the swim segment;
  (ii) Swim caps are provided by ITU or the Local Organising Committee;
  (iii) If an athlete chooses to wear two caps, the second swim cap must be unbranded and the official swim cap must be on the outside from the moment of the athletes' line-up procedure starts;

f）出发前 10 分钟，运动员须在出发区准备完毕。

g）出发前 5 分钟，运动员须在出发区就位。

h）出发前 1 分钟，运动员须入水或在出发线就位。

i）当运动员就位，出发程序将启动，并发出“On your marks!”（“各就位”）口令。

j）出发信号（鸣笛）将在本时段准确的出发时间响起。

k）“有效出发”中的抢跑（跳）者将不会被重新召回出发线。

l）抢跑（跳）者将在第一次换项时接受时间处罚。

m）如果运动员在出发程序开始前出发或在未指定的时段出发，将被取消比赛资格。

n）运动员晚于其被指定的时段出发必须得到出发技术官员的允许。

o）运动员的出发时间是指其被指定时段的出发时间，不得调整。

4.9 出发程序（滚动出发系统）

a）该出发系统主要用于参赛人数比较多的长距离比赛，也可用于不允许尾随的比赛（即使比赛并不是长距离比赛），或因出发场地空间较小运动员游泳时有安全隐患时。

b）该系统只能用于分龄组比赛。

c）出发形式不再是大规模集中出发。

d）出发技术官员可以在任何时候中断出发。

e）在出发时发生意外情况时，出发技术官员将决定运动员的出发时间。

f）如果任何运动员有两个或以上出发时间记录，第一个将被认定为有效时间。

g）运动员在其应出发时间前的任何组提前出发，将被取消资格。

h）运动员出发迟到需要得到出发技术官员的允许才能再出发。其出发时间为原出发组别第一名运动员的出发时间。

4.10 比赛装备

a）游泳帽

（1）运动员在游泳赛段必须佩戴正式游泳比赛的泳帽。

（2）泳帽由国际铁联或组委会提供。

（3）若运动员选择佩戴两个泳帽，第二个泳帽必须无商标，官方提供的泳帽须戴在最外面。

(iv) No sponsor logos are allowed on the official swim cap other than prescribed by ITU/ Local Organising Committee;
(v) Athletes may not alter the swim caps in any manner;
(vi) Failure to wear the official swim cap, or altering the official swim cap, may result in a penalty up to and including disqualification.

b.) Trisuits:
(i) Athletes must wear the approved trisuit for the non-wetsuit swims. If athletes choose to wear more than one trisuit, both have to comply with the specifications.
(ii) Trisuits must be 100% textile material, which is defined as materials consisting of natural and/or synthetic, individual and non-consolidated yarns used to constitute a fabric by weaving, knitting and/or braiding (this generally refers to suits made only from nylon or lycra that do not have any rubberized material such as polyurethane or neoprene);
(iii) When the use of wetsuits is forbidden, clothing covering any part of the arms and clothing covering any part of the legs below the knees is also forbidden with the exceptions outlined at 2.8.c.)(iii);
(iv) Trisuits must comply with the applicable Guidelines Regarding Authorised Identifications.

c.) Swimskins:
(i) Swimskins may be removed after the swim segment, except in the standard distance and shorter events.
(ii) Swimskins must be 100% textile material, which is defined as materials consisting of natural and/or synthetic, individual and non-consolidated yarns used to constitute a fabric by weaving, knitting and/or braiding (this generally refers to suits made only from nylon or lycra that do not have any rubberized material such as polyurethane or neoprene);
(iii) Swimskins must comply with the wetsuit section of the applicable Guidelines Regarding Authorised Identifications for middle and long distance events.

d.) Wetsuits:
(i) Wetsuits cannot exceed 5 mm thickness anywhere. If the wetsuit is made in two pieces, the combined thickness in the overlapping areas may not exceed the 5 mm thickness limit;
(ii) Propulsion devices that create an advantage for the athlete, or a risk to others, are forbidden;
(iii) The most external part of the wetsuits will fit to the athletes' body tightly while they are swimming;

（4） 除国际铁联和组委会官方指定之外，泳帽上不允许出现任何赞助商标志。

（5） 运动员不能以任何方式改动泳帽。

（6） 运动员不佩戴官方泳帽或随意改动官方泳帽将受到处罚，最严重的可被取消比赛资格。

b）比赛服

（1） 在不允许使用防寒泳衣的比赛中，运动员必须穿国际铁联认可的比赛服。如果运动员穿多套比赛服，则所有比赛服都必须符合规定。

（2） 比赛服必须为 100% 纺织料，即天然和 / 或合成、独立及非合并的纱线经过编织而成的纤维 [通常指不含类似聚亚安酯或氯丁（二烯）橡胶的尼龙或强力弹性纤维的衣料]。

（3） 在不允许使用防寒泳衣的比赛中，不允许比赛服覆盖肩膀以下的手臂部位和膝盖以下的小腿部位（2.8.c.）（iii）条款的情况除外）。

（4） 比赛服须遵守现行《国际铁联（比赛服）授权认证指南》。

c）泳 衣

（1） 除标准距离赛和更短距离比赛外，泳衣可在游泳比赛结束后脱换。

（2） 泳衣必须为 100% 纺织料，即天然和 / 或合成、独立及非合并的纱线经过编织而成的纤维 [通常指不含类似聚亚安酯或氯丁（二烯）橡胶的尼龙或强力弹性纤维的衣料]。

（3） 防寒泳衣须遵循现行《国际铁联（比赛服）授权认证指南》中关于中长距离赛事的防寒泳衣部分的规定。

d）防寒泳衣

（1） 防寒泳衣任何部位的厚度都不能超过 5 毫米。如果泳衣是由两部分组成，则结合处的厚度也不能超过 5 毫米的限制。

（2） 禁止使用可获利的推进设备，或可能伤害其他运动员的设备。

（3） 防寒泳衣的最外面部分在运动员游进过程中必须紧贴运动员身体。

(iv) A wetsuit may cover any part of the body except the face, hands and feet;
(v) There is no limitation regarding the length of the zipper.
(vi) Wetsuits must comply with the applicable Guidelines Regarding Authorised Identifications.
(vii) There is no limitation regarding the length of the zipper.
(viii) Wetsuits must comply with the applicable Guidelines Regarding Authorised Identifications.

e.) Illegal Equipment:
(i) Athletes must not use or wear:
- Artificial propulsion devices;
- Flotation devices;
- Gloves;
- Socks, except when use of wetsuits are mandatory;
- Wetsuits or any part of the wetsuits when they are forbidden;
- Non-certified swimsuits;
- Snorkels;
- Official race numbers (in non wetsuit swim only)
- Headphone(s), headset(s) or technical earplug(s), which are inserted or covering the ears, except ear protection plugs;
- Safety inflatable device (tube) which has been deployed. If deployed the athlete must retire from the race.

(ii) Any jewelry deemed to be a hazard to themselves or other athletes. (Athletes may be requested to remove any such items.)

5. CYCLING

5.1. General Rules:

a.) An athlete is not permitted to:
(i) Block other athletes;
(ii) Cycle with a bare torso;
(iii) Make forward progress without being in possession of the bike.
(iv) Use a different bike during the competition than the one checked-in.

b.) Dangerous Behaviour:
(i) Athletes must obey the specific traffic regulations for the event, unless a Technical Official advises otherwise;
(ii) Athletes leaving the field of play for safety reasons have to return to it without gaining any advantage. If an advantage is gained due to this action, the athlete will receive a time penalty to be served in the transition area for Age Groupers and at the run penalty box for everyone else.
(iii) Dangerous riding may result in a penalty. This includes but it not limited to passing another athlete on the wrong side.

（4） 防寒泳衣可以覆盖除脸部、手脚以外的任何部位。

（5） 对于拉链的长度没有限制。

（6） 防寒泳衣须遵循现行《国际铁联（比赛服）授权认证指南》。

e）非法装备

（1） 运动员不可以使用或穿着：

- 人造推进装置。
- 漂浮装置。
- 手套或袜子。
- 在规则不允许的情况下使用防寒泳衣或部分防寒泳衣。
- 未经认证的泳衣。
- 呼吸管。
- 官方号码布（仅在禁止使用防寒泳衣的游泳赛段）。
- 除护耳用具以外的，可置于耳道或覆盖耳朵的技术性耳塞、听筒、耳机。
- 可充气安全装置（管）。运动员一旦使用必须退出比赛。

（2） 任何可能对自己和他人造成伤害的珠宝首饰（运动员可能被要求移除）。

5. 自行车

5.1 总 则

a）运动员不允许：

（1） 阻挡其他运动员。

（2） 裸露躯干骑行。

（3） 脱离自行车进行比赛。

（4） 使用与检录时不同的自行车。

b）危险行为

（1） 除技术代表特别说明，运动员必须遵守具体的比赛交通规则。

（2） 如果运动员由于安全原因离开比赛场地，必须在没有获利的情况下回到比赛场地。如果因为这一行为而获利，则要接受时间处罚。分龄组运动员在转换区、其他运动员在跑步处罚区接受处罚。

（3） 危险骑行可能导致处罚。危险骑行行为包括但不限于在错误一侧超车。

5.2. Equipment:

a.) In general, UCI rules, as of January 1st of the current year, will apply during competition and also during familiarisation sessions and official training:

(i) UCI road race rules for draft-legal triathlon and duathlon competitions;

(ii) UCI time trial rules for draft-illegal triathlon and duathlon competitions;

(iii) UCI Mountain Bike (MTB) rules for winter triathlon, cross triathlon and cross duathlon competitions.

b.) The bicycle is a human powered vehicle with two wheels of equal diameter. The front wheel shall be steerable; the rear wheel shall be driven through a system comprising of pedals and a chain. Bicycles are referred to as bikes and will have the following characteristics in the following sections:

c.) For draft-legal competitions. Elite, U23, Junior and Youth:

(i) Frames:

- The frame of the bike shall be of a traditional pattern, i.e., built around a main triangle of three straight or tapered tubular elements, (which may be round, oval, flattened, teardrop shaped or otherwise in cross-section) such that the form of each element encloses a straight line. The elements of the frame shall be laid out such that the joining points shall follow the following pattern: the top tube connects the top of the head tube to the top of the seat tube; the seat tube (from which the seat post shall extend) shall connect to the bottom bracket shell; the down tube shall connect the bottom bracket shell to the bottom of the head tube. The rear triangles shall be formed by the chain stays, the seat stays and the seat tube with the seat stays anchored to the seat tube at points falling within the limits laid down for the slope of the top tube. The maximum height of the elements shall be 8 cm and the minimum thickness 2.5 cm. The minimum thickness shall be reduced to 1 cm for the chain stays and the seat stays. The minimum thickness of the elements of the front fork shall be 1 cm; these may be straight or curved. The maximum ratio of any two dimensions in a cross section of any tube is 1:3;
- The bike will be no more than 185 cm long, and 50 cm wide;
- The bike will measure between 24 cm and 30 cm from the ground to the center of the chain wheel axle;
- There will be no less than 54 cm and no more than 65 cm between a vertical line passing through the centre of the chain wheel axle and a vertical line through the centre of the front wheel axle;
- Fairings are prohibited. Any device, added or blended into the structure, that is destined to decrease, or which has the effect of decreasing, resistance to air penetration or artificially to accelerate propulsion, such as a protective screen, fuselage form fairing or the like, shall be prohibited;

5.2 比赛装备

a）总体上，国际自行车联盟规则（以比赛当年 1 月 1 日版本为准）适用于比赛、熟悉比赛路线训练和官方训练。

（1） 国际自行车联盟的公路赛规则适用于允许尾随的铁人三项和骑跑两项比赛。

（2） 国际自行车联盟的计时赛规则适用于不允许尾随的铁人三项和骑跑两项比赛。

（3） 国际自行车联盟的山地车规则适用于冬季铁人三项，越野铁人三项和越野骑跑两项比赛。

b）自行车由相同直径的两个轮子组成且人力驱动。前轮须可转向，后轮则通过脚蹬和车链组成的系统驱动。自行车必须具备以下特征：

c）允许尾随的比赛（优秀组、23 岁以下组、青年组和少年组运动员）：

（1） 车 架

- 自行车框架必须是传统样式的，即车架的主三角由三条边呈均匀或逐渐变细的管状（其横截面可以是圆形、椭圆形、扁平状、泪珠状等）构件以直线的形式包绕而成。车架的主三角三条边的结合处需满足以下要求：上管连接头管顶部和座管顶部，座管连接至底部的中轴套管，下管连接中轴套管和头管底部。车架的后三角由后下叉、后上叉和座管构成，其中后上叉应固定在座管顶部与上管的连接处。各个部件的厚度最大为 8 厘米，最小为 2.5 厘米，后下叉和后上叉的最小厚度为 1 厘米，前叉的最小厚度为 1 厘米，这些部件可以是直的或者弯曲的。任何两个部件连接处的截面尺寸的最大比例为 1:3。
- 自行车的长度不超过 185 厘米，宽度不超过 50 厘米。
- 从地面到牙盘轴心的距离应在 24 至 30 厘米之间。
- 牙盘轴心垂线与前轮轴心垂线的距离应不小于 54 厘米，不大于 65 厘米。
- 禁止使用整流罩。禁止使用任何附加或混合在主体结构上、用于减小阻力或增加推进力的装置，如保护遮板、整流装置或类似装置。

- Bikes provided with the UCI Road Race homologation label (Code RD) are always allowed in ITU draft legal events, even if they contravene any of the previous bullets in this 5.2 c) (i) insert.
- Bikes provided with the UCI Time Trial homologation label (Code TT) are forbidden unless they comply with the condition listed above.

(ii) Saddle position for U23 and Elite events:

- There will be a vertical line touching the front-most point of the saddle which will be no less than 5 cm for the men, and 2 cm for the women, behind a vertical line passing through the centre of the chain wheel axle, and an athlete must not have the capability of adjusting the saddle beyond these lines during competition.
- The expected ratio between E (Femur) and F (Tibia) is around 56% to 44%. Where the athlete's ratio is nearer to 50/50 an exception will be considered.
- Exceptions to this rule may be requested 30 days prior to the competition by the National Federation of the athlete to a panel composed of:
  - One person designated by ITU Technical Committee;
  - One person designated by ITU Coaches Committee;
  - One person designated by ITU Medical and Anti-Doping Commttee.

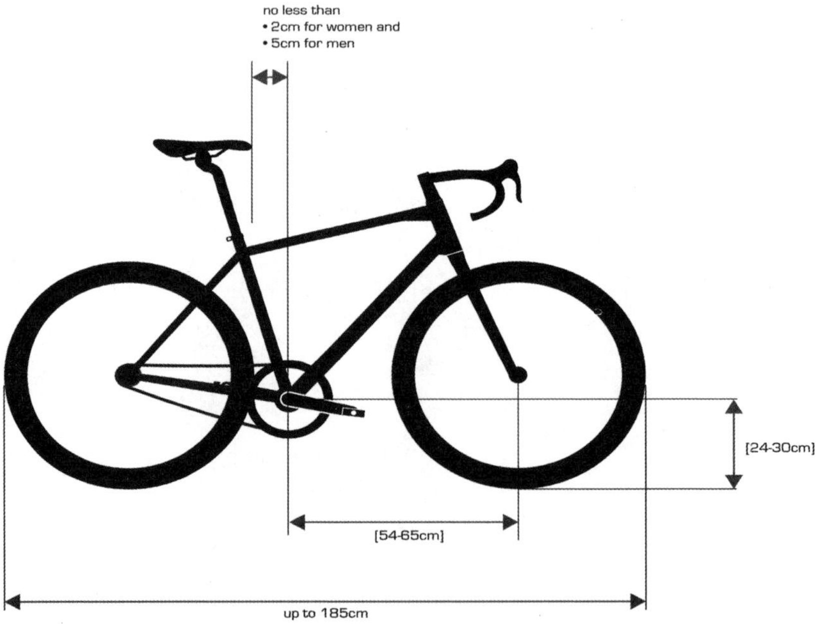

- 带有国际自行车联盟（UCI）公路赛认证标签（认证码 RD）的自行车，即便不符合 5.2 c（1）前 5 点的要求，也可在允许尾随的比赛中使用。
- 带有国际自行车联盟（UCI）计时赛认证标签（认证码 TT）的自行车禁止使用，除非其符合上述条件。

（2） 优秀组和 23 岁以下组的车座位置

- 车座最前端垂线须在牙盘轴心垂线之后，车座最前端垂线与牙盘轴心垂线的距离，男运动员的大于 5 厘米，女运动员的大于 2 厘米，并且运动员不能在比赛过程中调节车座超出上述距离范围。
- 估计普通人群股骨与胫骨的比例约为 65%:44% 左右，但运动员该比例大约是 50%:50%，因此需要考虑特殊情况。
- 对本规则例外情况的申请须在赛前 30 天由运动员所属国家会员协会向由以下成员构成的专家委员会提出：
  —国际铁联技术委员会指定的人选
  —国际铁联教练员委员会指定的人选
  —国际铁联医学和反兴奋剂委员会指定的人选

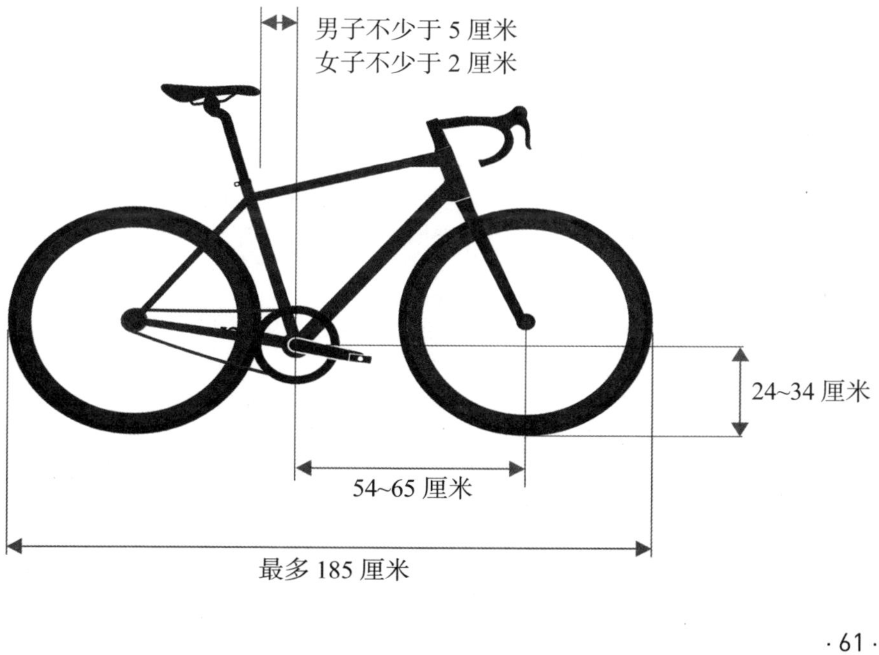

(iii) Non-traditional or unusual bikes:

- Non-traditional or unusual bikes or equipment shall be illegal unless details have been submitted to the ITU Technical Committee for approval at least 30 days before the Event.
- Provided all other criteria of the ITU rules are met then full details of the equipment including images must be supplied to the ITU Technical Committee. The procedure is outlined in Appendix P.
- A catalogue of all previously submitted equipment will be available on the website with confirmation as to whether it has been accepted or rejected. A form is available on the ITU website for athletes wishing to submit equipment for approval.

(iv) Logos and race number stickers:

- Only logos of bicycle related products may appear on the athlete's bicycle;
- Logos may not interfere with, or hinder the placement of, the bicycle race number on the bicycle frame;
- Bike race number stickers, provided by ITU or the Local Organising Committee, must be placed on the bike as instructed, without any alteration;

d.) For draft-illegal events, and Age Group draft-legal events:

(i) Frames:

- The bike will be no more than 185 cm long, and 50 cm wide;
- The bike will measure between 24 cm and 30 cm from the ground to the center of the chain wheel axle;
- There will be no less than 54 cm and no more than 65 cm between a vertical line passing through the center of the chain wheel axle and a vertical line through the center of the front wheel axle;
- The frame of the bike shall be of a traditional pattern, i.e., built around a closed frame of straight or tapered tubular elements (which may be round, oval, flattened, teardrop shaped or otherwise in cross-section). Bikes built around a diamond shape (no saddle down tube) or with a rear triangle which does not connect at the top of the down tube/top tube section are considered acceptable.
- Bikes provided with the UCI Time Trial homologation label (Code TT) are always allowed in ITU draft-illegal events, even if they contravene any of the previous bullets in this 5.2 d.) (i) insert.

(ii) Saddle-position:

- There will be a vertical line touching the front-most point of the saddle which will be no more than 5 cm in front of, and no more than 15 cm behind, a vertical line passing through the centre of the chain wheel axle, and an athlete must not have the capability of adjusting the saddle beyond these lines during competition;

（3） 非传统的或特异的自行车

- 除非自行车的详细资料在比赛前至少 30 天前提交国际铁联技术委员会审批，非传统或特异的自行车或装备都是违反比赛规则的。
- 如果该车符合国际铁联的规则的标准，包括自行车图片在内的所有的详细资料必须提供给国际铁联技术委员会。相关程序见附件 P。
- 所有曾提交的自行车资料及其被认定情况将公布在国际铁联网站上，运动员也可能在网站上下载装备审批申请表。

（4） 标识和比赛号码贴

- 只有与自行车相关的产品标识可以出现在运动员的自行车上。
- 标识不得阻碍或隐藏自行车框架上的自行车号码。
- 运动员必须按要求将国际铁联或当地组委会提供的自行车号码粘贴在自行车上，且不得做任何改动。

d）不允许尾随的比赛、分龄组允许尾随的比赛：

（1） 车 架

- 自行车的长度不超过 185 厘米，宽度不超过 50 厘米。
- 从地面到牙盘轴心的距离应在 24 至 30 厘米之间。
- 牙盘轴心垂线与前轮轴心垂线的距离应不小于 54 厘米，不大于 65 厘米。
- 自行车架必须是传统样式的，即由均匀或逐渐变细的管状构件（其横截面可以是圆形、椭圆形、扁平状、泪珠状等）构成的封闭结构。菱形车架结构的自行车（没有座管）或上管与下管顶部没有连接的后三角形车架结构自行车允许参赛。
- 带有国际自行车联盟（UCI）计时赛认证标签（认证码 TT）的自行车，即便不符合 5.2 d(1)前 4 点的要求，也可在不允许尾随的比赛中使用。

（2） 车座位置

- 车座最前端垂线与牙盘轴心垂线的距离，向前不能超过 5 厘米，向后不能超过 15 厘米，并且运动员不可在比赛过程中调节车座超出上述距离范围。

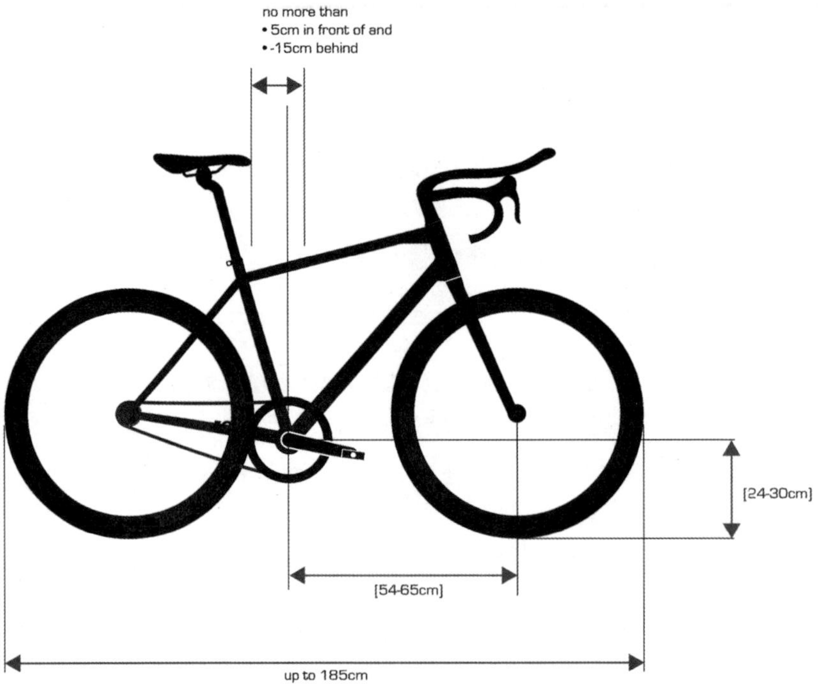

(iii) Non-traditional or unusual bikes:

- Non-traditional or unusual bikes or equipment shall be illegal unless details have been submitted to the ITU Technical Committee for approval at least 30 days before the Event. Provided all other criteria of the ITU rules are met then full details of the equipment including images must be supplied to the ITU Technical Committee. The procedure is outlined in Appendix P. A catalogue of all previously submitted equipment will be available on the website with confirmation as to whether it has been accepted or rejected. A form is available on the ITU website for athletes wishing to submit equipment for approval.

(iv) Logos and race number stickers:

- Only logos of bicycle related products may appear on the athlete's bicycle;
- Logos may not interfere with, or hinder the placement of, the bicycle race number on the bicycle frame;
- Bike race number stickers, provided by ITU or the Local Organising Committee, must be placed on the bike as instructed, without any alteration.

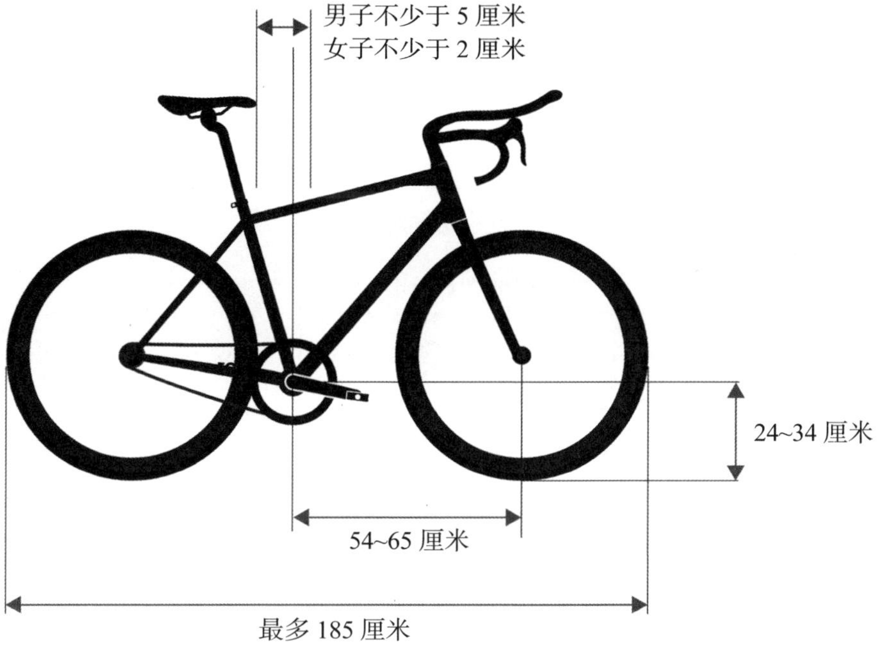

（3） 非传统的或特异的自行车

- 除非自行车的详细资料在比赛前至少 30 天前提交国际铁联技术委员会审批，非传统或特异的自行车或装备都是违反比赛规则的。如果该车符合国际铁联的规则的标准，包括自行车图片在内的所有的详细资料必须提供给国际铁联技术委员会。相关程序见附件 P。所有曾提交的自行车资料及其被认定情况将公布在国际铁联网站上，运动员也可能在网站上下载装备审批申请表。

（4） 标识和比赛号码贴

- 只有与自行车相关的产品标识可以出现在运动员的自行车上。
- 标识不得阻碍或隐藏自行车框架上的自行车号码。
- 运动员必须按要求将国际铁联或当地组委会提供的自行车号码粘贴在自行车上，且不得做任何改动。

e.) Wheels:

(i) No wheel may contain any mechanisms, which are capable of accelerating it;

(ii) Tubular tyres must be well glued, the levers of the quick releases must be closed tightly onto the hubs and wheels must be fixed properly onto the frame;

(iii) There must be a brake on each wheel;

(iv) Wheels can be replaced only at official wheel stations, where provided;

(v) Technical Officials at the wheel station will give the proper wheel to the athlete. The athlete is responsible for replacing the wheel in the forks. Wheels designated specifically for other athletes or teams cannot be used;

(vi) For Elite, U23, Junior and Youth draft-legal competitions, wheels are allowed to be used if they are included in the current UCI approved non-standard wheels lists. (Both list applicable, the one contains wheels approved prior 1st January 2016 and the other after this date.) Wheels not on this list must comply to the following criteria:

- A diameter between 70 cm maximum and 55 cm minimum, including the tyre;
- Both wheels must be of equal diameter;
- Wheels shall have at least 20 metal spokes;
- The maximum rim dimension will be 25 mm. on each side;
- The rim must be alloy;
- All components must be identifiable and commercially available.

(vii) For Age Group draft-legal competitions, wheels must have the following characteristics:

- Wheels shall have at least 12spokes;
- Disc wheels are not allowed.

(viii) For draft-illegal competitions, covers are allowed on the rear wheel. However, this provision may be changed by the Technical Delegate in the interest of safety, i.e. high-winds.

f.) Handlebars:

(i) For Elite, U23, Junior and Youth draft-legal competitions, the following handlebar rules will apply:

- Only traditional drop handlebars are permitted. The handlebars must be plugged;
- Clip-ons, including the bridge, must not exceed the foremost line of the brake levers;
- Clip-ons must have a solid factory bridge or be touching each other;
- Brake levers or gear levers must not be attached to the clip-ons The height difference between the highest point of the handlebar and the lowest inner part of the elbow rest cannot exceed 10 cm;

e）车 轮

（1） 车轮不可带有具备加速能力的机械装置。

（2） 管状轮胎胶合良好，碗组紧致，车轮正确安装固定在车架上。

（3） 每个车轮都必须有单独的刹车。

（4） 车轮只允许在官方的备用车轮站进行更换。

（5） 备用车轮站的技术官员将合适的车轮交给运动员。运动员自行负责更换。运动员不可使用其他运动员或参赛队的备用车轮。

（6） 对于优秀组、23 岁以下组、青少年组中允许尾随的比赛，如果在现行国际自行车联盟（UCI）批准的非标准车轮清单之列，均可以使用（2016 年 1 月 1 日以前或以后的批准的车轮清单均可）。不在车轮清单之列的车轮必须具备以下特征：

- 直径（包括车胎在内）介于 55 厘米至 70 厘米之间。
- 两个车轮的尺寸必须相同。
- 车轮至少有 20 根金属辐条。
- 每个轮圈最大宽度为 25 毫米。
- 轮圈的材质必须为合金。
- 所有的车轮组件必须为可识别品牌并可以在市场上买到的。

（7） 分龄组允许尾随的比赛中，车轮必须具有以下特征：

- 车轮必须有至少 12 根辐条；
- 禁止使用园盘轮。

（8） 对于不允许尾随的比赛，后轮允许覆盖。但技术代表可出于安全原因修改此项规则，如：强风天气。

f）车 把

（1） 对于优秀、23 岁以下、青年和少年组允许尾随的比赛，以下车把规则适用：

- 只允许使用传统的下弯式车把，车把端口必须封闭。
- 附加把，包括桥接装置，不得超过刹车把手的最前端。
- 附加把必须使用工厂出产的桥接装置连接，或相互接触。
- 刹车控制杆和变速控制杆不能安装在附加把上，附加把的最高点与肘垫内侧最低点之间的高度差不超过 10 厘米。

- Water bottles and water bottle holders may not be mounted onto the handlebars or clip-on.

(ii) For Age Group draft-legal competitions, the following handlebar rules will apply:

- Only traditional drop handlebars are permitted. The handlebars must be plugged;
- Clip-ons are not allowed.

(iii) For draft-illegal competitions, the following rules on handlebars apply:

- Only handlebars and clip-on bars not extending beyond the leading edge of the front wheel will be permitted. Clip-on bars in two pieces do not need to be bridged. All tube ends have to be plugged.

g.) Helmets:

(i) Helmets must be approved by a national accredited testing authority recognised by a National Federation affiliated with ITU;

(ii) Helmet must be used in all official activities when the athlete rides the bike: competition, familiarisation and training sessions;

(iii) An alteration to any part of the helmet, including the chin strap, or the omission of any part of the helmet, including an outer cloth cover, is prohibited;

- 车把或附加把上不得放置水瓶或水瓶架。

（2） 分龄组允许尾随的比赛中，以下车把规则适用：

- 只有传统下弯式的车把可以使用，车把末端必须封闭。
- 不允许使用附加把。

（3） 对于不允许尾随的比赛，车把必须符合以下规则：

- 车把和附加把不得超过前轮前沿。分为两部分的附加把不需连结在一起。所有的管状装置的末端均必须封闭。

g）头 盔

（1） 头盔须经过国际铁联会员协会认可的国家级检测机构的认可。

（2） 当运动员骑车参加任何官方活动时必须戴头盔：比赛、熟悉路线和培训会议。

（3） 不允许对头盔的任何部位进行改装，包括安全扣、外织物层，不能移除头盔的任何部分。

(iv) The helmet must be securely fastened and fit properly at all times and any garment worn underneath must not affect the fit when the athlete is in possession of the bike, which means from the time they remove their bike from the rack at the start of the bike leg, until after they have placed their bike on the rack at the finish of the bike leg;

(v) If an athlete moves the bike off the course for any reason, the athlete may not unfasten or remove the helmet until after he/she has moved outside the boundary of the bike course route and has dismounted the bike; and he/she must fasten the helmet securely on the head before returning onto the bike course or before remounting the bike;

(vi) Helmet race number stickers, provided by ITU or the Local Organising Committee, must be placed on the front and both sides of the helmet, without any alteration. No other stickers are allowed;

(vii) There must be a clearance around the official helmet number sticker of 1.5cm to ensure the number is clearly visible;

(viii) The helmet can be any colour or design.

h.) Platform Pedals:

(i) Platform pedals are allowed, provided a quick-release mechanism is fitted to ensure the release of the feet in case of a fall.

i.) Disc brakes:

Disc brakes are allowed.

j.) Illegal Equipment:

(i) Illegal equipment includes, but is not limited to:

- Headphone(s), headset(s), technical earplug(s) or smart helmets which are inserted or covering the ears;
- Glass containers;
- Mirrors;
- Bike or parts of the bike not complying with these rules;
- Uniform not complying with the applicable Guidelines Regarding Authorised Identifications.

k.) Any equipment or devices carried during the bike segment or added to the bike are subject to approval by the Head Referee before the competition, must be securly mounted, not endanger any athlete or give unfair advantage;

l.) For cameras and video cameras, in addition to requiring approval from the Head Referee, all the images and footage taken will be copied by ITU. The use of those images for commercial purpose is subject to approval by ITU.

（4） 运动员接触自行车的整个过程，即自运动员从车架上取下自行车，直到自行车比赛结束运动员将自行车放回车架上，都必须以安全合理的方式系紧头盔，且头盔下的穿戴物不得影响这种安全合理的方式的实现。

（5） 运动员由于任何原因需要离开赛道，必须在离开赛道并下车后方可解开头盔；在重新进入赛道或重新上车之前必须将头盔戴好并扣紧安全带。

（6） 由国际铁联或当地组委会提供的头盔贴必须贴于头盔的前面和两侧，不得做任何改动。不允许使用其他头盔贴。

（7） 必须保证官方头盔贴周围 1.5 厘米范围内整洁，以保证头盔号清晰可见。

（8） 头盔可以是任何颜色或设计。

h）卡式脚蹬

（1） 可以使用卡式脚蹬，但须确保运动员摔倒时脚可以快速脱离脚蹬。

i） 碟 刹

碟刹可以使用。

j） 违反规则的装备

（1） 违反规则的装备包括但不限于：

- 可置于耳道或覆盖耳朵的技术性耳塞、听筒、耳机、智能头盔。
- 玻璃制容器。
- 镜子。
- 不符合本规则的自行车或自行车的一部分。
- 不符合现行《授权认证指南》的比赛服。

k）自行车赛段运动员携带或者安装到自行车上的任何设备或装置，均须赛前取得裁判长的批准。必须安全地固定，不能对任何运动员形成危险或获得不公平利益。

l） 使用相机或摄像机除了须得到裁判长的批准以外，所有由此获得的图片和视频均须交国际铁联复制。若需将这些图片和视频用于商业用途，则须得到国际铁联执委会的批准。

5.3. Bike Check:

a.) A bike check may include all items listed in 5.2.

b.) A visual bike check will take place upon Check-in to the transition area before the competition. Technical Officials will check that bikes comply with the ITU Competition Rules;

c.) Athletes may request approval from the Head Referee after the Athletes' Briefing if their bike is legal;

d.) Each registered athlete may only check one bike into their transition;

e.) All athletes must rack their bike before Transition Area closes. Any athlete unable to do this must inform the Head Referee.

5.4. Overlapping:

a.) Elite, U23, Junior and Youth, athletes who have been lapped during the bike segment will be withdrawn from the competition by the Technical Officials. Technical Officials may anticipate this decision, for safety reasons, if the athlete is closer than 100 meters ahead from the leader and the Technical Official is totally sure that the overlapping will happen. This provision can be modified by the Technical Delegate, following the procedure outlined in 1.5.

5.5. Drafting:

a.) General Guidelines:

(i) There are two kinds of competitions, depending on the allowance of drafting:

- Draft-legal competitions;
- Draft-illegal competitions.

(ii) The competitions will be draft-legal or illegal according to this table:

	Junior and Youth	U23	Elite	Age Group	Paratriathlon
TRIATHLON					
Team Relay	Legal	Legal	Legal	/	/
Sprint Distance	Legal	Legal	Legal	Both options	Illegal
Standard Distance	/	Legal	Legal	Illegal	Illegal
Middle and Long Distance	/	/	Illegal	Illegal	Illegal
DUATHLON					
Team Relay	Legal	Legal	Legal	/	/
Sprint Distance	Legal	Legal	Legal	Both options	Illegal
Standard Distance		Legal	Legal	Illegal	Illegal
Middle and Long Distance	/	/	Illegal	Illegal	Illegal
AQUATHLON	/				
WINTER TRIATHLON (all distances)	Legal				
CROSS TRIATHLON AND DUATHLON (all distances)	Legal				
AQUABIKE	/	/	/	Illegal	/

5.3 验 车

a）自行车的验车内容包括 5.2 中所有条款。

b）自行车目测检查在赛前进入转换区时进行。技术官员将根据本规则进行检查。

c）为确保自行车符合规则，运动员必要时可在技术会上向裁判长申请对自行车进行检查，以便进行必要的调整。

d）一名运动员只能送检一辆自行车。

e）所有运动员必须在转换区关闭前将车放好，否则运动员必须报告裁判长。

5.4 套 圈

a）优秀组、23 岁以下组、青年组和少年组运动员在自行车赛段被套圈将由技术官员指令其退出比赛。出于安全的原因，如果领先运动员距离可能被套圈运动员不到 100 米而技术官员可以确认该运动员肯定会被套圈，技术官员可以提前执行退赛决定。技术代表有权根据本规则 1.5 的程序修改这条规则。

5.5 尾 随

a）总 则

（1） 根据是否允许尾随的规则，比赛分为两类：

- 允许尾随的比赛。
- 不允许尾随的比赛。

（2） 下表将比赛分为允许尾随和不允许尾随：

	少年组 青年组	23 岁 以下组	优秀组	分龄组	伤残运动员
铁人三项					
团体接力	允许尾随	允许尾随	允许尾随	/	/
短距离	允许尾随	允许尾随	允许尾随	不允许尾随	不允许尾随
标准距离	/	允许尾随	允许尾随	不允许尾随	不允许尾随
中、长距离	/	/	不允许尾随	不允许尾随	不允许尾随
骑跑两项					
团体接力	允许尾随	允许尾随	允许尾随	/	/
短距离	允许尾随	允许尾随	允许尾随	不允许尾随	不允许尾随
标准距离	/	允许尾随	允许尾随	不允许尾随	不允许尾随
中、长距离	/	/	不允许尾随	不允许尾随	不允许尾随
游跑两项	/				
冬季铁人三项（所有距离）	允许尾随				
越野铁人三项和骑跑两项（所有距离）	允许尾随				
游骑两项	/	/	/	不允许尾随	/

b.) Draft legal events:
  (i) It is forbidden to draft off a different gender athlete;
  (ii) It is forbidden to draft off an athlete being in a different lap;
  (iii) It is forbidden to draft off a motorbike or vehicle.

c.) Draft-Illegal events:
  (i) It is forbidden to draft off another athlete or motor vehicle. Athletes must reject attempts by others to draft;
  (ii) An athlete is entitled to any position on the course, provided they get to that position first and without contacting others. When taking a position, an athlete must allow reasonable space for others to make normal movements without making contact. Adequate space must be available before passing;
  (iii) An athlete who approaches from any position to take advantage of the draft, bears responsibility for avoiding the draft;
  (iv) To draft is to enter the bicycle or vehicle drafting zone:
    - Middle and long distance draft zone: the bicycle draft zone will be 12 meters long measured from the leading edge of the front wheel. An athlete may enter the draft zone of another athlete, but must be seen to be progressing through that zone. A maximum of 25 seconds will be allowed to pass through the zone of another athlete;
    - Standard and shorter distance events bicycle draft zone: the bicycle draft zone will be 10 meters long measured from the leading edge of the front wheel. An athlete may enter the draft zone of another athlete, but must be seen to be progressing through that zone. A maximum of 20 seconds will be allowed to pass through the zone of another athlete;
    - Motorbike draft zone: the draft zone behind a motorbike will be 12 meters long. This applies also for draft legal events;
    - Vehicle draft zone: The draft zone behind a vehicle will be 35 meters long and applies to every vehicle on the bike segment. This applies also for draft legal events.
  (v) Entry into the bicycle drafting zone: An athlete may enter a bike draft zone in the following circumstances:
    - If the athlete enters the draft zone, and progresses through it within the allotted time in the overtaking manoeuvre;
    - For safety reasons;
    - 100 meters before and after an aid station or transition area;
    - At an acute turn;
    - If the Technical Delegate excludes a section of the course because of narrow lanes, construction, detours, or for other safety reasons.

b）允许尾随的比赛中：

（1） 不同性别的运动员不允许尾随。

（2） 不允许尾随不同圈的运动员。

（3） 不允许尾随摩托车或机动车。

c）不允许尾随的比赛中：

（1） 禁止尾随其他运动员或机动车，运动员须拒绝其他运动员的尾随企图。

（2） 运动员有权在首先进入、并不与其他运动员发生身体接触的条件下，进入比赛路线上的任何一个位置。当进入一个新位置的时候，运动员必须为其他运动员的正常行进留出合理的空间。超车时应有充分的空间。

（3） 处于其他运动员尾随区的运动员有义务避免尾随的发生。

（4） 运动员进入其他比赛运动员自行车尾随区或机动车尾随区，视为尾随：

- 中、长距离比赛自行车尾随区：自行车尾随区从运动员前轮边缘起向后12米的距离。运动员可以进入另一名运动员的尾随区，但必须是明显在超越该名运动员。穿越其他运动员尾随区的时间限制为25秒。
- 标准距离和短距离比赛自行车尾随区：自行车尾随区从运动员前轮边缘起向后10米的距离。运动员可以进入另一名运动员的尾随区，但必须是明显在超越该名运动员。穿越其他运动员尾随区的时间限制为20秒。
- 摩托车尾随区：摩托车尾随区为摩托车后12米长的区域。此规则适用于所有允许尾随的项目。
- 机动车尾随区：机动车尾随区为机动车后35米长的区域，此规则适用于自行车赛段所有机动车，也适用于所有允许尾随的项目。

（5） 可以进入自行车尾随区的特殊情况：运动员可以在下列情况下进入另外一名运动员的尾随区：

- 运动员超车时进入尾随区，并在时限内穿越尾随区。
- 出于安全的原因。
- 饮水站或转换区前后100米。
- 在急转弯处。
- 技术代表特别指定的部分路线区域：如窄道、施工、绕道或出于其他安全原因。

(vi) Overtaking:
- An athlete is passed when another athlete's front wheel is ahead of theirs;
- An overtaken athlete must drop out of the draft zone of the passing athlete by continuously make rearward progress out of the draft zone of the passing athlete. Re-passing by an overtaken athlete prior to dropping out of the draft zone will result in a drafting violation;
- Overtaken athletes who remain within the draft zone of the passing athlete for more than the allotted time will be given a drafting violation;
- Athletes must keep to the side of the course and not create a blocking incident. Blocking is where an athlete who is behind cannot pass due to the leading athlete being poorly placed on the course;
- The Technical Delegate will instruct the athletes during the briefing on which side they must pass another athlete when mounted on their bicycle.

(vii) See the diagrams below for events where right hand side road rules apply.

Standard and shorter distances: 10m
Middle and longer distances: 12m

5.6. Penalties for drafting:

a.) It is forbidden to draft in a competition declared as draft-illegal;

b.) Technical Officials will notify the athletes who draft they are subject to a time penalty. This notification must be clear and unambiguous;

c.) The athlete sanctioned has to stop in the next penalty box and must stay there for a specific time depending on the competition distance. One minute for the sprint distance, two minutes for standard distance and five minutes for middle and long distance;

d.) It is the athlete's responsibility to stop in the next penalty box. Failing to stop will result in a disqualification;

e.) A second drafting offence will lead to a disqualification in standard distance events or shorter;

f.) The third drafting offence will lead to disqualification for middle and long distance events.

g.) Drafting violations cannot be appealed.

（6） 超 越

- 运动员的前轮被其他运动员的前轮超过时，此名运动员即被超越。
- 一旦被超越，被超越运动员必须逐渐退出领先运动员的尾随区。如被超越的运动员在未退出尾随区时就再次加速超越，将导致尾随犯规。
- 如被超越的运动员在规定时间内仍处于超越运动员的尾随区中，将导致尾随犯规。
- 运动员必须保持在比赛路线的一侧，不可制造阻挡的局面。阻挡是指后方的运动员由于前方运动员在赛道上处于不恰当的位置而无法超越的情况。
- 技术代表应在技术会上向运动员说明应从哪一侧超越其他运动员。

（7） 下图说明的情况适用于“右上行”交通规则。

5.6 对尾随的处罚

a） 在不允许尾随的比赛中禁止尾随。

b） 对于违规尾随的运动员，技术官员将清晰、明确地通知其接受时间处罚。

c） 接到处罚通知的运动员须在下一个处罚区停下，并根据不同的比赛距离接受一定时间的处罚：短距离 1 分钟，标准距离 2 分钟，中、长距离 5 分钟。

d） 运动员有义务在下一个处罚区停止比赛并接受处罚，否则将被取消比赛资格。

e） 在标准距离和短距离比赛中，第 2 次尾随犯规将被取消比赛资格。

f） 在中、长距离比赛中，第 3 次尾随犯规将被取消比赛资格。

g) 尾随犯规不可申诉。

5.7. Blocking:

a.) Athletes must keep to the side of the course and not create a hazard by blocking other athletes on the course. Blocking is where an athlete who is behind an athlete cannot pass due to the leading athlete being poorly placed on the course. Athletes blocking will receive a yellow card to be served at the next bike penalty box.

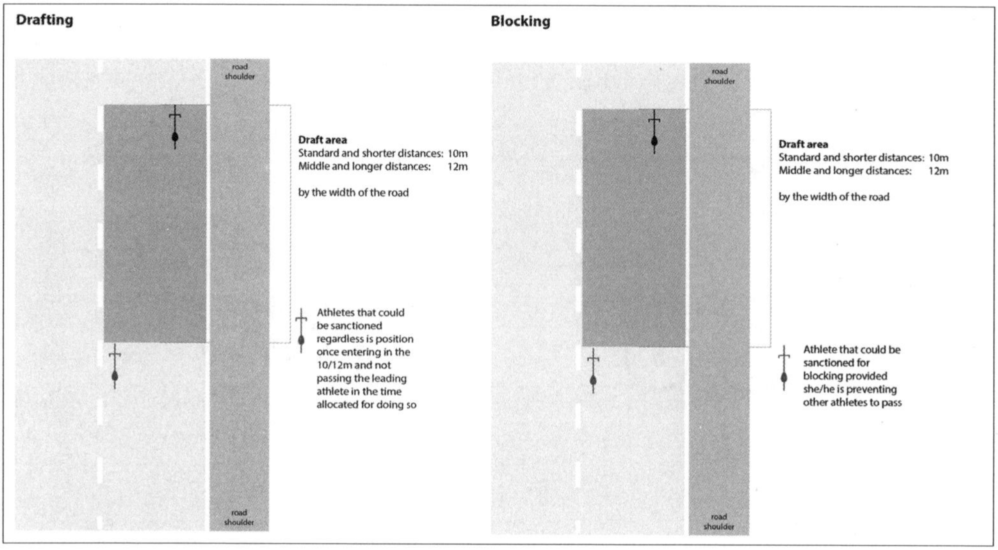

6. RUNNING

6.1. General Rules:

a.) The athletes will:

(i) Run or walk;

(ii) Wear the official race number (applicable always in the Age Group events. For other events, the Technical Delegate can make it mandatory and athletes will be informed in the race briefing);

(iii) Not crawl;

(iv) Not run with a bare torso;

(v) Not run with a bike helmet on;

(vi) Not use posts, trees or other fixed elements to assist manouvering curves;

(vii) Not be accompanied by any non-competing athletes, team members, team managers or other pacemakers on the course or alongside the course;

(viii) Not run together and/or take pace from other athlete/s who is/are one or more laps ahead (Applicable only to Elite, U23, Junior, Youth athletes and Paratriathletes).

5.7 阻 挡

a）运动员必须靠边行进，且不能阻挡其他运动员，以避免危险的情形。当领先运动员由于行进位置不当使其后的运动员无法通过即形成阻挡。运动员阻挡将在下一个自行车处罚区受到黄牌处罚。

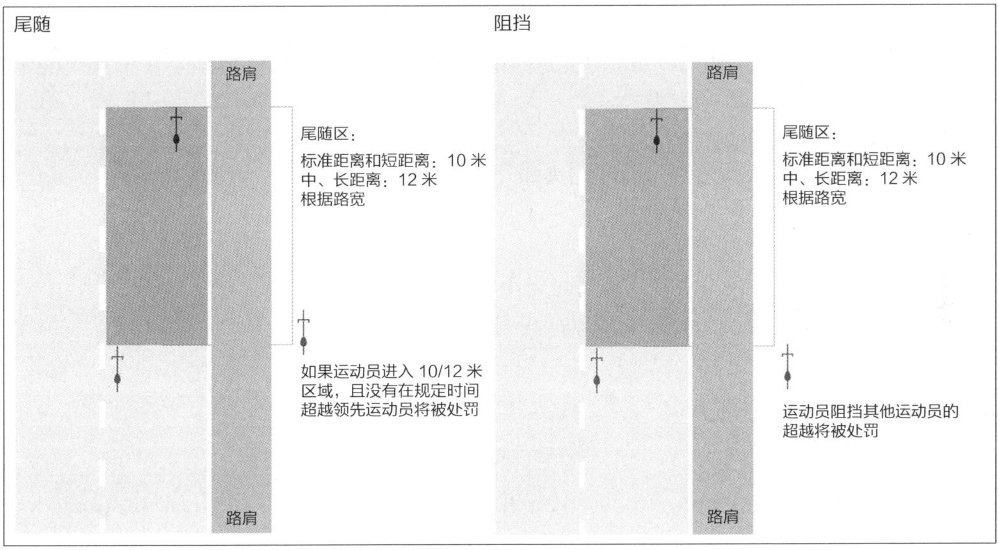

6. 跑 步

6.1 总 则

a）运动员：

（1） 可以跑或走。

（2） 佩戴号码布（适用于分龄组比赛，其他比赛中技术代表有权决定是否必须佩戴号码布，并在技术会上通知运动员）。

（3） 不可以爬行。

（4） 不可以裸体跑。

（5） 不可以戴头盔跑。

（6） 不可以借助杆、树或者其他固定物体协助转弯。

（7） 不可以由不参赛运动员、队友、领队或其他领跑人员在赛道上或赛道边上伴随跑。

（8） 不可以与其他领先一圈或多圈的运动员一起和 / 或同步调跑步（仅适用于优秀组、U23 组、青年组、少年组和伤残组运动员）。

6.2. Finish Definition:

a.) An athlete will be judged as finished, the moment any part of the torso crosses a vertical line extending from the leading edge of the finish line.

6.3. Safety Guidelines:

a.) The responsibility of remaining on the course rests with the athlete. Any athlete, who appears to Technical Officials or Medical personel as presenting a danger to themselves or others, may be removed from the competition;

b.) Athletes can't be accompanied by any non-competing person in the finish chute.

6.4. Illegal Equipment:

a.) Headphone(s), headset(s) or technical earplug(s), which are inserted or covering the ears;

b.) Glass containers;

c.) Uniform not complying with the ITU Guidelines Regarding Authorised Identification.

7. TRANSITION AREA

7.1. General Rules:

a.) All athletes must have their helmet securely fastened from the time they remove their bike from the rack before the start of the bike leg, until after they have placed their bike on the rack after the finish of the bike leg;

b.) Athletes must use only their designated bike rack and must rack their bike:

(i) For a traditional bike rack, the bike must be racked as follows:

- For the first transition: in an upright position with the front of the saddle hooked over the horizontal bar so the front wheel is pointing to the middle of the transition lane. Technical Officials may apply exceptions;
- For the second transition: In any direction, with both sides of the handlebar, both brake levers or the saddle within 0.5 m of the rack number or name plate. The bike must be racked in a way that does not block or interfere with the progress of another athlete.

(ii) In case of an individual bike rack, the bike must be racked in the first transition by the rear wheel and in the second transition by either of the wheels.

6.2 到达终点的定义

a）运动员躯干的任何部分穿过终点线前沿垂直线时，即被认为到达终点。

6.3 安全规则

a）能否在赛道上继续比赛取决于运动员。任何被技术官员或医务人员认为对其自身或他人构成危险的运动员将被停止比赛。

b) 在终点冲刺通道，运动员不能由非参赛运动员陪跑。

6.4 不符合比赛规则的装备

a）可置于耳道或覆盖耳朵的技术性耳塞、听筒、耳机。

b）玻璃制容器。

c）不符合国际铁联《授权认证指南》的比赛服。

7. 转换区

7.1 总 则

a）运动员接触自行车的整个过程都必须戴好头盔。即，从自行车比赛开始运动员从车架上取下自行车，直到自行车比赛结束运动员将自行车放回车架上。

b）运动员必须使用指定的车架位置，并将自行车放上车架：

（1） 如果是传统车架，自行车必须按照如下要求放置：

- 第一换项：自行车须直立放置，车座悬挂车架上，自行车前轮朝向转换区中央通道。技术官员可以申请例外情况。
- 第二换项：在任何方向上，双侧车把、刹车手把或车座须距离车架号码或信息牌 0.5 米以内。自行车的放置不能阻挡或妨碍其他运动员的比赛。

（2） 如果使用独立的自行车架，则第一换项须架起后轮，第二次换项可架起任意车轮。

c.) Athletes must place within 0.5m of the bin all equipment to be used at a later stage in the event. If a bin is not provided, the 0.5m will be measured from the point on the ground immediately below the rack number or name plate. The bin, if provided, must be within 0.5m from the rack number or name plate. All equipment already used must be deposited in the bin, exceptions are the bike shoes, which may remain fixed on the pedals. A piece of equipment is considered deposited in the bin when one part of the equipment is inside the bin. Only equipment to be used during the competition can be left in transition. All other belongings and equipment are to be removed before competition start;

d.) If an athlete wishes to use the same shoes in a duathlon for the second run these do not have to be placed in the bin in transition one, however, only one pair of running shoes may be on the floor at any time during the competition. Running shoes must be located within 0.5m of the athlete's bin (rack number/name plate).

e.) Bike shoes, glasses, helmet, and other bike equipment can be placed on the bike in Transition 1;

f.) Athletes must not impede the progress of other athletes in the transition area;

g.) Athletes must not interfere with another athlete's equipment in the transition area;

h.) Cycling is not permitted inside the transition area, except during the cycling segment. Mount and dismount lines are part of the transition area;

i.) Athletes must mount their bicycles after the mount line by having one complete foot contact with the ground after the mount line.

j.) Athletes must dismount their bicycles before the dismount line by having one complete foot contact with the ground before the dismount line.

k.) While in the transition area (before the mount line and after the dismount line) the bike can be pushed only by the athlete's hands.

l.) If during the mount or dismount manoeuvre, the athlete loses their shoe(s) or other equipment, they will be collected by the Technical Officials and no penalty will be applied.

m.) Nudity or indecent exposure is forbidden;

n.) Athetes can not stop in the flow zones of the transition area;

o.) Marking positions in the transition area is forbidden. Marks, towels and objects used for marking purposes will be removed and the athletes will not be notified;

p.) The helmet strap must remain unfastened in the transition area while the athlete is completing the first segment.

c）运动员必须把后续赛段需要使用的所有比赛装备放置在距离物品盒 0.5 米之内的地方。如果没有提供物品盒，上述装备需放置在距离车架号码或信息牌中心投影点 0.5 米之内。如果提供物品盒，则物品盒须放置在距离车架号码或信息牌 0.5 米之内。所有使用过的装备必须放在物品盒内。只要某一比赛装备的一部分放在物品盒内，这件装备就被认定为放在物品盒内。只有在比赛中需要用到的装备方可放置在转换区内，其他所有物品和装备须于比赛开始前转移出转换区。

d）在骑跑两项比赛中，如果运动员在第二个跑步赛段使用同一双鞋，他们在第一换项时就可以将鞋不放在物品盒里，但是，比赛期间盒外地面只能有一双鞋。跑步鞋必须放置在离运动员物品盒（车架号或姓名牌）0.5 米的范围内。

e）骑行鞋、眼镜、头盔以及其他的自行车装备可以放在自行车上。

f）运动员在转换区内不可阻止其他运动员的比赛。

g）运动员在转换区内不可动用其他运动员的比赛装备。

h）除自行车赛段，在转换区内不允许骑行。上车线和下车线是转换区的一部分。

i）运动员必须在规定的上车线之后上车且有一只脚在上车线后与地面接触一次。

j）在下车线之前下车，且一只脚在下车线前与地面接触一次。

k）在转换区内（上车线之前和下车线之后），运动员必须用手推行自行车。

l）如果运动员在上车与下车的过程中有鞋或其他装备掉落的情况，技术官员应该记录但不处罚。

m）不允许裸体和下流暴露行为。

n）运动员不可在转换区通道内停留。

o）禁止在转换区内做标记。标记、毛巾或用作标记目的物品将被移除，并不会通知运动员本人。

p）在运动员完成第一赛段比赛时，在转换区内头盔的搭扣应为打开状态。

8. COMPETITION CATEGORIES

8.1. World Championships:

a.) ITU may organise World Championships in the distances and categories shown in this chart:

	Elite	U23	Junior	Age Group	Paratriathlon
TRIATHLON					
Team Relay	Yes	Yes (U23/Jr combined)		/	/
Sprint Distance	Yes	Yes	Yes	Yes	Yes
Standard Distance	Yes	Yes	/	Yes	Yes
Middle Distance	Yes	/	/	Yes	Yes
Long Distance	Yes	/	/	Yes	Yes
DUATHLON					
Team Relay	Yes	/	Yes	/	/
Sprint Distance	Yes	Yes	Yes	Yes	Yes
Standard Distance	Yes	Yes	/	Yes	Yes
Middle Distance	Yes	/	/	Yes	Yes
Long Distance	Yes	/	/	Yes	Yes
AQUATHLON					
Standard Distance	Yes	Yes	Yes	Yes	Yes
Long Distance	Yes	/		Yes	Yes
WINTER TRIATHLON					
Team Relay	Yes	/	Yes	/	/
Sprint Distance	/	/	Yes	Yes	Yes
Standard Distance	Yes	Yes	/	/	/
CROSS TRIATHLON AND DUATHLON					
Team Relay	Yes	/	Yes	/	/
Sprint Distance	/	/	Yes	/	Yes
Standard Distance	Yes	Yes	/	Yes	Yes
AQUABIKE					
Standard Distance	/	/	/	Yes	/
Long Distance	/	/	/	Yes	/

b.) National Federations and Continental Confederations should include each of these categories in their National and Continental Championships.

8. 比赛类别

8.1 世界锦标赛

a）国际铁联可以按照以下表格中所列的距离和类别组织世界锦标赛：

	优秀组	23 岁以下组	青年组	分龄组	伤残组
铁人三项					
团体接力	有	有（23 岁以下组与青年组整合）		/	/
短距离	有	有	有	有	有
标准距离	有	有	/	有	有
中、长距离	有	/	/	有	有
骑跑两项					
团体接力	有	/	有	/	/
短距离	有	有	有	有	有
标准距离	有	有	/	有	有
长距离	有	/	/	有	有
游跑两项					
标准距离	有	有	有	有	有
长距离	有	/	/	有	有
冬季铁人三项					
团体接力	有	/	有	/	/
短距离	/	/	有	有	有
标准距离	有	有	/	/	/
越野铁人三项和骑跑两项					
团体接力	有	/	有	/	/
短距离	/	/	有	/	有
标准距离	有	有	/	有	有
游骑两项					
标准距离	/	/	/	有	/
长距离	/	/	/	有	/

b）各会员协会与洲际联合会应在其全国锦标赛和洲际锦标赛上设置上述类别。

9. PRIZES AND AWARDS

9.1. Prize Money:

a.) General Rules:

(i) Prize money for the ITU Events shall be distributed equally between men and women in both amount and depth, according to the ITU Prize Money Percentage Breakdown, as outlined in Appendix H.

(ii) Prize money will be paid regardless of the points cut-off percentage time of the winner.

9.2. Awards:

a.) Athletes or team members who place first, second or third at any event will be awarded an official podium medal (gold, silver, bronze);

b.) In addition, teams may receive a medal and/or trophy for first, second and third positions.

9. 奖 励

9.1 奖 金

a）总 则

（1） 国际铁联比赛的奖金应按照国际铁联奖金分配表（见附件 H）等额、等范围分配给男子和女子运动员。

（2） 奖金的发放不按照优胜者成绩的比例设限。

9.2 奖牌和奖杯

a） 所有国际铁联比赛中取得前 3 名的运动员或团队将在官方正式颁奖台获颁奖牌（金牌、银牌和铜牌）。

b） 此外，获得前 3 名的团体将获得奖牌和 / 或奖杯。

9.3. Prizes, Points and Awards in combined events/categories:

a.) In case of events which take place together or different categories competing together in the same wave, the awards, prize money and points will be distributed as follows:

Events taking place together:	Awards (medals) to:	Prize money to:	Points to:
Elite and U23	- Elite awards for all -U23 awards for U23	- Overall	- Overall
Elite, U23 and Junior	- Elite awards for all -U23 awards for U23 -Junior awards for Junior	- Overall	- Overall
U23 and Junior	-U23 awards for U23 -Junior awards for Junior	- Overall	- Overall
All categories	- Elite awards for all -Categories awards per categories	- Overall	- Overall
Triathlon Continental Championships with athletes from other continents	-Award for the athletes from the continent	-All are eligible	-Athletes from the continent
Multisport Continental Championships with athletes from other continents	-Award for the athletes from the continent	-All are eligible	- Overall
Continental Cups	- Overall	- Overall	- ITU points: overall -Continental points: Athletes from the continent

b.) Athletes from other continents can participate in Continental Championships provided that the competition is not full with the athletes from the host continent. In this case, points and medals are going to athletes from the host continent, but prize money is distributed to the athletes in the overall results. The exceptions to this paragraph are the Duathlon and Long distance Triathlon Continental Championships that are part of the World Series as well: in this case points are distributed to the overall results.

9.3 混合赛事的奖金、积分和奖品

a）同时举行的赛事或不同类别赛事同时出发的情况下，奖品、奖金和积分分配办法如下：

同场举行的赛事	奖品（奖牌）	奖金	积分
优秀组和 U23 组	优秀组发给所有运动员 U23 组发给 U23 组运动员	总排名	总排名
优秀组、U23 组和青年组	优秀组发给所有运动员 U23 组发给 U23 组运动员 青年组发给青年组运动员	总排名	总排名
U23 组和青年组	U23 组发给所有运动员 青年组发给青年组运动员	总排名	总排名
所有组别	优秀组发给所有运动员 其他组别发给本组运动员	总排名	总排名
有其他洲的运动员参赛的铁人三项洲际锦标赛	本大洲的运动员	所有符合条件的运动员	本大洲的运动员
有来自其他洲的运动员参赛的其他分项洲际锦标赛	本大洲的运动员	所有符合条件的运动员	总排名
洲际杯赛	总排名	总排名	国际铁联积分：总排名 洲际排名积分： 本大洲的运动员

b）如果东道主大洲的运动员人数不足以填满出发名单，其他大洲的运动员也可以参加该洲际锦标赛。在这种情况下，积分和奖牌由东道主大洲的运动员获得，但奖金将依据总排名进行发放。例外情况是被同时列为世界系列赛的骑跑两项和长距离铁人三项洲际锦标赛，这种情况下的积分将依据总排名来计算。

10. EVENTS

10.1. Wave starts:

a.) To ensure the safety of the athletes, there are limits on the quantity of athletes starting at the same time. The Technical Delegate may apply lower limits than the indicated, according to the event conditions:

	WTS WPS	WTS Grand Final	World Cup	Other Standard and shorter distances triathlons	Middle and Long Distance Triathlon. All events (*)	Cross Triathlon. All events	DuathlonAll events
Elite	55	65	65	70	100	100	100
U23	n/a	70	n/a	70	n/a	100	100
Junior	n/a	70	n/a	70	n/a	100	100
Youth	n/a	n/a	n/a	70	n/a	n/a	n/a
Semi-final/ Final (any category)	90	n/a	90	90	n/a	n/a	n/a
Paratriathlon	70	110	70	80	80	80	80
AG	n/a	200	n/a	200	500	500	500

(*) Long distance triathlon may have larger start groups if they are in water start events and after Technical Delegate approval.

b.) Athletes from the same age group can be divided in two or more wave starts provided:

(i) Both/all waves will have the similar number of athletes assigned;

(ii) Athletes from the same National Federation will be split in all groups randomly, assigning the similar number to each of the waves;

(iii) National Federations with only one athlete will be entered to one or the other wave, in order to keep the numbers balanced. The same principle will apply to the excess resulting from National Federations with odd number of athletes;

(iv) The champion will be the athlete with quickest time, no matter in which wave he/she is starting in;

(v) The result list of the Age Groups affected will contain the athletes of both waves sorted by times;

(vi) The waves containing athletes from the same age group will be scheduled one immediately after the other;

(vii) These waves will not include athletes from a different Age Group.

10.2. Swim:

a.) The Technical Delegate may modify the distance of the swim segment or even cancel the swim, depending on the speed of the current.

10. 赛 事

10.1 出发分组

a）为确保运动员的安全，同一时间开始比赛的运动员人数受以下限制。技术代表可以根据比赛条件确定比该标准更低的出发人数限制：

	世界系列赛（WTS）/ 世界伤残人系列赛（WPS）	世界系列赛（WTS）总决赛	世界杯（World Cup）	其他标准 / 短距离铁人三项比赛	中 / 长距离铁人三项比赛（*）	越野铁人三项比赛	骑跑两项比赛
优秀组	55	65	65	70	100	100	100
23 岁以下组	n/a	70	n/a	70	n/a	100	100
青年组	n/a	70	n/a	70	n/a	100	100
少年组	n/a	n/a	n/a	70	n/a	n/a	n/a
半决赛 / 决赛（任何类别）	90	n/a	90	90	n/a	n/a	n/a
伤残组	70	100	70	80	80	80	80
分龄组	n/a	200	n/a	200	500	500	500

（）如果在水中出发且得到技术代表的允许，长距离铁人三项出发人数可以更多。*

b）同一年龄组的运动员可以分为两组或以上出发：

（1） 每组运动员数量相同。

（2） 来自同一会员协会的运动员将被随机分到两组，每组的运动员数量相等。

（3） 为保持每组人数平衡，会员协会仅有一名运动员参赛的将被分到任意组。同样的规则也运用在拥有奇数数量运动员的协会中。

（4） 无论在哪一组出发，完成时间最短的运动员将成为冠军。

（5） 分在不同组的同一年龄组运动员的成绩编排在一起。

（6） 同一年龄组的出发时间相邻安排。

（7） 不同年龄组的运动员不安排在一组比赛。

10.2 游 泳

a）技术代表可根据水流速度修改游泳距离甚至有权取消游泳比赛。

b.) Water quality:

(i) Samples of the water collected from three different locations on the swim course will be separately analysed and the poorest results will determine if the swim can take place. The swim will be allowed if the following values are below the level of tolerance in the different types of water:

- Sea and transition water:
  - PH between 6 and 9;
  - Entero-cocci not more than 100 per 100 ml (ufc/100ml);
  - Escherichiacoli E. Coli not more than 250 per 100 ml (ufc/100ml);
  - Absence of Red Tide Algal bloom.
- Inland water:
  - PH between 6 and 9;
  - Entero-cocci not more than 200 per 100 ml (ufc/100ml);
  - Escherichiacoli E. Coli not more than 500 per 100 ml (ufc/100ml);
  - The presence of Blue-Green Algal blooms/scum (cyanobatteria) not more than 100.000 cells/ml.
- All units have to be ufc/100 ml or nmp/100 ml. (ufc→Colony Forming Units: nmp→ Most Probable Number)

(ii) If the water quality test shows values out of the tolerance limits as indicated above, the swim will be cancelled, unless the ITU Medical and Anti-Doping Committee permits.

10.3. Transition:

a.) The Technical Delegate will determine the position of the mount and dismount lines. Both lines will be considered as part of the transition area.

10.4. Bike:

a.) A 10% tolerance margin will be accepted for the distance of the bike segment provided that it has been approved by the Technical Delegate. In the middle and long distance events, this tolerance is limited to 5%;

b.) There must be a minimum number of penalty boxes as follows:

- Standard distance or shorter events: one every 10 km;
- Middle and long distance events: one every 30 km.

10.5. Support team:

a.) National Federation's Quota: Every National Federation has a support team quota according to these charts:

b）水 质

（1） 游泳比赛水域的水质应进行分开检测，水样应取自游泳水域内三个不同的区域，其中水质检测结果最差的数据将作为决定是否举行游泳比赛的依据。检测结果须符合以下条件方可举行游泳比赛：

- 海水和过渡水
  - PH 值在 6 至 9 之间。
  - 每 100 毫升水中肠球菌（Entero-cocci）的含量不超过 100（ufc/100ml）。
  - 每 100 毫升水中大肠杆菌（Escherichiacoli E. Coli）的含量不超过 250（ufc/100ml）。
  - 不含赤潮藻华。
- 内陆水
  - PH 值在 6 至 9 之间。
  - 每 100 毫升水中肠球菌（Entero-cocci）的含量不超过 200（ufc/100ml）。
  - 每 100 毫升水中大肠杆菌（Escherichiacoli E. Coli）的含量不超过 500（ufc/100ml）。
  - 蓝藻（Blue-Green Algal）含量不超过 100000（cells/ml）。
- 所有的单位必须为 ufc/100ml 或 nmp/100ml（ufc 为菌落数，nmp 为最大概率数）。

（2） 除非国际铁联医务委员会批准，如果水质监测结果显示超过以上数值，则取消游泳比赛。

10.3 转换区

a） 技术代表决定上车线和下车线的位置，上车线和下车线均构成转换区的一部分。

10.4 自行车

a） 自行车赛段距离的误差不得超过 10%，并须经技术代表同意。中长距离比赛自行车赛段距离的误差不得超过 5%。

b） 自行车处罚区的数量不得少于以下标准：

- 标准距离或短距离比赛：每 10 公里一个。
- 中、长距离的比赛：每 30 公里一个。

10.5 保障团队

a） 协会名额分配：每个会员协会保障团队人员数量依照下表进行配备：

(i) Elite events:

Athletes	1 to 3	4 to 6	7 or more
Coaches	2	3	4

(ii) U23 events (U23 not mixed with other categories):

Athletes	1 to 6	7 or more
Coaches	2	3

(iii) Junior events:

Athletes	1 to 6	7 or more
Coaches	2	3

(iv) Youth events:

Athletes	1 to 6	7 or more
Coaches	2	3

(v) Elite Paratriathlon Events:

Athletes	1 to 3	4 to 6	7 or more
Coaches	2	3	4

(vi) Multisport Festival (Age Group only):

Total number of athletes across all events	1 to 50	51 to 100	More than 101
Coach	2	3	4

(vii) Age Group events:

Athletes	1 to 50	51 to 100	101 to 150	More than 151
Coaches	2	4	6	8

(viii) Delegation support:

Athletes	1 to 50	51 to 100	More than 101
Bike mechanic/Ski man	1	2	3
Medical	1	1	1
NF Representatives *	2	2	2

** Only in case no Congress held in conjunction with the event.*

b.) Head of Delegation:

(i) National Federations with athletes in every category of Elite, U23, Junior in both genders, will be provided with an extra accreditation with coach access for all events during the World Triathlon Series Grand Final.

(ii) National Federations with athletes in all four events - Duathlon, Aquathlon, Cross Triathlon and Long Distance Triathlon – in Elite category in both genders, will be provided an extra accreditation with coach access for all events during the Multisport World Championships Festival.

（1）优秀组

运动员	1~3 人	4~6 人	7 人或以上
教练员	2 人	3 人	4 人

（2）23 岁以下组（U23 不与其他项目混合）

运动员	1~6 人	7 人或以上
教练员	2 人	3 人

（3）青年组比赛

运动员	1~6 人	7 人或以上
教练员	2 人	3 人

（4）少年组

运动员	1~6 人	7 人或以上
教练员	2 人	3 人

（5）优秀伤残组

运动员	1~3 人	4~6 人	7 人或以上
教练员	2 人	3 人	4 人

（6）分项运动大会（分龄组）

参赛总人数	1~50 人	51~100 人	101 人及以上
教练	2 人	3 人	4 人

（7）分龄组比赛

运动员	1~50 人	51~100 人	101~150 人	151 人及以上
教练员	2 人	4 人	6 人	8 人

（8）代表团保障人员

运动员	1~50 人	51~100 人	101 人及以上
机械师	1 人	2 人	3 人
队医	1 人	1 人	1 人
协会代表 *	2 人	2 人	2 人

** 只在比赛未单设项目代表团的情况下。*

b）代表团团长

（1） 在世界系列赛总决赛时，国家会员协会的优秀组、23 岁以下组、青年组的男、女队将分别获得一张额外的教练员证件。

（2） 在多项运动世界锦标赛时，国家会员协会在骑跑两项、游跑两项、越野铁人三项和长距离铁人三项的所有优秀组男、女队将分别获得一张额外的教练员证件。

c.) All the personnel registered as part of the support team will receive an accreditation with access according to their role;

d.) National Federations are responsible for entering their support personnel in the ITU online entry system. ITU will approve the support personnel according to the quota seven days prior to the event. No additions will be admitted after this deadline.

10.6. Start times:

a.) The minimum time difference between waves will be:

	Inter gender start time difference (1)	Elite/AG start time difference (2)
Continental Cup Sprint	45 min	1h
Continental Cup Standard	1h 30 min	2h
World Cup Sprint	1h 45 min	1h 30 min
World Cup Standard	2h 45 min	2h 30 min
World Triathlon Series Sprint	1h 45 min	1h 45 min
World Triathlon Series Standard	2h 45 min	2h 45 min
Duathlon Standard Distance	1h 30 min	2h 30 min
Triathlon and Duathlon Middle and Long Distance	5 min	5 min
3x Team Relay	1h 45 min	n/a

(1) This will be applicable whether the men or the women's event starts first.

(2) This will be applicable for Age Group waves starting after the Elite events. Elite events starting after the Age Group Events will only start once the Age Group Events have finished.

b.) The Technical Delegate can decide to reduce the above indicated differences in Continental Cup and Duathlon standard distance events provided that the men and the women will not be on the bike segment simultaneously;

c.) The Technical Delegate can decide to reduce the above indicated differences in Continental Cups and Duathlon standard distance events to a minimum of five minutes if one of the events has fewer than 10 athletes competing, and enough officials to control any potential drafting between male and female athletes;

d.) The Technical Delegate can also require different start times by asking for a specific regulation, as indicated under section 1.6;

e.) Events not included in the previous chart will need the approval of the Technical Delegate prior to publishing the start times.

10.7. Modified events:

a.) When a competition cannot be held in the original format due to force majeure, all the points for all the rankings related, including Olympic Qualification List points, will be reduced depending on the final conditions under which the event took place:

c）根据不同的人员角色，所有注册的保障团队成员将会得到参赛证件，并拥有相应的通行权限。

d）会员协会有义务通过国际铁联在线报名系统为其保障人员进行参赛注册，国际铁联将根据上述名额分配办法于赛前 7 天审批各协会申请，该截止日期之后不再接受增加人员的申请。

10.6 出发时间

a）不同出发批次的最短出发间隔时间如下：

	不同性别 出发时间间隔注（1）	优秀组 / 分龄组 出发时间间隔注（2）
短距离洲际杯赛	45 分钟	1 小时
标准距离洲际杯赛	1 小时 30 分钟	2 小时
短距离世界杯赛	1 小时 45 分钟	1 小时 30 分钟
标准距离世界杯赛	2 小时 45 分钟	2 小时 30 分钟
短距离世界系列赛	1 小时 45 分钟	1 小时 45 分钟
标准距离世界系列赛	2 小时 45 分钟	2 小时 45 分钟
骑跑两项标准距离比赛	1 小时 30 分钟	2 小时 30 分钟
铁人三项和骑跑两项中、长距离比赛	5 分钟	5 分钟
团体接力赛	1 小时 45 分钟	n/a

注（1）：无论男子运动员或女子运动员先出发，都适用此表。

注（2）：优秀组比赛之后的分龄组比赛同样适用。分龄组比赛后的优秀组比赛必须在分龄组比赛完成之后才能进行出发。

b）技术代表有权决定减少洲际杯赛和骑跑两项标准距离比赛的出发时间间隔，但要确保男、女运动员不会同时处于自行车赛段。

c）如果某一组别参赛运动员人数不足 10 人，并且有足够的技术官员可以控制可能发生的男、女运动员之间的尾随行为，则技术代表有权决定将洲际杯赛和骑跑两项标准距离比赛的出发时间间隔减少到最少 5 分钟。

d）技术代表也可依据 1.6 的规定申请特别规则，安排不同的出发时间。

e）上表没有包含的比赛，需经技术代表批准后方可公布出发时间。

10.7 比赛距离或形式发生调整的赛事

a）如果某场比赛因不可抗力原因无法按照既定模式举行，则包括奥运会资格排名积分在内的所有与排名有关的积分数将根据最终比赛情况酌情折减：

(i) If the event remains as a triathlon or the multisport originally planned, but any of all of the segments are shortened according to the ITU Competition Rules, 100 % of the points will be awarded;
(ii) If the event becomes another ITU multisport competition according to the ITU Competition Rules in terms of distances and conditions, 75 % of the points will be awarded;
(iii) If a triathlon event becomes a duathlon and the swim is replaced by a running segment with similar duration of the cancelled swim, 75% of the points will be awarded;
(iv) If the event becomes another ITU multisport competition with deviations from the ITU Competition Rules in terms of distances and conditions, 50 % of the points will be awarded.

10.8. Cut-off time:

a.) Technical Delegate may determine a cut-off time for the entire competition or any intermediate point;
b.) If there is a cut-off time, it must be announced at least 30 days before registration closed.

11. TECHNICAL OFFICIALS

11.1. General:

a.) The duties of the Technical Officials are to conduct the competition are in accordance with the ITU Competition Rules;
b.) ITU Technical Officials are:
(i) Technical Officials;
(ii) Paratriathlon Specific Technical Officials;
(iii) Chair of the Competition Jury.
c.) Technical Officials must be at least 19 years old on the 31st of December in the year of the competition they are working on;
d.) To hold a competition under these Competition Rules, it is necessary to have the presence of:
(i) A Technical Delegate; and
(ii) A Head Referee.

11.2. ITU Technical Officials:

a.) The Technical Officials at all ITU competitions are:
(i) The ITU Technical Delegate (TD) ensures all aspects of the ITU Competition Rules and ITU Event Organisers' Manual are fulfilled. Local Organising Committees will modify the competition conditions, as per the indications of the Technical Delegate at any time. Accredited coaches will be informed about the modifications;
(ii) The Assistant Technical Delegate (ATD) assists the Technical Delegate with his/her duties;

（1） 如果比赛形式仍为铁人三项或最初计划的多分项，只是某一或者全部赛段的比赛距离按照国际铁联规则进行了缩减，则积分数保持全额不变。

（2） 如果比赛形式按照国际铁联规则改变成为其他分项的比赛，则积分数折减为全额的 75%。

（3） 如果铁人三项比赛改为骑跑两项，游泳赛段由持续时间与游泳赛段类似的跑步赛段取代，则积分数折减为全额的 75%。

（4） 如果比赛未按照国际铁联规则在比赛距离或形式上发生改变，则积分数折减为全额的 50%。

10.8 关门时间

a） 技术代表可以决定整个比赛和任何赛段的关门时间。

b）如果有关门时间，至少在比赛报名前 30 天公布。

11. 技术官员

11.1 总 则

a） 技术官员的职责是使比赛按照国际铁联规则进行。

b） 国际铁联技术官员是指：

（1） 技术官员。

（2） 伤残铁人三项技术官员。

（3） 仲裁委员会主席。

c） 技术官员在其执裁当年的 12 月 31 日前必须年满 19 岁。

d） 为保证规则的执行，有必要设置：

（1） 技术代表。

（2） 裁判长。

11.2 国际铁联技术官员

a） 国际铁联比赛中的技术官员包括：

（1） 国际铁联技术代表（TD）负责确保国际铁联规则及国际铁联比赛操作手册中的各项内容得到实施。比赛当地组委会（LOCs）应按照技术代表的指示随时完善比赛条件，将相关修改内容告知注册教练员。

（2） 技术代表助理（ATD）负责协助技术代表。

(iii) The Head Referee checks the certification of the Technical Officials, makes the results official by signing them and makes final judgments on rule violations;

(iv) The Chief Race Official (CRO) assigns and monitors the work of all Technical Officials;

(v) Technical Officials are assigned to Registration, Start, Finish, Transition Area(s), Pre-transition Area, Swim, Swim exit, Bike, Run, Wheel Stations, Aid Stations, Technology, Penalty Boxes, Lap Counter, Protocol, Race Control Office, Video Review, and Vehicle Control. An adequate number of Technical Officials will be assigned to each area and will be responsible for the enforcement of ITU Competition Rules within their assigned jurisdiction. A Technical Official may be assigned in more than one position. Additional positions may be created if necessary;

(vi) Technical Officials can be accredited as Bike Check Officials to conduct technological fraud control. Complete procedure can be found in Appendix N.

(vii) The Competition Jury is appointed by the Technical Delegate;

(viii) The ITU Medical Delegate, appointed by the ITU Medical and Anti-Doping Committee, is responsible for all medical and anti-doping issues on behalf of ITU.

11.3. Paratriathlon Specific Technical Officials:

a.) The Chief Classifier is a classifier responsible for the direction, administration, co-ordination and implementation of classification matters;

b.) Classifiers will be responsible for determining the Sport Class and Sport Class Status of the Paratriathletes from PTS2 to PTS5, PTWC1 and PTWC2 Paratriathletes;

c.) Classifiers certified by the International Blind Sports Federation and International Paralympic Committee will be responsible to determine the sport class and sport class status of the PTVI1, PTVI2 and PTVI3 Paratriathletes;

d.) ITU Paratriathlon Classification Rules are included in Appendix G.

11.4. Competition Jury:

a.) The ITU Technical Delegate will appoint the members of the Competition Jury as follows:

(i) For Olympic Games and the Elite competitions of the World Triathlon Series Grand Final the Competition Jury consists of five people being selected from:

- The Technical Delegate or the Assistant Technical Delegate, who chairs the Competition Jury;
- A member of the ITU Executive Board;
- A representative of the host National Federation;
- A representative from the ITU Technical Committee;
- A representative from the ITU Medical and Anti-Doping Committee.

（3） 裁判长（Head Referee）负责技术官员的资格认证，签署正式比赛成绩以及对犯规行为做最终裁决。

（4） 裁判长助理（Chief Race Official）负责分配并监督所有技术官员的工作。

（5） 技术官员（Technical Official）负责检录、出发、终点、转换区、预备转换区、游泳、起水区、自行车、跑步、备用车轮站、饮水站、技术、处罚区、计圈、仪式、竞赛控制及车辆控制等岗位的工作。每个比赛区域都将分配到足够数量的技术官员，并由他们在各自权限范围内确保国际铁联规则的实施。一名技术官员可被委派多于一个岗位，必要的情况下可以增设岗位。

（6） 须确定验车技术官员以防止技术欺诈。相关程序见附件 N。

（7） 仲裁委员会由技术代表指定。

（8） 国际铁联医务代表由国际铁联医务委员会指派，代表国际铁联负责所有医务和反兴奋剂事宜。

11.3 伤残铁人三项比赛技术官员

a） 主分级师有责任对运动员分级工作进行指导、管理、协调和实施。

b） 分级师负责鉴定从 PT2—PT5、PTWC1 和 PTWC2 级伤残运动员的伤残级别、伤残级别状态。

c） 由国际盲人体育联合会（International Blind Sports Federation）和国际残疾人奥林匹克委员会（International Paralympic Committee）认证的分级师，将负责鉴定 PTVI1、PTVI2、PTVI3 运动员的伤残级别和伤残级别状态。

d） 伤残运动员铁人三项比赛的分级规则见附件 G。

11.4 仲裁委员会

a） 国际铁联技术代表将按照以下原则指定仲裁委员会成员

（1） 奥运会、世界铁人三项系列赛总决赛优秀组比赛的仲裁委员会由 5 人组成:

- 技术代表或技术代表助理，作为仲裁委员会主席。
- 国际铁联执行委员会成员 1 名。
- 东道主会员协会代表 1 名。
- 国际铁联技术委员会代表 1 名。
- 国际铁联医务和反兴奋剂委员会代表 1 名。

(ii) For all the other ITU Events and other Games that do not include the Olympic Games, the Competition Jury consists of three people being selected from:
- The Technical Delegate or the Assistant Technical Delegate, who chairs the Competition Jury;
- A member of the ITU Executive Board or any Committees or Commissions, or if none are present, a member of the Continental Confederation's Executive Board or any Committees or Commission, or staff liaisons, or if none are present, a representative from the host National Federation;
- A representative from the host National Federation.

(iii) The Competition Jury can invite experts to the hearing, whereby they may have voice but no vote.

b.) Being a member of the Competition Jury in one event is not compatible with:

(i) Being a Technical Official in the same event other than the Technical Delegate;

(ii) Being an accredited coach in the same event;

(iii) Being an athlete competing in the same event.

c.) Duties of the Competition Jury:

(i) The Competition Jury rules on all appeals and all protests;

(ii) The Competition Jury has the authority to modify the competition results as a consequence of its decision on the appeal or protest. This results modification is a Field of Play decision;

(iii) The Competition Jury must be available starting before the Athletes' Briefing until after the end of competition;

(iv) The Competition Jury Chair is responsible for filing a written statement on all appeals and decisions reached.

d.) Competition Jury meetings schedule:

(i) Competition Jury will meet, at a minimum:
- After the race briefing;
- One hour before the start of the event;
- After the last finisher.

(ii) Additionally, in the Age Group events, the Competition Jury will meet, at a minimum:
- After the first finisher;
- After the finish of the first half of the field.

e.) Competition Jury Integrity:

(i) The Competition Jury observes the following principles:
- Give equal weight to the evidence and testimony provided by all;

（2） 对于国际铁联所有的比赛以及除奥运会以外的其他比赛仲裁委员会由 3 人组成：

- 技术代表或技术代表助理，即仲裁委员会主席。
- 国际铁联执行委员会成员 1 名，或国际铁联任何委员会成员 1 名，或洲际联合会执委会成员 1 人，或洲际联合会任何委员会会员 1 名，或参会联络人员 1 名，如若上述无法实施，则在东道主会员协会选出代表 1 名。
- 东道主会员协会代表 1 名。

（3） 比赛仲裁委员会可以邀请相关专家听意见、提建议，但其没有投票表决权。

b）仲裁委员会成员不得兼任下列职务

（1） 技术代表除外的，同一赛事的技术官员。

（2） 同一赛事的注册教练员。

（3） 同一赛事的参赛运动员。

c）仲裁委员会的职责

（1） 对一切申诉和抗议做出裁决。

（2） 仲裁委员会有权根据其对申诉或抗议的裁决对比赛成绩进行修正。该成绩修改为赛场决定（译者注：由技术官员或仲裁委员会对国际铁联规则所做出的应用与解）。

（3） 仲裁委员会必须从运动员技术会前至比赛结束后在岗。

（4） 仲裁委员会主席负责就所有裁决撰写书面声明。

d）仲裁委员会例会

（1） 仲裁委员会至少须在以下时间召开会议：

- 技术会后。
- 比赛开始前一小时。
- 最后一名运动员完成比赛后。

（2） 分龄组比赛中，仲裁委员会至少须在以下时间召开会议：

- 第一名运动员完成比赛后。
- 完成比赛半程后。

e）仲裁的公正性

（1） 仲裁委员会应遵守以下原则：

- 公平衡量一切证据和证词。

- Recognize that honest testimony can vary and be in conflict as a result of personal observation or recollection;
- Have an openminded approach until all evidence has been submitted;
- Recognise an athlete is innocent until the alleged violation has been established to the complete satisfaction of the Competition Jury.

(ii) Conflict of interest:

- The Chair of the Competition Jury decides if any member has a conflict of interest;
- In the case of conflict of interest or absence or any other reason the Chair of the Competition Jury can replace the member who has the conflict of interest. The Chair of the Competition Jury can appoint the replacement at his/her discretion. The Competition Jury will remain with the same number of members that it originally had;
- The Chair of the Competition Jury is deemed not to have a conflict of interest.

11.5. Technology Tools:

a.) Technical Officials may use any kind of electric, electronic, magnetic, or other technological support to acquire data or evidence on rule infractions as supporting evidence.

11.6. Volunteer Certification:

a.) All volunteers, who are assigned to areas of responsibility on the Field of Play, must be educated to ITU's minimum standard. Education kits obtained from ITU will cover key areas of Field of Play responsibility.

11.7. Health:

a.) ITU encourages Technical Officials to undergo an annual health evaluation.

11.8. Technical Officials' Certification:

a.) All documents related to the procedures and regulations on Technical Officials' certification as well as the list of certified Technical Officials can be found under - http://www.triathlon.org/development/technical_officials/certification

12. PROTESTS

12.1. General:

a.) A protest is against the conduct of an athlete, Technical Official, or the conditions of the competition. An athlete or an National Federation designate may file a protest with the Head Referee provided the protest has not been previously observed by the Technical Officials and ruled upon by the Head Referee.

- 认识到由于个体观察和记忆不同，诚实的证词也会出现多样性和矛盾性。
- 接受并获取全面的证据。
- 在对犯规的判罚得到仲裁委员会所有成员一致认可之前，都认为运动员是清白的。

（2） 利益关系：

- 仲裁委员会主席决定是否某个成员存在利益关系。
- 如因存在利益关系或缺席或其他理由，仲裁委员会主席可自主任命相关替换成员，更换后仍需保持与之前一样的委员人数。
- 仲裁委员会主席视为不存在利益关系。

11.5 技术手段

a）国际铁联官员可利用任何电动的、电子的、磁性的或其他技术手段协助获取犯规数据或证据作为支撑依据。

11.6 志愿者资格认证

a）被分配负责比赛区域（FOP）范围内工作的所有志愿者应通过培训达到国际铁联最低级别的标准。国际铁联将提供培训的要点。

11.7 健 康

a）国际铁联鼓励技术官员进行年度体检。

11.8 技术官员认证

a）任何与技术官员认证相关的程序性和规则性文件以及认证合格的技术官员名单可查询以下链接：

http://www.triathlon.org/development/technical_officials/certification

12．抗 议

12.1 总 则

a）抗议是针对运动员、技术官员行为或比赛的环境和条件而言。运动员或会员协会代表可向裁判长提出抗议，如果此抗议事先尚未得到裁判的判决。

12.2. Protests Concerning Eligibility:

a.) Protests concerning the eligibility of an athlete shall be made to the Head Referee before the Athletes' Briefing. The Competition Jury will decide on this in a meeting scheduled immediately after the Athletes' Briefing.

12.3. Protests Concerning the Course:

a.) Protests concerning the safety of the course or its variance to the regulations must be made to the Head Referee no later than twenty-four (24) hours before the start of the competition.

2.4. Protests Concerning the Competition:

a.) An Elite, Youth, Junior, U23 athlete and Paratriathlete, who protests against another athlete or Technical Official, must do so to the Head Referee within five (5) minutes of his/her finish time. In case of a protest that is initiated within this period, the time limit will be extended by fifteen (15) more minutes.

b.) An Age Group athlete, who protests against another athlete or Technical Official, must do so to the Head Referee within fifteen (15) minutes after the last athlete finished the competition. In case of a protest that is initiated within this period, the time limit will be extended by thirty (30) more minutes from the time the athlete initiated the protest.

12.5. Protests Concerning Equipment:

a.) Protests concerning an athlete's equipment on an Elite, Youth, Junior, U23 and Paratriathlon competition, which infringes on the conditions set out in the ITU Competition Rules, must be delivered to the Head Referee within five (5) minutes of his/her finish time. In case of a protest that is initiated within this period, the time limit will be extended by fifteen (15) more minutes.

b.) Protests concerning an athlete's equipment on an Age Group competition, which infringes on the conditions set out in the ITU Competition Rules, must be delivered to the Head Referee within fifteen (15) minutes after the last athlete finished the competition. In case of a protest that is initiated within this period, the time limit will be extended by thirty (30) more minutes from the time the athlete initiated the protest.

12.6. Protests Concerning Timing and Results:

a.) Protests concerning errors in the results, which are not reflecting the decisions made by the Head Referee or the Competition Jury, may be delivered in writing by the athlete or the National Federation to the ITU Technical Delegate within thirty (30) days after the competition.

12.2 对参赛资格的抗议

a）对某名运动员参赛资格的抗议应在运动员技术会前提交给裁判长。仲裁委员会将在运动员技术会后立即召开会议做出裁决。

12.3 对比赛路线的抗议

a）对比赛路线安全或不符合规则之处提出的抗议必须至少在赛前 24 小时书面提交给裁判长。

12.4 对比赛的抗议

a）优秀、少年、青年、23 岁以下组的参赛运动员和伤残铁人三项运动员对其他运动员或技术官员提出的抗议，应在完成比赛后 5 分钟内提交给裁判长。如果在此期间产生抗议，则抗议时限可延长 15 分钟。

b）分龄组的运动员如对其他运动员或技术官员提出抗议，应在参赛最后一名运动员结束比赛后 15 分钟内提交给裁判长。如果在此期间产生抗议，则抗议时限可从运动员提出抗议起延长 30 分钟。

12.5 对比赛装备的抗议

a）对某名参加优秀、少年、青年、23 岁以下组和伤残铁人三项比赛的运动员不符合规则的器材装备的抗议应在完成比赛后 5 分钟内提交给裁判长。如果在此期间产生抗议，则抗议时限可延长 15 分钟。

b）对某名分龄组比赛的运动员不符合规则的器材装备的抗议，应在参赛最后一名运动员结束比赛后 15 分钟内提交给裁判长。如果在此期间产生抗议，则抗议时限可从运动员提出抗议起延长 30 分钟。

12.6 对计时和成绩的抗议

a）对为体现裁判长和仲裁委员会决定的成绩错误的抗议，可由运动员或会员协会在赛后 30 天内以书面形式向国际铁联技术代表提出。

12.7. Contents of a Protest:

a.) The protest related to 12.1, 12.2, 12.3, 12.4 and 12.5 must be accompanied by a deposit of $50 USD, or its equivalent, and will be refunded if the protest is successful. If the protest is denied, there will be no refund and the money will be retained by ITU. Protest forms may be obtained from the Head Referee. A sample of the protest form is included in Appendix B:

(i) Information to be included:
- The alleged rule violated;
- The location and approximate time of the alleged violation;
- Persons involved in the alleged violation;
- A statement, including a diagram of the alleged violation, if possible;
- The names of witnesses who observed the alleged violation.

12.8. Protest Procedures:

a.) The following procedure will be followed in the event of a protest:

(i) Protests will be filed with the Head Referee, signed by the protester, within the time limits specified above;

(ii) The Head Referee will announce on the notice board in the finish area that a protest has been filed;

(iii) The protester and the accused and/or their national coach or representative must be present. If the protester does not attend, the protest hearing may be postponed or cancelled. The Competition Jury will determine if absence from the hearing is valid;

(iv) Failure of any party to attend the hearing may justify the Competition Jury in making a decision without them;

(v) A representative for either the protester or the accused may be designated to appear if approved by the Chair of the Competition Jury;

(vi) The hearing will not be open to the public;

(vii) The Competition Jury Chair will explain the process and everyone's rights;

(viii) The Competition Jury Chair will read the protest;

(ix) The protester and the accused will be given adequate time to give their accounts of the incident;

(x) Witnesses (up to two each) may speak for up to three (3) minutes each;

(xi) The Competition Jury will hear the evidence and render a decision, by simple majority;

(xii) The decision will be posted immediately and delivered in writing to the parties upon request;

(xiii) The Competition Jury will produce minutes of the meeting, including the Competition Jury's decision, which must be approved by all members of the Competition Jury, by the end of the meeting. The minutes will be submitted to ITU.

12.7 抗议的内容

a）与上述 12.1、12.2、12.3、12.4、12.5 有关的抗议在提交抗议书的同时需交纳抗议费 50 美元或其他等额币种，如抗议成功，此费用将予以退还；如抗议不成功，则此费用将由国际铁联保留。抗议书可从裁判长处获得，抗议书的样本见附件 B。

（1） 抗议书的内容包括：

- 犯规情况。
- 犯规时间及地点。
- 犯规涉及的人员。
- 相关陈述，如可能可包含图表说明。
- 证人姓名。

12.8 抗议的程序

a）抗议应遵循以下程序：

（1） 抗议书应由抗议人签字，并在上述条款说明的时间范围内提交给裁判长。

（2） 裁判长将在终点的公告牌上公布抗议。

（3） 原告和被告或各自国家（地区）教练或代表必须出席听证会。如果原告没有出席听证会，则听证会可延期或取消。仲裁委员会将决定原告的缺席是否有效。

（4） 任何一方当事人缺席听证会，仲裁委员会均有权在该方缺席的情况下做出裁决。

（5） 经仲裁委员会主席认可，原告或被告可由其代表出席听证会。

（6） 听证会不公开举行。

（7） 仲裁委员会主席将说明相关过程和每个人的权利。

（8） 由仲裁委员会主席宣读抗议书。

（9） 应给予原告和被告充分的时间陈述本方观点。

（10） 双方证人（各 2 人）各有 3 分钟时间陈词。

（11） 仲裁委员会将根据各方证词，按简单多数原则做出裁决。

（12） 裁决立即公布，并以书面形式通知各当事人。

（13） 在会议结束时，仲裁委员会须形成备忘录，备忘录包括仲裁委员会的决议并须得到竞赛委员会的批准。备忘录将提交国际铁联。

12.9. Results revision process:

a.) National Federations, Continental Confederations or ITU can request the revision of the results based on new evidence. This request will be addressed to the ITU Technical Committee, who decides if a results revision case will be opened.

b.) A revision panel appointed by the ITU Technical Committee consisting of three members including at least one ITU Technical Committee member will make a proposal to ITU Technical Committee.

c.) ITU Technical Committee will decide on the results revision case by maintaining or modifying the results.

d.) The revised results will be announced, published and the athletes informed.

e.) Decisions of the ITU Technical Committee as an outcome of the results revision process can be subject to appeal by a Level 2 appeal process.

13. APPEALS

13.1. Appeal Jurisdiction:

a.) An appeal is a request for a review of a decision made by the Head Referee (Level 1), the Competition Jury or any ITU panel (Level 2) and the ITU Medical and Anti-Doping Committee solely with regards to eligibility (Level 3) or the ITU Arbitration Tribunal (Level 3). A sample of the Appeal Form is available in Appendix C.

b.) Decisions from any Competition Jury and any ITU panel may be appealed to the ITU Arbitration Tribunal, except:

(i) Decisions made by the ITU Anti-Doping Hearing Panel;

(ii) Field of Play decisions.

13.2. Level 1 Appeal Procedure:

a.) The following procedure will be followed in the event of a Level 1 Appeal until the medal ceremony:

(i) A Representative of a National Federation or an athlete may appeal the decision of the Head Referee to the Competition Jury. The appropriate appeal form can be obtained from the Head Referee;

(ii) Appeals will be filed in writing to the Head Referee, signed by the appellant and will be accompanied by a fee of $50 USD or equivalent. It will be refunded if the appeal is successful. If the appeal is denied, there will be no refund and the money will be retained by ITU;

(iii) The Head Referee will post information on the notice board that an appeal has been filed.

12.9 成绩修正程序

a）基于新的证据，国家会员协会、洲际联合会或国际铁联可以要求修正成绩。该要求需要提交给国际铁联技术委员会决定。

b）成绩修正小组由国际铁联技术委员会任命，由三人组成且至少一人是国际铁联技术委员会成员，并由其向技术委员会提议。

c）国际铁联技术委员会将决定是否修正成绩。

d）修正的成绩将公开发布并通知运动员。

e）作为成绩修正过程的结果，对于国际铁联的决定可以通过二级申诉的方式进行申诉。

13. 申 诉

13.1 申诉权限

a）申诉是指对裁判长的决定（一级申诉）、对仲裁委员会或国际铁联申诉委员会的决定（二级申诉）以及国际铁联医学和反兴奋剂委员会有关参赛资格的决定（三级申诉）或对国际铁联仲裁法庭（三级申诉）的判决提出重新审查的请求。申诉表的样本见附件 C。

b）仲裁委员会和国际铁联申诉委员会的决定可以被申诉至国际铁联仲裁法庭，除了：

（1）决定是由国际铁联反兴奋剂听证小组做出的。

（2）赛场决定（译者注：由技术官员或仲裁委员会对国际铁联规则所做出的应用与解）。

13.2 一级申诉程序

a）一级申诉应遵循以下程序（时间截止到颁奖仪式）：

（1）国家会员协会代表或运动员可针对裁判长的判罚结果向仲裁委员会提出申诉。申诉表格可从裁判长处领取。

（2）书面申请由申请人签字并提交给裁判长，每次申诉应交纳申诉费 50 美元或其他等额币种，如果申诉成功此费用将退还申诉人，若申诉不成功则不予退还并由国际铁联保留。

（3）裁判长将在终点的公告牌上公布申诉。

b.) The following procedure will be followed in the event of a Level 1 Appeal after the medal ceremony till 48 hours after the end:

(i) A Representative of a National Federation or an athlete may appeal the decision of the Head Referee to the ITU Appeal Panel. The appropriate appeal form can be obtained from the Head Referee;

(ii) Appeals will be filed in writing to the Head Referee, signed by the appellant and will be accompanied by a fee of $50 USD or equivalent. It will be refunded if the appeal is successful. If the appeal is denied, there will be no refund and the money will be retained by ITU.

13.3. Level 1 Appeal Timelines:

a.) Appeals against decision taken by the Head Referee between the Athletes'/ Team Managers' briefing and the start of the competition:

(i) An Elite, Youth, Junior, U23 athlete/team and Paratriathlete or National Federation representative on behalf of such athlete, who appeals a Head Referee's decision taken between the Athletes' briefing and the start of the competition must do so to the Head Referee within five (5) minutes after the announcement of the Head Referee's decision. In case of an appeal that is initiated within this period, the time limit will be extended by fifteen (15) more minutes.

(ii) An Age Group athlete or National Federation representative on behalf of such athlete, who appeals a Head Referee's decision taken between the Athletes' briefing and the start of the competition must do so to the Head Referee within fifteen (15) minutes after the announcement of the Head Referee's decision. In case of an appeal that is initiated within this period, the time limit will be extended by thirty (30) more minutes.

b.) Appeals against decision taken by the Head Referee during the competition before the athlete finishing:

(i) An Elite, Youth, Junior, U23 athlete/team and Paratriathlete or National Federation representative on behalf of such athlete, who appeals a Head Referee's decision taken before the athlete finished the competition must do so to the Head Referee within five (5) minutes of his/her finish time. In case of an appeal that is initiated within this period, the time limit will be extended by fifteen (15) more minutes. For team competitions, this time limit is related to the final team time;

(ii) An Age Group athlete or National Federation representative on behalf of such athlete, who appeals a Head Referee's decision taken before the athlete finishes the competition must do so to the Head Referee within fifteen (15) minutes after the last athlete finishes the competition. In case of an appeal that is initiated within this period, the time limit will be extended by thirty (30) more minutes from the time the athlete initiated the appeal;

b）如下程序将在一级申诉之后进行（时间从颁奖仪式之后 48 小时内）：

（1） 国家会员协会代表或运动员可针对裁判长的判罚结果向国际铁联申诉委员会提出申诉。申诉表格可从裁判长处领取。

（2） 书面申请由申请人签字并提交给裁判长，每次申诉应交纳申诉费 50 美元或其他等额币种，如果申诉成功此费用将退还申诉人，若申诉不成功则不予退还并由国际铁联保留。

13.3 一级申诉时间表

a）运动员技术会或领队会至比赛出发之前的针对裁判长的申诉：

（1） 优秀组、青年组、少年组、U23、残疾人组运动员 / 组或国家会员协会代表针对裁判长决定的申诉，应在裁判长宣布决定之后 5 分钟内向裁判长提出。如果在此期间产生申诉，则申诉时限可再延长 15 分钟或更长。

（2） 分龄组运动员或者国家会员协会代表针对裁判长决定的申诉，应在裁判长宣布决定之后 15 分钟内向裁判长提出。如果在此期间产生申诉，则申诉时限可再延长 30 分钟或更长。

b）比赛期间至比赛结束之前的针对裁判长的申诉：

（1） 优秀组、青年组、少年组、U23、残疾人组运动员 / 组或国家会员协会代表针对裁判长决定的申诉，应在他 / 她比赛结束 5 分钟之内向裁判长提出。如果在此期间产生申诉，则申诉时限可再延长 15 分钟或更长。团体比赛以全队完成时间为依据。

（2） 分龄组运动员或者国家会员协会代表针对裁判长决定的申诉，应在最后一名运动员完成比赛 15 分钟内向裁判长提出。如果在此期间产生申诉，则申诉时限可基于申诉时间再延长 30 分钟或更长。

c.) Appeals against decision taken by the Head Referee after the athlete finishes the competition:
   (i) An athlete/team or National Federation representative on behalf of such athlete, who appeals a Head Referee's decision made after the athlete finishes the competition but before 48 hours after the end of competition must do so within five (5) days after the end of the competition;

d.) Appeals 48 hours or more after the end of the competition:
   (i) Any decisions on violations are managed by the ITU Technical Committee through the results review process;

e.) Competition Jury existence:
   (i) Appeals between the time of the Athletes'/Team Managers' briefing and the medal ceremonies will be managed by the Competition Jury;
   (ii) Appeals after the medal ceremonies will be managed by the ITU Appeal Panel with representative from the ITU Technical Committee, ITU Sport Department and the Technical Delegate of the event or if such not available the representative of the LOC.

13.4. Level 1 Appeal Content:

a.) An appeal will contain:
   (i) Competition name, location, date;
   (ii) Appellant's name, address, phone, fax, email;
   (iii) Witness(es) name(s);
   (iv) Alleged decision appealed;
   (v) Facts of the violation;
   (vi) Rationale/summary of appeal.

13.5. Level 1 Appeal Hearing in case of a Competition Jury:

a.) The appellant and the accused and/or their national representative must be present. If the appellant does not attend, the appeals hearing may be postponed or cancelled. The Competition Jury will determine if absence from the hearing is valid;
b.) Failure of any party to attend the hearing may justify the Competition Jury in making a decision without them;
c.) A representative for either the appellant or the accused may be designated to appear if approved by the Chair of the Competition Jury;
d.) The hearing will not be open to the public;
e.) The Competition Jury Chair will explain the process and everyone's rights;
f.) The Competition Jury Chair will read the appeal;
g.) The appellant and the accused will be given adequate time to give their accounts of the incident;
h.) Witnesses (up to two each) may speak for up to three (3) minutes each;
i.) The Competition Jury will hear the evidence and render a decision, by simple majority;
j.) Affected athletes may be heard by the Competition Jury and will be informed about the decision;

c）运动员比赛后针对裁判长的申诉：

（1） 在完成比赛后 48 小时之内，运动员或国家会员协会代表对裁判长的决定提出申诉，必须在完成比赛后 5 天之内提出。

d）比赛完成 48 小时之后的针对裁判长的申诉：

（1） 有关犯规的所有裁决由国际铁联技术委员会依据成绩审核的结果确定。

e）比赛仲裁委员会裁决：

（1） 运动员技术会或领队会至颁奖仪式之间提出的申诉由比赛仲裁委员会裁决。

（2） 颁奖仪式后出现的申诉由国际铁联技术委员会、国际铁联体育部和比赛技术代表或作为备选的当地组委会代表组成的申诉小组裁决。

13.4 一级申诉内容

a）申诉的内容包括

（1） 比赛名称、地点、日期。

（2） 申诉人姓名、地址、电话、传真、电子邮箱。

（3） 证人姓名。

（4） 申诉所针对的决定。

（5） 犯规情况。

（6） 申诉内容摘要。

13.5 一级申诉听证会（比赛仲裁委员会）

a） 原告和被告或各自国家（地区）代表必须出席听证会。如果原告没有出席听证会，则听证会可延期或取消。仲裁委员会将决定上述人员的缺席是否有效。

b） 任何一方当事人缺席听证会，仲裁委员会均有权在该方缺席的情况下做出裁决。

c） 经仲裁委员会主席认可，原告或被告可由其代表出席听证会。

d） 听证会不公开举行。

e） 仲裁委员会主席将说明相关过程和每个人的权利。

f） 由仲裁委员会主席宣读申诉书。

g） 应给予原告和被告充分的时间陈述本方观点。

h） 双方证人各有 3 分钟时间陈词。

i） 仲裁委员会将根据各方证词，按简单多数原则做出裁决。

j） 仲裁委员会可能听取被影响的运动员陈述，并通知其仲裁结果。

k.) The decision will be posted immediately and delivered in writing to the parties upon request;
l.) The Competition Jury will produce minutes of the meeting, including the Competition Jury's decision, which must be approved by all members of the Competition Jury, by the end of the meeting. The minutes will be submitted to ITU.

13.6. Level 1 Appeal Hearing in case of an ITU Appeal Panel:

a.) The appellant and the accused and/or their national representative may be present. If the appellant does not attend in person or by any other mean of communication, the appeals hearing may be postponed or cancelled. The Appeal Panel will determine if absence from the hearing is valid;
b.) Failure of any party to attend the hearing may justify the Appeal Panel in making a decision without them;
c.) A representative for either the appellant or the accused may be designated to be heard if approved by the Chair of the Appeal Panel;
d.) The hearing will not be open to the public;
e.) The Appeal Panel Chair will explain the process and everyone's rights;
f.) The Appeal Panel Chair will read the appeal;
g.) The appellant and the accused will be given adequate time to give their accounts of the incident;
h.) Witnesses (up to two each) may speak for up to three (3) minutes each;
i.) The Appeal Panel will hear the evidence and render a decision, by simple majority;
j.) Affected athletes will may be heard by the Appeal Panel and will be informed about the decision;
k.) The decision will be communicated immediately and delivered in writing to the parties upon request;
l.) The Appeal Panel will produce minutes of the meeting, including the Appeal Panel's decision, which must be approved by all members of the Appeal Panel, by the end of the meeting. The minutes will be submitted to ITU.

13.7. Level 2 Appeal Procedure:

a.) The following procedure will be followed in the event of a Level 2 Appeal:
(i) Decisions from any Competition Jury and any ITU panel (except the ITU AD Hearing Panel) may be appealed to the ITU Arbitration Tribunal;
(ii) Only appeals supported by National Federation will be admitted;
(iii) Appeals may be submitted up to thirty natural days after the Competition Jury met or within thirty natural days from the Competition Jury or Panel decision;
(iv) Appeals will be submitted in writing to the ITU Secretary General and will be accompained by a deposit of $ 500 USD. It will only be refunded if the appeal is successful.;

k）裁决立即公布，并以书面形式通知各当事人。

l）在会议结束时，仲裁委员会须形成备忘录，备忘录包括仲裁委员会的决议并须得到竞赛委员会的批准。备忘录将提交国际铁联。

13.6 一级申诉听证会（国际铁联申诉委员会）

a）原告和被告或各自国家（地区）代表必须出席听证会。如果原告没有出席听证会，则听证会可延期或取消。国际铁联申诉委员会将决定上述人员的缺席是否有效。

b）任何一方当事人缺席听证会，国际铁联申诉委员会均有权在该方缺席的情况下做出裁决。

c）经国际铁联申诉委员会主席认可，原告或被告可由其代表出席听证会。

d）听证会不公开举行。

e）国际铁联申诉委员会主席将说明相关过程和每个人的权利。

f）由国际铁联申诉委员会主席宣读申诉书。

j）应给予原告和被告充分的时间陈述本方观点。

h）双方证人（每方最多 2 人）各有 3 分钟时间陈词。

i）国际铁联申诉委员会将根据各方证词，按简单多数原则做出裁决。

j）国际铁联申诉委员会可能听取被影响的运动员陈述，并通知其仲裁结果。

k）裁决立即公布，并以书面形式通知各当事人。

l）在会议结束时，国际铁联申诉委员会须形成备忘录，备忘录包括国际铁联申诉委员会的决议并须得到国际铁联申诉委员会所有成员的认可。备忘录将提交国际铁联。

13.7 二级申诉程序

a）二级申诉应遵循以下程序：

（1）对比赛仲裁委员会或国际铁联申诉委员会（除国际铁联医学和反兴奋剂委员会）的决定可以向国际铁联仲裁法庭提出申诉。

（2）只有申诉得到国家会员协会的支持申诉才能被接受。

（3）申诉须在与比赛仲裁委员会会晤后的 30 天之内，或在比赛仲裁委员会或国际铁联申诉委员会做出决定的 30 天内提交。

（4）申诉须以书面的形式提交给国际铁联秘书长，同时提交 500 美金的申诉费。如果申诉成功，申诉费将退还。

(v) Level 2 appeal decisions may be appealed to CAS (Level 3 of Appeal)

13.8. Level 3 Appeal Procedure:

a.) The following procedure will be followed in the event of a Level 3 Appeal:

(i) The decision of the ITU Arbitration Tribunal or of the ITU Medical and Anti-Doping Committee (solely with regards to eligibility) may be appealed, as a final and last resort, to the Court of Arbitration for Sport (CAS), to the exclusion of any recourse to ordinary courts, within thirty (30) natural days from the decision of ITU Arbitration Tribunal.

(ii) Any decision taken by the said court (CAS) shall be without appeal and shall be binding on the parties concerned.

（5） 对二级申诉的申诉将诉诸国际仲裁法庭（三级申诉）。

13.8 三级申诉程序

a）三级申诉应遵循以下程序：

（1） 对国际铁联医学和反兴奋剂委员会（仅与参赛资格有关）或仲裁法庭的判决结果有异议可在国际铁联仲裁法庭做出裁决后的30日内，作为最终的解决方式，申诉至瑞士洛桑的国际体育仲裁法庭，而不可向普通民事法庭提出诉讼。

（2） 国际体育仲裁法庭做出的裁决为最终裁决，对当事各方有效。

ITU COMPETITION RULES: SPECIFIC DISCIPLINE COMPETITION RULES

14. INDOOR TRIATHLON

14.1. Definition:

a.) An Indoor triathlon consists of a triathlon, which takes place in a closed space such as a sports pavillion, which has a swimming pool, a cycling track and a running track.

14.2. Swim:

a.) Two athletes are allowed per lane of 2.5 meters wide.

14.3. Transition area:

a.) Following the swim there will be a ten (10) second "neutralized" time period that is compulsory for all athletes. The purpose of this period is to sponge excess water off the athletes. Water on the track makes it very slippery and dangerous for all athletes. Not complying with this rule will result in disqualification.

14.4. Bike Segment:

a.) The lapped athletes will be not removed from the race;

b.) Athletes can draft from others who are on a different lap.

15. MIDDLE AND LONG DISTANCE EVENTS

15.1. Medical Guidelines:

a.) Specific medical guidelines, including "hot weather" guidelines and medical evacuation plans will be developed by the Race Medical Director in conjunction with the ITU Medical Delegate.

15.2. Distances:

a.) The course should have demanding hills and challenging technical aspects. A 5% tolerance margin will be accepted for the distance of the bike course, provided it has been approved by the Technical Delegate.

15.3. Penalties:

a.) Details about penalties are outlined in section 3.

15.4. Coaches Stations:

a.) In elite races, coaches will have a designated space available on the bike and run segments in order to supply athletes with their own food and beverages.

国际铁人三项联盟竞赛规则：分项竞赛规则

14. 室内铁人三项

14.1 比赛形式

a）室内铁人三项比赛一般在设有游泳池、场地自行车馆和田径场的体育馆举行。

14.2 游 泳

a）2.5 米宽的泳道每道允许 2 名运动员比赛。

14.3 转换区

a）到达游泳终点后，所有运动员必须停留 10 秒钟，其目的是使用海绵吸干运动员身上的水分。水会让自行车赛道变得很滑，对所有运动员造成危险。违反此规则的运动员将被取消比赛资格。

14.4 自行车

a）被套圈的运动员可以继续比赛。

b）运动员可以尾随其他处于不同圈数的运动员。

15. 中、长距离铁人三项

15.1 医疗保障方案

a）比赛医务主任与国际铁联医务代表共同制定详细的医疗保障方案，包括“炎热天气”和急救疏散方案等。

15.2 比赛距离

a）比赛路线应包含高难度的坡道和技术难度。经技术代表同意，自行车路线的距离允许有 5% 的偏差。

15.3 处 罚

a）处罚具体细节见第 3 章。

15.4 教练员指导区

a）自行车和跑步赛道上将分别设置教练员指导区，教练员们可以在这些区域为运动员提供自备的食品和饮料。

15.5. Special Needs Station:

a.) Additional stations on the bike and or run may be provided for special needs;

b.) Any items given out at these stations will be the handed out by volunteers supplied by the Local Organising Committee;

15.6. Transition area:

a.) In the transition area, Technical Officials or Local Organising Committee staff may assist athletes by receiving and placing their bikes and handing out their equipment. This service must be equal for all athletes;

b.) Athletes are allowed to replace their uniforms in the transition area. If the athlete needs to become nude to do it, this action needs to be done inside the tent provided by the Local Organising Committee for this purpose. All the uniforms used by the athlete have to comply with the ITU Competition Rules;

c.) Wetsuits must be removed in the designated area;

d.) For the events where bag drop system is in place, all equipment must be deposited inside the proper bag provided by the Local Organising Committee. The only exception is the bike shoes that may remain attached to the pedals at all times.

15.7. Uniform:

a.) Front zipper is allowed;

b.) Zipper can be undone to the point of the end of the breastbone (sternum) during the competition, with the exception of the last 200 meters of the run, when it needs to be zipped up.

15.8. Outside Assistance:

a.) Medical assistance, food and liquid are permitted at aid stations, special needs stations or at coaches' stations;

b.) Bike catchers may be provided;

c.) Bike Mechanic support may be provided at the approved locations and by the approved vehicles;

d.) The Local Organising Committee may provide helpers to remove wetsuits;

e.) All other outside assistance is prohibited.

15.5 特别补给区

a）骑行或跑步时可在特别区进行补给。

b）在补给区分发的任何物品都应由当地组织委员会的志愿者完成。

15.6 转换区

a）在转换区内，技术官员或当地组委会成员可以协助运动员放车和传递比赛装备，但应同等对待所有运动员。

b）运动员在转换区内可以更换比赛服，如果运动员需要裸体换衣，需在当地组委会提供的专用帐篷内进行，运动员所穿着的所有比赛服都必须符合国际铁联规则。

c）防寒服必须在指定区域更换。

d）在所有设有备包放置系统的赛事中，所有装备必须在当地组织委员会提供的包中正确放置。只有骑行鞋可一直绑在脚蹬上。

15.7 比赛服

a）允许使用前置拉链。

b）比赛期间该拉链最多可拉下至胸骨末端，但在跑步赛段的最后 200 米必须拉上。

15.8 场外援助

a）补给站、特别补给站或教练指导区可提供医疗救助、食物和饮品。

b）可提供辅助自行车协放人员。

c）指定服务车辆在指定地点提供自行车维修服务。

d）当地组织委员会可提供人员帮助更换防寒泳衣。

e）禁止其他场外援助。

16. TEAM AND RELAY EVENTS

16.1. Types of Events:

a.) ITU may organise Team Events in the distances and categories shown in this table:

	Type of competition
Triathlon	3 x Same Gender / 4 x Mixed
Triathlon LD	Adding 3 best times
Duathlon	3 x Same Gender / 4 x Mixed
Duathlon LD	Adding 3 best times
Winter	3 x Same Gender / 4 x Mixed
Cross Triathlon	3 x Same Gender / 4 x Mixed
Cross Duathlon	3 x Same Gender / 4 x Mixed
Corporate Triathlon	Corporate

16.2. Continental Championships and National Federation Events:

a.) Continental Confederations and National Federations should include each of these team competitions in their championships.

16.3. Definitions:

a.) **Mixed relay:** A team is composed of 4 athletes: 2 men and 2 women, who will compete in the following order: woman, man, woman, man. Each of them will cover a complete triathlon, cross triathlon, duathlon, cross duathlon or winter triathlon. The total time for the team is from the start of the 1st team member to the finish of the 4th athlete. Time is continuous and the timing does not stop between athletes. ITU may allow mixed nation teams for specific competitions;

b.) **3x relay:** A team is composed of 3 athletes of same gender. Each of them will cover a complete triathlon, cross triathlon, duathlon, cross duathlon or winter triathlon. The total time for the team is from the start of the 1st team member to the finish of the 3rd athlete. Time is continuous and the timing does not stop between athletes. ITU may allow mixed nation teams for specific competitions;

c.) **Corporate:** A team is composed of 3 athletes regardless of gender. The first athlete will cover the swim segment, the second one the bike segment and the third one the run segment. The total time for the team is from the start of the 1st team member to the finish of the 3rd athlete. Time is continuous and the timing does not stop between athletes. ITU may allow mixed nation teams for specific competitions;

d.) **Team competiton based on the individual results**: The total team time is the addition of the 3 best times of the athletes from the same nation and gender. In case of a tie, the time of the third team member will determine the team result;

16. 团体和接力赛

16.1 比赛组别和距离

a）国际铁联可按照以下类别和距离举办团体比赛：

	比赛形式
铁人三项	3 × 同性接力 /4 × 混合接力
长距离铁人三项	取最好的 3 项个人成绩加和
骑跑两项	3 × 同性接力 /4 × 混合接力
长距离骑跑两项	取最好的 3 项个人成绩加和
冬季铁人三项	3 × 同性接力 /4 × 混合接力
越野铁人三项	3 × 同性接力 /4 × 混合接力
越野骑跑两项	3 × 同性接力 /4 × 混合接力
单项接力铁人三项	单项接力

16.2 洲际锦标赛和会员协会比赛

a）洲际联合会和会员协会应在其洲际锦标赛和全国锦标赛上设置上述团体赛事。

16.3 比赛形式

a）**混合接力：**每个参赛队由 4 名运动员组成：2 名男子和 2 名女子，比赛顺序为：女、男、女、男；每名运动员均须完成一个完整的铁人三项 / 骑跑两项 / 冬季铁人三项比赛；各队完成时间的计算方式为：从第 1 名队员出发开始直至第 4 名队员完成比赛，时间连续不间断计算。国际铁联允许特许比赛中可由不同国别运动员联合组队。

b）**3 人接力：**每个参赛队由 3 名同性别的运动员组成，每名运动员均须完成一个完整的铁人三项 / 骑跑两项 / 冬季铁人三项 / 越野铁人三项 / 越野骑跑两项比赛；各队完成时间的计算方式为：从第 1 名队员出发开始直至第 3 名队员完成比赛，时间连续不间断计算。国际铁联允许特许比赛中可由不同国别运动员联合组队。

c）**单项接力：**每个参赛队由 3 名运动员组成，不限性别；第 1 名运动员完成游泳赛段，第 2 名运动员完成自行车赛段，第 3 名运动员完成跑步赛段；各队完成时间的计算方式为：从第 1 名队员出发开始直至第 3 名队员完成比赛，时间连续不间断计算。国际铁联允许特许比赛中可由不同国别运动员联合组队。

d）**基于个人赛的团体赛：**取同一个队、同性别的 3 名成绩最好的运动员的完成时间相加得团体总成绩。如果总成绩相同，则比较第 3 名运动员的成绩。

16.4. Results:

a.) When National Federations are allowed to enter more than one team, only the team with the best finishing position will be listed in the results and eligible for awards (medals) and prize money.

16.5. Eligibility:

a.) The general eligibility rules apply. The minimum age is 15 years.

b.) Athletes who are competing under ITU flag are not eligible to be included in any team

16.6. Uniform:

a.) The ITU Guidelines Regarding Authorised Identification apply. All members of a team must wear the same country uniform.

16.7. Team Relay Briefing:

a.) Team relay briefing. A briefing for the coaches will be conducted the day before the event.

16.8. Team Composition:

a.) The team coach will declare the team composition at the team relay briefing. All team compositions will be `published after the team relay briefing;

b.) Two hours before the competition start, the coach can communicate a different team composition to the Technical Delegate, otherwise the team composition communicated at the team relay briefing will remain in force.

16.9. Competition Day Check-In:

a.) All the team members must check in together.

b.) Team members can use the same bike.

16.10. Relay Exchange:

a.) The relay exchange from one team member to another will take place inside the exchange zone, which is 15 meters long;

b.) The exchange is completed by the in-coming athlete, using their hand to contact the body of the out-going athlete within the relay zone;

c.) If the exchange occurs unintentionally outside the exchange zone, the team will receive a penalty of 10 seconds, which must be served in the penalty box. If the relay Exchange was done intentionally outside the relay zone, the team will be disqualified.

d.) If the exchange is not completed, the team will be disqualified;

e.) Prior to the relay exchange, the athletes will wait in a pre-relay exchange area until the Technical Official tells them to enter the exchange zone.

16.11. Penalty Box:

a.) Infringements due to starting before the official start time and leaving the helmet strap fastened in transition area infringements will be served by the athlete who infringes the rule;

b.) All time penalties will be penalised with 10 seconds and are to be served at the penalty box. These penalties can be served by any team member currently competing on the field of play.

16.12. Finish:

a.) Only the last team member is allowed to cross the finish line.

16.4 比赛成绩

a） 当每个会员协会可报多个队时，只有成绩最好的队可计成绩和获奖。

16.5 运动员参赛资格

a） 适用通用的参赛资格规则。最低参赛年龄为 15 岁。

b）代表国际铁联参赛的运动员不能参加任何队。

16.6 比赛服

a） 适用《国际铁联（比赛服）授权认证指南》。同一个参赛队的所有成员须穿着同样颜色和样式的比赛服。

16.7 接力赛技术会

a）比赛前一天将召开由教练员参加的接力赛技术会。

16.8 队伍组成

a） 各队教练员在接力赛技术会上提名参赛队员。在接力比赛技术会后接力成员的名单将被公布。

b） 比赛开始前 2 小时，各队教练员可通知技术代表更换参赛队员，否则以接力赛技术会上提供的名单为准。

16.9 比赛日检录

a）同一个参赛队的所有成员须一起检录。

b）参赛队所有成员可以使用同一辆自行车。

16.10 接 力

a） 队员之间的接力在“接力区”完成，接力区长 15 米。

b） 接力方式为：完成比赛的运动员用手接触后一名运动员的身体。

c） 如果交接棒确因失误发生在“接力区”之外，则相关的参赛队必须在处罚区接受 10 秒的处罚。如果有意在接力区外交接棒，取消成绩。

d） 如果接力未能在“接力区”内完成，则相关的参赛队将被取消比赛成绩。

e）接力之前，运动员将在“预接力区”等待，直到技术官员通知其进入接力区。

16.11 处罚区

a） 运动员在出发信号发出前出发或者在转换区未打开头盔搭扣的犯规行为将由犯规运动员接受处罚。

b） 其他时间处罚均为 10 秒并将在处罚区进行。任何一名在赛场上比赛的运动员均可接受时间处罚。

16.12 完成比赛

a） 只有各队的最后一名运动员可通过终点线。

17. PARATRIATHLON

17.1. General:

a.) Paratriathlon, as per the ITU Constitution, is governed by the ITU Competition Rules. This section contains the rules which affect only paratriathlon.

17.2. Paratriathlon Sport Classes:

a.) ITU Paratriathlon has implemented an evidence-based classification system to group impairments into sport classes according to the extent of activity limitation they cause the athlete when performing in the sport of paratriathlon;

b.) There are nine (9) sport classes, as defined in Appendix G:

(i) PTWC1: Most impaired wheelchair users. Athletes must use a recumbent handcycle on the bike course and a racing wheelchair on the run segment;

(ii) PTWC2: Least impaired wheelchair users. Athletes must use a recumbent handcycle on the bike course and a racing wheelchair on the run segment;

(iii) PTS2: Severe impairments. In both bike and run segments, amputee athletes may use approved prosthesis or other supportive devices;

(iv) PTS3: Significant impairments. In both bike and run segments, the athlete may use approved prosthesis or other supportive devices;

(v) PTS4: Moderate impairments. In both bike and run segments, the athlete may use approved prosthesis or other supportive devices;

(vi) PTS5: Mild Impairments. In both bike and run segments, the athlete may use approved prosthesis or other supportive devices;

(vii) PTVI1: Includes athletes who are totally blind, from no light perception in either eye, to some light perception One guide is mandatory throughout the race. Must ride a tandem during the bike segment.

(viii) PTVI2: Includes athletes who are more severe partially sighted athletes. One guide is mandatory throughout the competition. Must ride a tandem during the bike segment.

(ix) PTVI3: Includes athletes who are less severe partially sighted athletes. One guide is mandatory throughout the competition. Must ride a tandem during the bike segment.

17. 伤残铁人三项

17.1 总 则

a）依据国际铁联章程，伤残铁人三项受国际铁联竞赛规则约束。本章节所含规则只适用于伤残铁人三项。

17.2 伤残铁人三项运动级别

a）国际铁联采用循证分级系统，根据运动员参加伤残铁人三项运动时其伤残所造成的行动受限程度进行运动分级。

b）共有 9 个运动级别，如附录 G 所述：

（1） PTWC1：最重度伤残轮椅使用者。运动员在自行车赛道中必须使用倚靠式手摇三轮车，在跑步赛段中必须使用竞速轮椅。

（2） PTWC2：轻度伤残轮椅使用者。运动员在自行车赛道中必须使用倚靠式手摇三轮车，在跑步赛段中必须使用竞速轮椅。

（3） PTS2：极重度伤残。在自行车和跑步赛段中，截肢运动员可使用经过许可的假肢或其他辅助性设备。

（4） PTS3：重度伤残。在自行车和跑步赛段中，运动员可使用经过许可的假肢或其他辅助性设备。

（5） PTS4：中度伤残的。在自行车和跑步赛段中，运动员可使用经过许可的假肢或其他辅助性设备。

（6） PTS5：轻微伤残的。在自行车和跑步赛段中，运动员可使用经过许可的假肢或其他辅助性设备。

（7） PTVI1：包括双眼均无光感知能力的完全失明的，和具有些微光感知能力的运动员。比赛全程必须有引导员陪同，在自行车赛段中必须使用双人自行车。

（8） PTVI2：包括严重的视力障碍运动员，比赛全程必须有引导员陪同，在自行车赛段中必须使用双人自行车。

（9） PTVI3：包括轻度的视力障碍运动员，比赛全程必须有引导员陪同，在自行车赛段中必须使用双人自行车。

17.3. Paratriathlon Medal Events:

a.) There will be six (6) medal events as follows:

(i) PTWC: PTWC1 and PTWC2 sport class athletes competing together;

(ii) PTS2;

(iii) PTS3;

(iv) PTS4;

(v) PTS5;

(vi) PTVI: PTVI1, PTVI2 and PTVI3 sport class athletes competing together.

17.4. Classification:

a.) Paratriathlon Classification Rules can be found in Appendix G;

b.) All Paratriathletes competing at an ITU sanctioned competition must have an international paratriathlon classification to ensure they meet the minimal eligibility criteria for competition and are assigned an appropriate sport class. Paratriathletes requiring classification will need to:

(i) be available to attend an International Classification appointment with an ITU designated Classification Panel prior to the competition;

(ii) provide, at time of classification, the "ITU PI Medical Diagnostics Form" or "ITU VI Medical Diagnostics Form" signed by the appropriate medical personnel, a passport sized photo and any other relevant medical documentation.

c.) Paratriathletes competing at an ITU event, where classification is not available, will be informed through their National Federation to submit specific medical documentation to ITU, no later than six weeks before competition, so that a provisional classification can be assigned to them;

d.) When an athlete's sport class changes, a revision of the past results can be requested. ITU will study each request on a case to case basis and decide whether the relevant competition results need to be modified.

17.5. Eligible classes and Competition formats:

a.) All Paratriathletes are allowed to compete in triathlon, duathlon and aquathlon events. Only Paratriathletes from sport classes PTS2, PTS3, PTS4 and PTS5 are allowed to compete in winter triathlon, cross triathlon and cross duathlon events;

b.) All Paratriathletes may start all together, or grouped in waves. Athletes from the same sport class and gender must start in the same wave;

c.) The Paratriathlon World Championships, the Paratriathlon Continental Championships and the World Paratriathlon Events taking place on Sprint distance will have a time limit of 2 hours;

d.) In a Duathlon event, a paratriathlon competition should be organised at least in two wave starts with a difference of at least one (1) minute. PTWC1 and PTWC2 athletes should start in the first wave and the rest of the athletes in the second wave;

e.) At the discretion of the technical delegate the competition format may be changed;

17.3 伤残铁人三项奖牌赛

a）共有如下 6 个奖牌赛事：

（1） PTWC：PTWC1 和 PTWC2 运动级别运动员共同竞赛。

（2） PTS2。

（3） PTS3。

（4） PTS4。

（5） PTS5。

（6） PTVI：PTVI1、PTVI2 和 PTVI3 级运动员共同竞赛。

17.4 分 级

a）伤残铁人三项分级规则见附录 G。

b）所有参加国际铁联批准的比赛项目的伤残运动员必须进行国际伤残铁人三项分级，以保证他们符合参赛的最低合格标准并被分配到合适的运动级别。要求进行分级的伤残铁三运动员需要：

（1） 在赛前参加一次与国际铁联指定的分级小组举行的国际分级见面会。

（2） 在进行正式分级时提供由合格医务人员签字的《国际铁联身体伤残医学诊断表》或《国际铁联视力伤残医学诊断表》、一张护照尺寸的照片和其他相关医学文件。

c）伤残铁三运动员参加不提供分级服务的国际铁联比赛时，将由其会员协会告知其最迟在开赛 6 周前向国际铁联提交个人医学档案，以对其进行临时性分级。

d）当运动员的分级发生变更时，运动员可对其以往成绩提出修正要求。国际铁联将会对修正要求进行基于具体情况的调查研究，并决定相关成绩是否需要进行调整。

17.5 资格级别和比赛模式

a）所有伤残铁三运动员都可参加铁人三项、骑跑两项和游跑两项。只有 PTS2、PST3、PTS4 和 PTS5 级别的伤残铁三运动员可以参加冬季铁人三项、越野铁人三项和越野骑跑两项。

b）所有伤残铁三运动员可以一起出发，也可分组按批次出发。同一级别和同一性别的运动员应当在同一批次出发。

c）伤残铁人三项世界锦标赛、伤残铁人三项洲际锦标赛和世界伤残铁人三项赛事的短距离比赛将有两小时的时间限制。

d）骑跑两项比赛中，伤残铁三运动员的比赛中应当组织至少两波间隔为至少一分钟的起跑。PTWC1 和 PTWC2 级的运动员应在第一波出发，剩下的运动员在第二波出发。

e）根据技术代表的判断，比赛模式可以变更。

f.) Athletes in different classes may compete together by using the staggered start called "Interval Start System":

(i) In competitions where all classes start together, the relevant compensation time will be added to the final times of the athletes competing in the classes, as follows:

	PTWC1 Men	PTWC2 Men	PTWC1 Women	PTWC2 Women
Sprint triathlon	0:00	+3:00	0:00	+3:58
Sprint duathlon	0:00	+2:44	0:00	+3:36

	PTVI1 Men	PTVI2/PTVI3 Men	PTVI1 Women	PTVI2/PTVI3 Women
Sprint triathlon	0:00	+3:16	0:00	+3:42
Sprint duathlon	0:00	+2:58	0:00	+3:22

* In case a triathlon is modified to a duathlon, duathlon values will be used.

(ii) In races utilizing the "Interval Start System", the start list should be prepared according to the example shown in Appendix L2;

(iii) If an athlete is reclassified into a different class following observation, their finishing time will be adjusted according to the designated compensation times;

(iv) In order to avoid overlapping or issues due to time constraints, the Head Referee may allow a mass start;

(v) Any protests that are filed regarding the starting order and/or compensation times, shall take place according to ITU Article. 12., "Protest of Eligibility."

17.6. Paratriathletes' briefing:

a.) Please see the rules at 2.7 b.) regarding the Paratriathletes briefing.

b.) All guides and personal handlers must be registered at the briefing;

f）不同级别的运动员可以同时出发，可以采用“间隔出发制”交错出发：

（1） 在所有级别同时出发的比赛中，相应补时将被计入在该级别的运动员的最终成绩中，如下表：

	PTWC1 男子	PTWC2 男子	PTWC1 女子	PTWC2 女子
短程铁人三项	0:00	+3:00	0:00	+3:58
短程骑跑两项	0:00	+2:44	0:00	+3:36

	PTVI1 男子	PTVI2/PTVI3 男子	PTVI1 女子	PTVI2/PTVI3 女子
短程铁人三项	0:00	+3:16	0:00	+3:42
短程骑跑两项	0:00	+2:58	0:00	+3:22

** 铁人三项调整为骑跑两项时，将采用骑跑两项的计分。*

（2） 采用间隔出发制的比赛中，出发名单应按照附录 L2 中的示例做好准备。

（3） 若运动员在考察后被重新分到不同的级别中，他们的完成时间将按照指定的补时进行调整。

（4） 为避免重叠交叉或比赛时限的问题，裁判长可允许进行集体出发。

（5） 任何与出发顺序或补时有关的抗议将按国际铁联第 12 章“对参赛资格的抗议”执行。

17.6. 伤残铁三运动员赛前技术会

a） 参见规则 2.7 b) 关有伤残运动员技术会内容。

b） 所有引导员和个人助理都必须在技术会上登记报到。

c.) All Paratriathletes will pick up their own race packet following the briefing. The race packet will include:
 (i) PTWC1 and PTWC2: red swim cap, 3 race number stickers for the helmet, 1 race number sticker for the handcycle, 1 race number sticker for the racing wheelchair, 1 race number sticker for the daily wheelchair, 1 official race number for the athlete and 1 official race number for the personal handler;
 (ii) PTS2, PTS3, PTS4 and PTS5; red, yellow or green swim cap, 3 race number stickers for the helmet, 1 race number sticker for the bike, 3 race number stickers for the prosthesis/aiding devices, 1 official race number for the athlete or 4 sets of body marking, and 1 official race number for the personal handler if authorised;
 (iii) PTVI1: 1 orange swim cap for the athlete and 1 white swim cap for the guide, 6 race number stickers for the helmets, 1 race number sticker for the bike, 1 official race number or 4 sets of body marking for the athlete and 1 official race number for the guide with the word "GUIDE" written on it.
 (iv) PTVI2 and PTVI3: 1 green swim cap for the athlete and 1 white swim cap for the guide, 6 race number stickers for the helmets, 1 race number sticker for the bike, 1 official race number or 4 sets of body marking for the athlete and 1 official race number for the guide with the word "GUIDE" written on it.

17.7. Paratriathlon Personal Handlers

a.) Securing qualified personal handlers shall be the responsibility of the paratriathlete, and they should all be identified and receive credentials from the ITU Technical Officials at the Paratriathlon Briefing;

b.) Personal handlers are to be allotted as follows:
 (i) Up to one (1) personal handler for sport classes PTS2, PTS3, PTS4 and PTS5. The classification process will determine for each athlete the allowance of using one handler in the competitions. The approval for already classified athletes will be done by an Approval Panel composed of:
  - ITU Head of Classification;
  - A member of the ITU Paratriathlon Committee;
  - A person designated by Sport Department.
 (ii) Up to one (1) personal handler for sport class PTWC;
 (iii) No personal handlers for sport class PTVI1, PTVI2 and PTVI3 (Guides may act as the personal handler for this sport class).

c.) Personal handlers are specifically allowed to assist Paratriathletes by:
 (i) Helping with prosthetic devices or other assistive devices;
 (ii) Lifting Paratriathletes in and out of handcycles and wheelchairs;
 (iii) Removing wetsuits or clothing;

c）所有伤残运动员将在技术会后领取参赛包，包内含有：

（1） PTWC1 和 PTWC2 级：红色泳帽，3 张头盔号码贴，1 张手摇自行车号码贴，1 张竞速轮椅号码贴，1 张日常轮椅号码贴，1 张运动员的官方号码布和 1 张个人助理的官方号码布。

（2） PTS2、PTS3、PTS4 和 PTS5 级：红色、黄色或绿色泳帽，3 张头盔号码贴，1 张自行车号码贴，3 张用于假肢或辅助设备的号码贴，1 张运动员的官方号码布或 4 套身体标识贴，1 张给获得授权的个人助理的官方号码布。

（3） PTVI1 级：1 个运动员的橙色泳帽，1 个引导员的白色泳帽，6 张头盔号码贴，1 张自行车号码贴，1 张运动员的官方号码布或者 4 套身体标识贴，1 张给引导员的印有“GUIDE”字样的官方号码布。

（4） PTVI2 和 PTVI3 级：1 个运动员的绿色泳帽，1 个引导员的白色泳帽，6 张头盔号码贴，1 张自行车号码贴，1 张运动员的官方号码布或者 4 套身体标识贴，1 张给引导员的印有“GUIDE”字样的官方号码布。

17.7 伤残铁人三项个人助理

a）伤残铁三运动员有责任确保个人助理符合资格要求，个人助理必须在伤残铁人三项赛前技术会上获得认证，且接收来自国际铁联技术官员的认证凭证。

b）个人助理应按以下原则分配：

（1） PTS2、PTS3、PTS4 和 PTS5 级运动员最多可有 1 名个人助理。分级程序将决定是否允许每一名运动员在比赛中使用个人助理。已分级运动员的审批将由包含以下人员的审批小组进行：

- 国际铁联分级主管。
- 1 名国际铁联伤残铁人三项委员会委员。
- 体育部指定的人员。

（2） PTWC 级运动员最多有 1 名个人助理随同。

（3） PTVI1、PTVI2、PTVI3 级运动员无个人助理随同（引导员可在该级别中作为个人助理。

c）个人助理具体可对伤残铁三运动员进行如下辅助：

（1） 帮助安装运动员的假肢或操作其他辅助设备。

（2） 帮助伤残铁三运动员上、下手摇式自行车和轮椅。

（3） 脱下防寒泳衣或服装。

(iv) Repairing bikes and helping Paratriathletes with other equipment at the transition area or at the official wheel station. PTVI1, PTVI2 and PTVI3 guides can help to repair the bike along the whole bike course, without receiving external help;

(v) Racking the bikes in transition.

d.) All personal handlers shall be subject to the ITU Competition Rules in addition to further regulations deemed appropriate or necessary by the Head Referee;

e.) Any action taken by a personal handler, which propels the Paratriathletes forward may result in a disqualification;

f.) One personal handler can assist ~~a~~ maximum of one athletes~~;~~

g.) All personal handlers shall be located within two (2) meters of their athletes' transition spot during the competition. Permission from a Technical Official is required in order to move outside that zone.

17.8. Paratriathlon Registration Process:

a.) Briefing registration:

(i) Paratriathletes have to sign the attendance list in order to enter the briefing room. At this stage, they must communicate to the Registration Officials whether they will have their own personal handler;

(ii) Paratriathletes must attend the briefing with their personal handler;

(iii) Immediately after the briefing, they will collect their race package and their personal handler will collect the personal handler's t-shirt, as provided by the Local Organising Committee.

b.) Paratriathletes' lounge check in:

(i) Paratriathletes and personal handlers must check in together;

(ii) Personal handlers need to present themselves with the official race number and the official personal handler's t-shirt;

(iii) If a Paratriathlete is present without his/her personal handler/s, he/she has to wait until the personal handler/s arrive. If the Paratriathletes wishes to register on his/her own, then the personal handler/s will not have access to the Field of Play;

(iv) Once a personal handler has been registered, they can only be replaced in exceptional circumstances and only after approval by the Technical Delegate;

(v) Two Timing chips will be delivered to all athletes during this process;

(vi) Equipment (prosthesis, crutches, etc) for the pre-transition area (must have a race number on it) and will be checked at the Paratriathletes' lounge.

（4） 在转换区或官方维修站帮助伤残铁三运动员维修自行车或安装调试其他设备。在不接受外部帮助的情况下，PTVI1、PTVI2、PTVI3 引导员可在整个自行车赛道帮助伤残铁三运动员维修自行车。

（5） 将自行车架在转换区。

d）除国际铁联竞赛规则外，所有个人助理还需服从裁判长要求的其他适当或必要的规则。

e）个人助理采取的任何助力伤残运动员的行动都可能导致运动员失去比赛资格。

f）1 名个人助理最多只能为 1 名运动员提供辅助。

g）比赛时，所有个人助理必须位于运动员转换点 2 米内。离开该区域需获得技术官员的许可。

17.8 伤残铁人三项报到流程

a）赛前技术会报到：

（1） 伤残铁三运动员需要在签到表上签名才能进入赛前技术会会场。同时运动员须向签到官员说明自己是否有个人助理随同。

（2） 个人助理须和伤残铁三运动员一同参加赛前技术会。

（3） 赛前技术会结束后运动员需立即领取参赛包，个人助理需领取个人助理的 T 恤衫，以上物资由当地组委会提供。

b）伤残铁三运动员休息室检录：

（1） 伤残铁三运动员及其个人助理必须一起检录。

（2） 个人助理需身着其官方号码布和官方个人助理 T 恤衫。

（3） 伤残铁三运动员需等待其个人助理抵达并一起检录，若伤残铁三运动员意图独自检录，则其个人助理无法进入比赛场地。

（4） 一经检录，只有在遇到特殊情况并由技术代表同意后方可更换个人助理。

（5） 该过程中将为每名运动员分发两块计时芯片。

（6） 用于预备转换区的装备（假肢、拐杖等）须贴有号码，并在运动员休息室接受检查。

17.9. Pre-Transition area conduct:

a.) If a pre-transition area exists, paratriathletes in PTWC1, PTWC2, PTS2, PTS3, PTS4 and PTS5 sport classes may remove their wetsuits in this area. Only personal handlers from athletes racing in the PTWC1 and PTWC2 sport class are allowed to assist their assigned Paratriathlete in this area, but cannot propel nor push the athlete forward;

b.) All PTWC1 and PTWC2 athletes must transfer in a day chair from pre-transition to transition. The wheelchairs provided by the PTWC1 and PTWC2 Paratriathletes for this area must have functional brakes;

c.) The closest available area to the swim exit area will always be used to line up the PTWC1 and PTWC2 wheelchairs according to their race number;

d.) There should be a dedicated space in the pre-transition area with numbered chairs from 1-9+0, to set up and display all prosthetic devices/crutches for Paratriathletes from the PTWC1, PTWC2, PTS2, PTS3, PTS4 and PTS5 sport classes (if required). PTS2, PTS3, PTS4 and PTS5 athletes must leave their prosthesis or crutches at the chair with the same number as the last digit of their race number. A minimum of two (2) Technical Officials will coordinate the distribution of these equipment devices to the athletes as they exit the water and receive notification of the race number from the Technical Official situated at the water exit. All of the equipment will be lined up in numerical order;

e.) No athletes' equipment can be left in the pre-transition area, once the athlete exits the pre-transition area.

f.) Adapted cleats and bike shoes with non-exposed cleats - that are mounted on prosthetic legs - are allowed in the pre-transition area, provided that the cleats are covered or enclosed by anti-slip material.

g.) Paratriathletes in PTS2 to PTS5 with an absent lower limb must use a prosthesis or crutches between Pre-Transition and Transition area 1. Hopping on one leg is not permitted from Pre-Transition to Transition area 1.

17.10. Transition Area Conduct:

a.) The Local Organising Committee shall provide a minimum of 16 swim exit assistants at swim exit area, who will be responsible for assisting the Paratriathletes from the swim exit to the pre-transition area. The final number of swim exit assistants shall be determined by the ITU Technical Delegate. Only these persons will be allowed to enter this area. Their training should be supervised by the ITU Technical Delegate;

b.) During the swim exit, the paratriathletes will receive assistance from the swim exit assistants according to their swim cap colours, as follows:

(i) Red: Paratriathlete needs to be lifted from the swim exit to the wetsuit removal area;

(ii) Yellow: Paratriathlete needs to be supported to walk/run from the swim exit to the wetsuit removal area;

17.9 预备转换区管理

a）若设有预备转换区，PTWC1、PTWC2、PTS2、PTS3、PTS4 和 PTS5 级的运动员在此区域脱去防寒泳衣。只有参加 PTWC1、PTWC2 级比赛的伤残铁三运动员的个人助理可以在此区域对各自指定的运动员进行辅助，但不能助力向前推行运动员。

b）所有 PTWC1、PTWC2 级运动员从预备转换区到达转换区时须乘坐日常轮椅。PTWC1、PTWC2 级运动员提供的用于该区域的轮椅必须有能正常使用的刹车。

c）在距离上水区最近的区域，将按照 PTWC1、PTWC2 级运动员的号码摆放他们的轮椅。

d）（如有需要）应当在预备转换区准备从 1~9+0 数字的椅子，设置专门区域用于摆放和展示所有 PTWC1、PTWC2、PTS2、PTS3、PTS4 和 PTS5 级伤残铁三运动员的假肢或拐杖。PTS2、PTS3、PTS4 和 PTS5 级运动员把假肢或拐杖放在其比赛号码最后一位数的椅子上。当运动员出水时，至少两名技术官员将在该区域协调相关器材的发放并接收上水区技术官员的报号提示。所有装备器材需按号码摆放好。

e）运动员离开预备转换区时，应将其所有的装备带离预备转换区。

f）预备转换区内允许使用安装在假肢上的有非暴露防滑钉的适应性运动钉鞋和自行车鞋，防滑钉应被覆盖或裹上防滑材料。

g）PTS2 到 PTS5 级的肢残运动员必须使用假肢或拐杖在预备转换区和第一换项区之间穿行。不允许单腿跳。

17.10 转换区管理

a）当地组委会应当在上水区安排至少 16 名上水助理人员，负责帮助上水区的伤残铁三运动员到达预备转换区。上水区的助理人员最终数量由国际铁联技术代表决定。只有这些人员才能进入该区域。对这些人员的培训应受国际铁联技术代表监督。

b）上水期间，上水助理将根据运动员泳帽颜色对伤残铁三运动员提供帮助：

（1） 红色：伤残铁三运动员需要从上水区抬至防寒泳衣更换区。

（2） 黄色：伤残铁三运动员需要被搀扶着走或跑到防寒泳衣更换区。

(iii) Green, orange or white: Paratriathlete does not need any assistance at the swim exit. White caps will be used for the guides.

c.) Swim exit assistants will assist the athletes to the best of their ability, in good faith and considering safety as the main principle;

d.) Bicycles, tandems or handcycles are not allowed from the swim exit to the transition area;

e.) All mobility equipment shall remain within each Paratriathlete's assigned space in the transition zone. All used swim caps, goggles, wetsuits, swim tethers, helmets in the box;

f.) Bike shoes must be left in the athlete assigned space in the transition area, before and after the bike segment;

g.) PTVI1, PTVI2 and PTVI3 positions in the transition area must be the closest to the mount line (women and men), followed by the rest of the sport classes PTS5, PTS4, PTS3, PTS2 and PTWC1 and PTWC2. PTWC1 and PTWC2 Paratriathletes are allowed to ride the handcycle inside the transition area;

h.) Each PTWC1 and PTWC2 paratriathlete will have an individual space of 4x2 meters. The athlete, the handlers and all the equipment will be inside this space, during manouvres in the transition area.

17.11. Paratriathlon Swimming Conduct / Equipment:

a.) For safety reasons, categories will be presented during the Paratriathletes' presentation at competition start in the following order: PTVI1, PTVI2, PTVI3, PTS5, PTS4, PTS3, PTS2, PTWC1 and PTWC2. For safety reasons, PTWC1 and PTWC2 paratriathletes should always enter the water after all other Paratriathletes are in place;

b.) The swim start shall be an "in-water" start;

c.) If the swim portion consists of multiple laps, Paratriathletes will not be required to exit the water between laps;

d.) Artificial propulsive devices including (but not limited to) fins, paddles, or floating devices of any kind are not allowed. All prosthetic and/or orthoses devices are considered propulsion devices except for the approved knee braces. Use of any such devices will result in disqualification;

e.) Any sharp objects, screws, prosthetic liners, or prosthetic devices that can be harmful are not allowed during the swim segment;

f.) Wetsuit use is determined by the chart below:

Swim length	Wetsuits mandatory below	Maximum stay in water
750 m	18 °C	45 mins
1500 m	18 °C	1h 10 mins
3000 m	18 °C	1h 40 mins
4000 m	18 °C	2h 15 mins

（3） 绿色、橙色或白色：伤残铁三运动员在上水区不需要任何辅助，白色泳帽仅用于引导员。

c） 上水助理应当以安全为首要原则，全心全力帮助运动员发挥出最佳水平。

d） 上水区和转换区之间不允许使用自行车、双人自行车和手摇式自行车。

e） 所有移动装备必须留在各伤残运动员所在转换区内的指定位置，所有使用过的泳帽、护目镜、防寒泳衣、泳绳和头盔放在箱子里。

f） 在自行车比赛前及比赛后，自行车鞋必须被放置在转换区内的指定位置。

g） 转换区内 PTVI1、PTVI2、PTVI3 级运动员（男子和女子）的位置必须离上车线最近，后面紧接着是 PTS5、PTS4 、PTS3 、PTS2 和 PTWC1、PTWC2 级运动员。PTWC1、PTWC2 级伤残铁三运动员可以在转换区内骑乘手摇式自行车。

h） 每名 PTWC1、PTWC2 级伤残铁三运动员将有一片 4 米 ×2 米的个人空间。在转换期间，运动员和个人助理及其所有装备都需在此区域内。

17.11 伤残铁人三项游泳比赛管理 / 装备

a） 出于安全考虑，伤残铁三运动员在比赛开始时将按以下类别分组出发：PTVI1、PTVI2、PTVI3 、PTS5、 PTS4 、PTS3 、PTS2 和 PTWC1、PTWC2。PTWC1、PTWC2 级运动员需在其他所有伤残铁三运动员就位后入水。

b）游泳比赛从水中出发。

c）若游泳部分包含多圈次，伤残铁三运动员不需要在圈次间离水。

d）人造推进设备包括（但不限于）脚蹼、桨板或其他任何类型的漂浮设备都不允许使用。除经许可的膝关节支架外，所有假肢和其他辅助设备将被认定为推进设备。使用任何一种此类设备都会被取消比赛资格。

e） 任何尖锐物体、螺丝刀、假肢衬垫，或其他任何可能造成伤害的假肢设备都不允许在游泳赛段使用。

f） 防寒泳衣使用参照下表：

游泳距离	低于该温度时强制使用防寒泳衣	水中停留最长时间
750 米	18℃	45 分钟
1500 米	18℃	1 小时 10 分钟
3000 米	18℃	1 小时 40 分钟
4000 米	18℃	2 小时 15 分钟

g.) If any paratriathlete has not completed the swim course within this time limit and is more than 100 meters short of the finish, they shall be removed immediately from the water;

h.) Wetsuits will not be permitted when the water temperature is 28 °Celsius or above;

i.) If the water temperature is between 30.1°C and 32.0°C, the maximum distance is 750 m and the maximum stay in water 20 minutes;

j.) The swim portion may be cancelled, if the official water temperature is higher of 32°C or lower than 15 °C. (Official water temperature is calculated, as indicated in the chart below):

(i) The temperatures above are not always the water temperature used in the final decision. If the water temperature is lower than 22°C and the air temperature is lower than 15°, then the adjusted value is to decrease the measured water temperature according to the next chart:

(*)		Air temperature (All values in °C)								
		15	14	13	12	11	10	9	8	7
Water Temperature (All values in °C)	22	18.5	18.0	17.5	17.0	16.5	16.0	15.5	15.0	Cancel
	21	18.0	17.5	17.0	16.5	16.0	15.5	15.0	Cancel	Cancel
	20	17.5	17.0	16.5	16.0	15.5	15.0	Cancel	Cancel	Cancel
	19	17.0	16.5	16.0	15.5	15.0	Cancel	Cancel	Cancel	Cancel
	18	16.5	16.0	15.5	15.0	Cancel	Cancel	Cancel	Cancel	Cancel
	17	16.0	15.5	15.0	Cancel	Cancel	Cancel	Cancel	Cancel	Cancel
	16	15.5	15.0	Cancel	Cancel	Cancel	Cancel	Cancel	Cancel	Cancel
	15	15.0	Cancel	Cancel	Cancel	Cancel	Cancel	Cancel	Cancel	Cancel

17.12. Paratriathlon Cycling Conduct / Equipment:

a.) Paratriathlon competitions are draft-illegal events. Winter Triathlon, Cross Duathlon and Cross Triathlon are draft legal events for Paratriathletes;

b.) In paratriathlon competitions, the term "bike" used herein shall include bicycles, tandems, or handcycles;

c.) All bikes shall be propelled by human force. Arms or legs can be used to propel the cycle, but not both. Any violation shall result in disqualification;

d.) Bike specifications for paratriathlon competitions are outlined in the ITU Competition Rules section 5.2;

e.) Bicycles, tandems, and handcycles must have two independent braking systems. Bicycles and tandems must have an independent brake on each wheel. Both brakes on the handcycles will act on the front wheel;

f.) Disc brakes are allowed;

g.) Paratriathletes with one upper limb impairment may use a splitter in the braking system and it is not considered as a bike adaptation;

h.) Protective shields, fairings or other devices, which have the effect of reducing resistance, are not allowed;

i.) Artificial handgrips and prosthetics can be fixed to the bike or to the athlete's body, but not both simultaniously

g）若有任何伤残铁三运动员在上述时间限制内没有完成游泳比赛且处在终点线外100米以上，则应该立即将其从水中带上岸。

h）水温在28℃或以上时，不允许使用防寒泳衣。

i）水温在30.1℃和32.0℃之间，最远距离为750米，在水中停留最长时间为20分钟。

j）若官方测定水温高于32℃或低于15℃，取消游泳比赛（官方水温按下表测算）。

（1）上述水温并不是做出最后决定时使用的数值。若水温低于22℃且气温低于15℃，测得水温则按下表进行下调。

		气温（℃）								
		15	14	13	12	11	10	9	8	7
水温（℃）	22	18.5	18.0	17.5	17.0	16.5	16.0	15.5	15.0	取消
	21	18.0	17.5	17.0	16.5	16.0	15.5	15.0	取消	取消
	20	17.5	17.0	16.5	16.0	15.5	15.0	取消	取消	取消
	19	17.0	16.5	16.0	15.5	15.0	取消	取消	取消	取消
	18	16.5	16.0	15.5	15.0	取消	取消	取消	取消	取消
	17	16.0	15.5	15.0	取消	取消	取消	取消	取消	取消
	16	15.5	15.0	取消	取消	取消	取消	取消	取消	取消
	15	15.0	取消	取消	取消	取消	取消	取消	取消	取消

17.12 伤残铁人三项自行车比赛管理 / 设备

a）伤残铁人三项是不允许尾随的比赛。伤残铁三运动员参加冬季铁人三项，越野骑跑两项和越野铁人三项时允许尾随。

b）在伤残铁人三项比赛中，此处使用的“自行车”一词包含了自行车、双人自行车或手摇式自行车。

c）所有自行车应由人力驱动。手或腿可用于驱动自行车，但不能同时驱动。违反此规定将取消比赛资格。

d）用于伤残铁人三项的自行车技术参数在《国际铁联竞赛规则》5.2中有描述。

e）自行车、双人自行车和手摇式自行车必须有两套独立的刹车系统。自行车和双人自行车的前后轮必须有独立的刹车。手摇式自行车的两个刹车都应作用于前轮。

f）允许使用碟刹。

g）单臂残疾的伤残铁三运动员可在刹车系统中使用分离器，且不被认为是对自行车进行改装。

h）不允许使用防护盾、整流罩或其他有减少阻力效果的设备。

i）可以将人工握把和假肢固定到自行车或运动员身体上，但不能同时固定在两者上。

j.) Except for handcycles (PTWC1 and PTWC2), a rider's position shall be supported solely by the pedals, the saddle and the handlebars;

k.) Paratriathletes with a lower limb above the knee amputation or limb defficency not wearing a prosthesis may use a support/socket for the thigh which is not considered an adaptation requiring approval.

l.) All requests for impairment adaptations to any bike or handcycle must be submitted by the corresponding National Federation in writing for ITU approval at least one (1) month before the event in which the athlete wishes to compete in, with a clear explanation and a minimum of 5 pictures using the form named "Equipment Adaptation Form" posted under: http://www.triathlon.org/about/downloads_category/paratriathlon. The solicitant will be informed by the ITU on the outcome of the request once the panel has reviewed the information. If accepted, the information will be incorporated to the "Approved Paratriathlon Impairment Adaptations on Bicycles" file under the same location;

m.) The ITU and the ITU Technical Officials shall not be liable for any consequences deriving from the choice of equipment and/or any adaptations used by Paratriathlete, nor for any defects it may have, or its non-compliance;

n.) No bike course shall have a maximum gradient of over 12% at the steepest section;

o.) If the use of the official race number is mandatory, it must be visible from the back.

17.13. Paratriathlon PTWC1 and PTWC2 Swimming Conduct/Equipment:

a.) Athletes may only use up to 3 bindings around the legs in any position. The bindings will be 10cm in width, as a maximum;

b.) The use of knee brace is permitted, provided the equipment provides neither flotation nor propulsion. If a wetsuit is worn, the brace shall be fitted to the outside of the wetsuit. The knee brace can cover half of the leg's surface as a maximum. The length cannot surpass the upper half of the thigh or the bottom half of the calf and has to be holding the knee/s area:

(i) Knee brace specifications:

- Material: PVC plastic or carbon-fiber with no floatability or propulsion capacity;
- It cannot have any space or chamber that traps air or any other kind of gas;
- The thickness is limited to 5mm as a maximum.

j）除 PTWC1、PTWC2 级手摇式自行车使用者外，骑手的位置应该由踏板、座垫和把手独立支持。

k）下肢膝关节以上截肢的或有肢体缺陷的伤残铁三运动员若未使用假肢，则可以使用大腿支架或插槽，这一改动不需要请求许可。

l）所有对自行车或手摇自行车的伤残适应性改造申请必须在运动员欲参加的比赛开赛至少一个月前由相关会员协会以书面形式提交给国际铁联审批，申请需使用下面地址中的“装备适应性改造表”并附上清晰的解释和至少 5 张照片：http://www.triathlon.org/about/downloads_category/paratriathlon。审核小组完成信息审查后，申请者将收到国际铁联的申请结果通知。若申请通过，相关信息将被录入同地址下的“认可的伤残铁人三项自行车伤残适应性改造列表”文件中。

m）国际铁联和国际铁联技术官员不对伤残铁三运动员选择的装备和进行的适应性改造及其缺陷与不适配性造成的任何后果负责。

n）自行车赛道最陡峭处的坡度不应超过 12%。

o）若强制使用官方号码布，则其必须从背面可视。

17.13 伤残铁人三项 PTWC1、PTWC2 级游泳比赛管理 / 装备

a）运动员在腿上任一处使用至多 3 条捆绑带，捆绑带最大宽度为 10 厘米。

b）在装备不提供浮力或推进力的情况下，允许使用膝关节支架。如果穿着了防寒泳衣，膝关节支架应当被固定在泳衣之外。膝关节支架最多覆盖腿部表面的一半。长度不能超过大腿的上半部分或小腿的下半部分且必须支撑住膝关节区域：

（1） 膝关节支架详细要求：

- 材质：不提供浮力或推进力的 PVC 塑料或碳纤维。
- 不能有可以存储空气或其他任何气体的空间或腔室。
- 厚度不得超过 5 毫米。

c.) The knee braces have to be approved by ITU. All requests must be submitted by the corresponding National Federation in writing for ITU approval at least (1) month before the event in which the athlete wishes to compete in, with a clear explanation and a minimum of 5 pictures using the form named "Knee Brace Approval Request Form" posted under the "Documents" section of the ITU website. The National Federation solicitant will be informed by the ITU on the outcome of the request once the panel has reviewed the information. If accepted, the information will be incorporated to the "Approved Knee Braces Catalogfile under the same location;

d.) The use of wetsuit bottoms is always permitted.

17.14. Paratriathlon PTWC1 and PTWC2 Cycling Conduct/Equipment:

a.) Paratriathletes must use an arm powered (AP) handcycle in a recumbent position;

b.) Specifications of a recumbent position handcycle are as follows:

(i) A handcycle shall be an arm powered, three-wheeled vehicle with an open frame of tubular construction, which conforms to the general principles of the International Cycling Union's (UCI) construction for bicycles (except that the chassis frame tubes need not be straight). For the seat or backrest construction, the maximum frame tube diameter may not exceed the maximum defined by the general principles of UCI;

(ii) The single wheel may be of a different diameter to the double wheels. The front wheel or wheels shall be steerable; the single wheel, either front or rear, shall be driven through a system comprising handgrips and a chain. The handcycle shall be propelled solely through a chainset and conventional cycle drive train, of crank arms, chainwheels, chain and gears, with handgrips replacing foot pedals. It shall be propelled by the hands, arms and upper body only;

(iii) The Paratriathlete must have clear vision. As such, the horizontal of the Paratriathlete's eye line must be above the center of the crank housing/crank set, when (s)he is sitting with his/her hands on the handlebars facing forward at full extent, the tip of his/her shoulder blades in contact with the backrest and his/her head in contact with the headrest, when applicable. From this position, conforming measurements are calculated as follows: (#1) The distance from the ground to the centre of the Paratriathlete's eyes and (#2) the distance from the ground to the centre of the crank housing (crank set). Measurement #1) must be equal or greater than measurement #2;

(iv) All handcycles must have a mirror fixed either to the athlete's helmet or at some point on the front of the bike to ensure rear-view vision is possible;

c）其关节支架必须获得国际铁联批准。所有申请必须在运动员欲参加的比赛开赛至少一个月前由相关会员协会以书面形式提交给国际铁联审批，申请需使用国际铁联网站文档区中的“膝关节支架许可申请表”并附上清晰的解释和至少 5 张照片。审订小组完成信息审查后申请者将收到国际铁联的申请结果通知。若申请通过，信息将被录入同一地址下的“审批通过的膝关节支架目录”文件中。

d）允许使用防寒泳衣下装。

17.14 伤残铁人三项 PTWC1、PTWC2 组自行车赛管理 / 装备

a）伤残铁三运动员必须使用手臂驱动的倚靠式手摇自行车。

b）倚靠式手摇自行车详细要求如下：

（1）手摇自行车应当是由手臂驱动，有三个轮子，以管状结构构筑起开放式框架的载具。同时还需要符合国际自行车联盟对自行车构成的基本原则（除了底盘框架管不需要是直的）。座位或靠垫架构部分，框架管最大直径不应超过国际自行车联盟在总则中规定的最大直径。

（2）独立轮和并立轮必须为不同直径。前轮应当是可控的；独立轮，无论是前轮还是后轮，应当由一个包含握把和链条的系统驱动。手摇自行车应当由一套独立的链组和由手摇柄、牙盘、链条、飞轮和用以替代踏板的握把组成的常规自行车装置驱动。手摇自行车应当只由手、臂和上肢驱动。

（3）伤残铁三运动员应当有清晰的视野。当运动员面朝前方手握自行车手把坐下，肩胛端与座位靠背接触，头与头部靠垫相接触时，运动员水平视线应当高于手摇柄的中心或手摇柄装置。在这一姿势下，符合规定的距离如下：（#1）地面到伤残铁三运动员两眼中间的距离，（#2）地面到手摇柄中心位置的距离。#1 应大于等于 #2。

（4）所有手摇自行车前端某处或运动员头盔上应当装有后视镜，以保证后方视野。

(v) The athlete must have the feet positioned in front of the knees during the bike segment;

(vi) Adjustments to handcycle may not be made during the competition;

(vii) Wheels of the handcycle may vary in diameter between a (ERTRO) 406 mm minimum and a 622 mm maximum, excluding the tyre. Modified hub attachments may be used if necessary. The width of handcycle double wheels may vary between 55 cm minimum and 70 cm maximum, measured at the centre of each tyre where the tyres touch the ground;

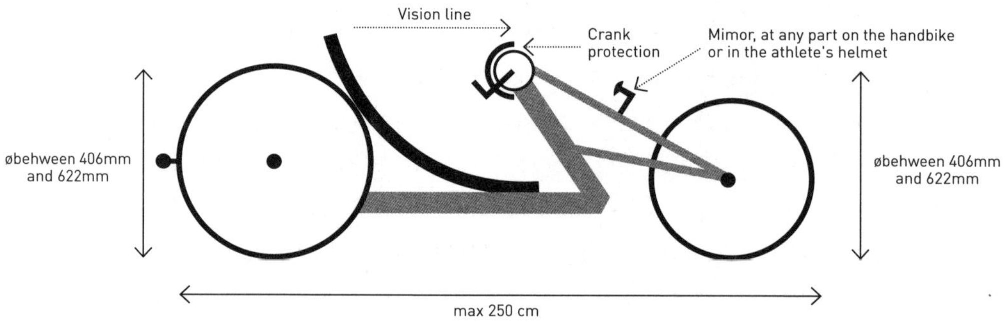

(viii) Disc wheels are allowed in the front and rear of the handcycles;

(x) Disc brakes are allowed on the rear wheels;

(xi) A handcycle shall not measure more than 250 cm in length or 75 cm in width;

(xii) The shifting device can either be within the extremities of the handlebars, or on the side of the Paratriathlete's body;

(xiii) The largest chain ring shall have a guard securely fitted to protect the Paratriathlete. This protection shall be made of solid material that is sufficiently robust and covers the chain ring fully over half of its circumference (180°) on the side facing the rider;

(xiii) Any fillets, or ribs, inserted at joints between tubes, shall be for strengthening purposes only. Non-functional, aerodynamic devices are not permitted for competition;

(xiv) A quick release body harness is permitted;

(xv) It is mandatory that a handcycle with two rear wheel should be equipped with a safety bar to prevent the front wheelof a following competitior from entering the space between the rear wheels;

（5） 自行车比赛时，运动员须将脚放在膝盖前方。

（6） 比赛期间不能对手摇自行车进行调整。

（7） 手摇自行车车轮直径可在 406 毫米到 622 毫米之间，不包括轮胎。如果需要可以使用改良的轮毂连接件。手摇自行车两并立轮的宽度在 55 厘米到 70 厘米之间，以两轮触地点中心位置的间距离为准。

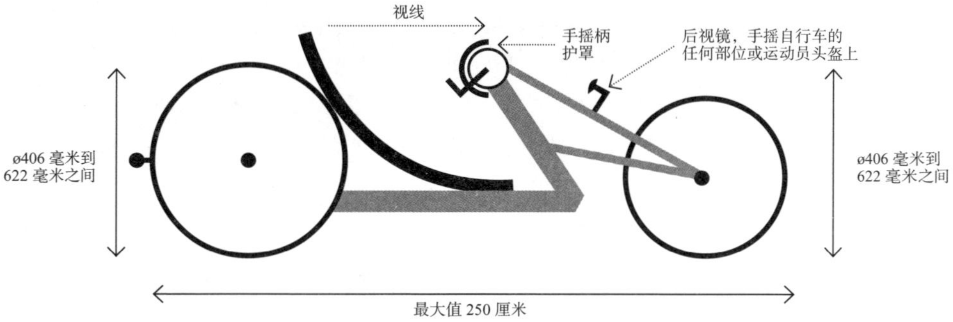

（8） 手摇自行车前轮和后轮允许使用碟盘轮。

（9） 允许在后轮上使用碟刹。

（10）手摇自行车长度不能超过 250 厘米，宽度不能超过 75 厘米。

（11）变速装置既可以位于握把上也可以位于伤残铁三运动员体侧。

（12）最大的牙盘上应当牢固地装上保护装置以保护运动员。该保护装置应当由有足够强度的硬质材料制成，足够结实，并能完全遮住面对骑手一侧的至少半周牙盘（超过 180° ）。

（13）任何在框架管连接处添加的绑带或肋材应只用于加强强度。非功能性、空气动力学设备不允许在比赛中使用。

（14）允许使用速脱式安全带。

（15）后轮采用并立轮的手摇自行车必须在车后方安装保险杠，以防止后方参赛者的前轮进入前车的后轮之间。

(xvi) A safety bar is required and must not exceed the width of each rear wheel tyre and all tube ends must be closed or plugged. The safety bar must be fitted 15 mm (+/- 2 mm) behind the wheels. It must be around tube (at least 18 mm in diameter) and made of adequately solid material to resist impact without bending or breaking. The distance between the ground and the bar axis must be 280 mm (+/- 10 mm). The structure and assembly of the safety bar must guarantee that normal bumps, which may be experienced during a competition, don't affect the safe functioning of the bar (see diagram);

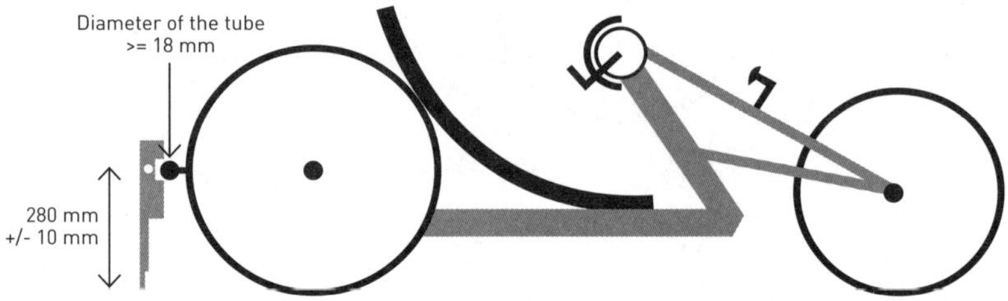

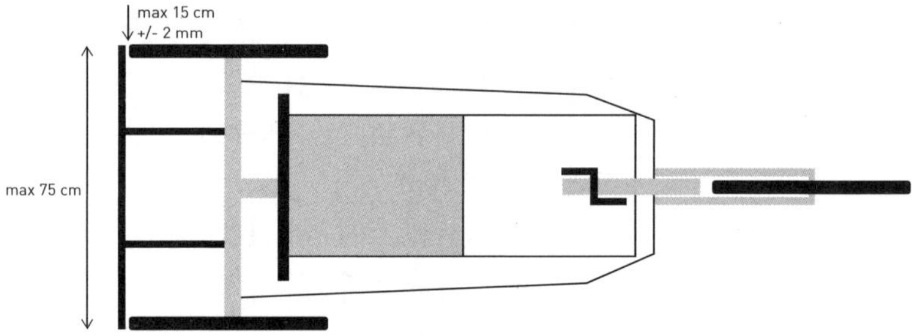

c.) The official race number will be placed at the back of the handcycle and will be visible from the back;

d.) The helmet must be fastened before getting onto the handcycle and it must remain fastened till the finish;

e.) Athletes must stop completely at the mount line exiting Transition 1 and at the dismount line on entering Transition 2. Once stopped, the Technical Official will say "Go" and the athlete can continue the competition. The wheelchair is considered correctly stopped if the front wheel stops immediately before the line. If the front wheel stops touching the line or beyond the line, a time penalty will be applied.

（16）车上必须装有保险杠，且宽度不能超过后轮。所有框架管末端必须被封闭或填充。保险杠必须被安装在后轮后 15 毫米（±2 毫米）。必须采用能够抵抗冲击且不弯曲或断裂的高强度硬质材料圆形管（直径至少 18 毫米）。保险杠的轴心距离地面必须为 280 毫米 ±10 毫米。保险杠的结构和组装必须保证比赛期间经常出现的碰撞不影响其安全防护功能（见图示）。

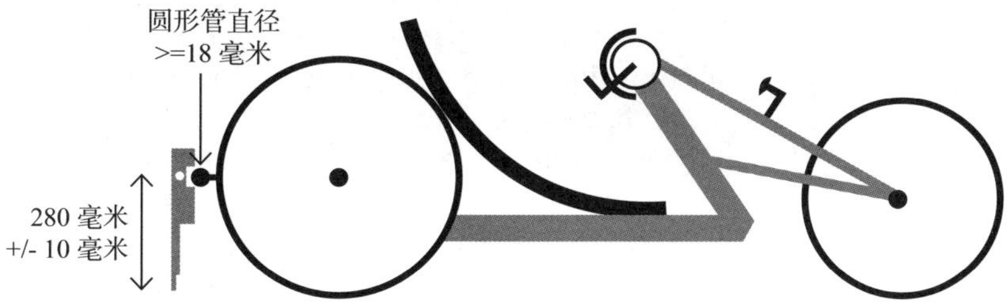

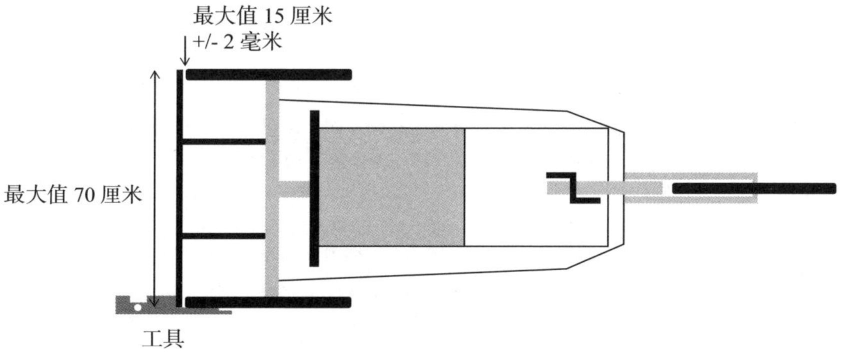

c）官方号码布应放置在手摇自行车后部，且从后方可视。

d）上车前须戴好头盔，且保持紧固直到比赛结束。

e）运动员在离开转换区 1 的上车线和进入转换区 2 的下车线处必须完全停止。一旦停止，需要由技术官员下达“出发”的指令才能继续比赛。轮椅前轮在触线前完全停止才被认为是停止达标，触线或压线者需接受时间处罚。

17.15. Paratriathlon PTWC1 and PTWC2 Running Conduct/ Equipment:

a.) All paratriathletes perform the run portion in a "racing wheelchair";

b.) The specifications of a "racing wheelchair" (hereafter referred to as "the chair") are as follows:

(i) The chair shall have two large wheels and one small wheel;

(ii) There should be a brake at the front wheel;

(iii) No part of the body of the chair may extend forwards beyond the hub of the front wheel and be wider than the inside of the hubs of the two rear wheels. The maximum height from the ground of the main body of the chair shall be 50 cm;

(iv) The maximum diameter of the large wheel, including the inflated tyre, shall not exceed 70 cm. The maximum diameter of the small wheel, including the inflated tyre, shall not exceed 50 cm;

(v) Only one plain, round, hand rim is allowed for each large wheel. No mechanical gears or levers that propel the chair shall be allowed;

(vi) Only hand operated, mechanical steering devices will be allowed;

(vii) Paratriathletes must be able to turn the front wheel manually to the left and right;

(viii) No part of the chair may protrude behind the vertical plane of the back edge of the rear tyres;

(ix) It will be the Paratriathlete's responsibility to ensure the wheelchair conforms to all the above rules and no event shall be delayed while adjustments are made to the chair;

(x) Paratriathletes must ensure that their lower limbs have enough support/bracing to prevent them from dragging or making contact with the ground during the event;

(xi) Paratriathletes shall wear the approved bike helmet at all times while seated in the chair.

c.) Propulsion by any other method except the Paratriathlete pushing on the wheels or push-rims will result in disqualification.

d.) It is forbidden to draft off a motorbike or vehicle and blue card will be used to inform the athletes. Drafting is entering the motorbike or vehicle drafting zone (penalties outlined in 5.6):

- Motorbike draft zone: the draft zone behind a motorbike will be 12 meters long.
- Vehicle draft zone: The draft zone behind a vehicle will be 35 meters long and applies to every vehicle.

e.) A Paratriathlete attempting to overtake another Paratriathlete carries the responsibility of ensuring full clearance of the chair being overtaken before cutting across. The Paratriathlete being overtaken has the responsibility not to obstruct or impede the passing Paratriathlete once the front wheel(s) of the passing chair is ahead of his/hers;

17.15 伤残铁人三项 PTWC1、PTWC2 级跑步比赛管理 / 设备

a）所有伤残铁三运动员应乘坐“竞速轮椅”完成跑步阶段比赛。

b）“竞速轮椅”（此后称轮椅）的详细要求如下：

（1） 轮椅应当具有两个大轮子和一个小轮子。

（2） 前轮应当有刹车。

（3） 轮椅车体不能超过前轮中心，不能宽于两后轮之间的距离。轮椅主体到地面的距离不超过 50 厘米。

（4） 包括已充气的轮胎，大轮最大直径不超过 70 厘米，小轮最大直径不超过 50 厘米。

（5） 两个大轮只能使用扁平的圆形手摇轮辋。不能安装可以驱动轮椅的机械装置或控制杆。

（6） 只能使用手动的机械转向装置。

（7） 伤残铁三运动员能够手动将前轮向左和向右转。

（8） 车体不能超出后轮胎的后边缘所在垂直面。

（9） 伤残铁三运动员有责任保证其轮椅符合以上所有规则，比赛不会因为调整轮椅而延后。

（10）伤残铁三运动员必须保证其下肢有足够的支撑或固定装置以防止其下肢拖到地面或在比赛期间与地面发生接触。

（11）伤残铁三运动员坐在轮椅上时须一直佩戴认证许可的头盔。

c）伤残铁三运动员推动轮子或轮毂之外的任何举动都将导致其比赛资格被取消。

d）禁止尾随摩托车或其他机动车，尾随将罚以蓝牌警告。进入摩托车或机动车尾随区域将视为尾随（处罚条例见 5.6）：

- 摩托车尾随区：摩托车向后 12 米的距离。
- 机动车尾随区：机动车向后 35 米的距离，适用于任何机动车辆。

e）尝试超越前方运动员的运动员有责任保证轮椅在碰撞前完全超越。尝试超越的运动员的轮椅前轮超过被超运动员的轮椅时，被超越的运动员有责任避免对其超越的阻碍。

f.) PTWC1 and PTWC2 athletes will be judged as finished, the moment in which the centre of the axle of the leading wheel reaches the vertical plane of the nearer edge of the finish line;
g.) The official race number will be placed at the back of the wheelchair and visible from the back;
h.) No run course shall have a maximum gradient of over 5% at the steepest section;

17.16. Paratriathlon PTS2, PTS3, PTS4 and PTS5 Running Conduct / Equipment:

a.) Athletes are permitted to use prosthesis provided that the prosthesis replaces a missing body part of the athlete. Athletes may only compete with prostheses, orthoses or other special adaptive equipment that has been checked and approved during the classification evaluation.
b.) The use of running blades is only allowed as long as they are mounted on a prosthetic leg.
c.) Athletes will wear a official race number or four sets of body decals, which will be visible from the front.

17.17. Paratriathlon PTVI1, PTVI2 and PTVI3 Conduct:

The following additional rules apply to all visually impaired (PTVI1, PTVI2 and PTVI3) paratriathletes and their guides:

a.) General:
(i) No guide dogs will be allowed at any time;
(ii) Each athlete must have a guide of the same gender and nationality. Both athlete and guide will hold a license from the same National Federation;
(iii) Each athlete is allowed a maximum of one (1) guide during each competition;
(iv) An athlete cannot act as a guide until a period of twelve (12) months has passed since his/her last sprint or standard distance elite triathlon ITU event or any elite triathlon event recognized by ITU on sprint or standard distance;
(v) All guides must comply with minimum age requirements as per the ITU Competition Rules Appendix A;
(vi) In the event of an injury or illness, and upon presentation of a medical certificate, a guide may be replaced up to 24 hours before the official start of the competition. No changes will be allowed after this deadline;
(vii) Guides are not allowed to pull or push the athletes;
(viii) Athlete and guide shall not be more than 1.5 meters apart during the swim segment and no more than 0.5 meters apart during any other segment of the competition;
(ix) Guides may not use paddleboards, kayaks, etc. (on the swim portion) or bicycles, motor bicycles, etc., (on the run portion) or any other mechanical means of transport.

f）PTWC1、PTWC2 级运动员的前轮轴触及终点线近端边缘所在的垂直面时被判定完成比赛。

g）官方号码布应放置在轮椅后方并从后侧方可见。

h）跑道最陡峭处的最大坡度不能超过 5%。

17.16 伤残铁人三项 PTS2、PTS3、PTS4 和 PTS5 级跑步比赛管理 / 装备

a）运动员可使用假肢替代失去的身体部分。运动员只能使用在分级评估期间经过检查并批准使用的假肢、矫正器械或其他特殊适应性装备。

b）刀片式假肢只能固定在假腿上使用。

c）运动员须佩戴官方号码布或贴上 4 套身体标识，且从前方可见。

17.17 伤残铁人三项 PTVI1、PTVI2、PTVI3 级比赛管理

以下附加规则适用于所有视力残疾（PTVI1、PTVI2、PTVI3）伤残铁三运动员及其引导员：

a）总 则

（1） 任何时间不得使用导盲犬。

（2） 每名运动员须有一名相同性别和相同国籍的引导员。运动员和引导员双方都须持有同一会员协会发放的许可证。

（3） 每次比赛中每名运动员最多允许有 1 名引导员陪同。

（4） 运动员不能在其参加过国际铁联优秀组短距离或标准距离赛事或其他任何国际铁联认可的优秀组短距离或标准距离赛事的 12 个月内作为引导员参与比赛。

（5） 所有引导员必须符合《国际铁联竞赛规则》附录 A 中的最低年龄要求。

（6） 引导员遇到伤病时，出具相应医学证明后可在比赛正式开始前最少 24 小时替换引导员，该截止时间后不允许做出任何变更。

（7） 引导员不允许推拉运动员。

（8） 运动员和引导员的距离在游泳赛段应不大于 1.5 米，在其他赛段距离应不大于 0.5 米。

（9） 引导员不得使用桨板、小艇等（在游泳赛段中）或自行车、摩托车等（跑步赛段中）或其他任何机械运输工具。

(x) All PTVI1 athletes must wear blackout goggles throughout the entire competition. Swim blackout goggles may be removed only once the athlete and guide have reached their bike position in Transition area 1. The bike/run blackout glasses must be used from Transition area 1 until the athlete and guide cross the finish line. Both the blackout goggles and glasses will be checked at registration and the athlete must ensure they do not allow light to enter through the main patched or painted area, nose piece, sides or bottom.

(xi) Athletes and guides are subject to ITU Anti-Doping Rules

b.) Swimming conduct:

(i) Each athlete must be tethered to their own guide during the swim;

(ii) At no time may a guide lead or pace the paratriathlete nor propel them forward by pulling or pushing;

(iii) The guide must swim next to the athlete within a maximum separation distance of 1.5m from the athletes' head to the guide's head. The tether must be elastic rope with bright or reflective color and up to 80 cm long measured with no tension. It can be fixed at any point of the athletes' body.

c.) Cycling conduct:

(i) All paratriathletes and guides must use a tandem bicycle. The specifications of the tandem bicycle are as follows:

- A tandem is a vehicle for two riders, with two wheels of equal diameter, which conforms to the general principles of UCI construction for bicycles. The front wheel shall be steerable by the front rider, known as the pilot. Both riders shall face forward in the traditional cycling position and the rear wheel shall be driven by both cyclists through a system comprising pedals and chains; the maximum sizes will be 2.70 meters long and 0.5 meters wide;
- The tandem top tube, and any additional strengthening tubes, may slope to suit the morphological sizes of the riders.

d.) Running conduct:

(i) Each athlete must be tethered during the run to his/her guide. The tether shall be made from non-elastic material and not store energy and/or offer a performance gain to the athlete.

(ii) The athlete may use an elbow lead during the run. The guide-runner is not allowed to push, pull or otherwise propel athletes in order to gain an advantage at any stage during a competition. A guide-runner may assist an athlete who has tripped or fallen to regain his/her footing and/or orientation as long as such assistance does not provide any advantage to the athlete towards his/her running direction.

（10） 所有 PTVI1 级运动员须在比赛全程使用黑色遮光护目镜。黑色遮光泳镜只能在运动员和其引导员到达其在转换区 1 的自行车停放点摘下一次。运动员在从转换区 1 到通过终点线期间必须全程使用骑行 / 跑步黑色遮光镜。所有黑色遮光护目镜和黑色遮光镜都将在注册时接受检查以保证光线不能从镜片、涂层区、鼻垫、边缘或底部穿过。

（11） 运动员和引导员必须遵守国际铁联反兴奋剂规定。

b）游泳比赛管理

（1） 游泳期间，每名运动员必须用绳索和其引导员连在一起。

（2） 任何时候引导员都不能带动伤残铁三运动员或以推、拉的方式推进运动员。

（3） 连接绳索必须是颜色明亮或明显反光的有弹性的绳索，且非延展状态下长度可超过 80 厘米，引导员必须在运动员体侧游泳，且两者头部距离不能超过 1.5 米。

c）自行车比赛管理

（1） 所有伤残运动员和引导员必须使用双人自行车。双人自行车详细要求如下：

- 双人自行车是一种供两人乘骑，有两个等直径轮子的，符合国际自行车联盟对自行车的总体规定要求的载具。前轮必须能由前方骑手控制，亦称驾驶员。两名骑手必须以传统骑行姿势面朝前方。后轮必须由两名骑手用一个包含踏板和链条的系统来驱动。自行车最大尺寸为 2.70 米长、0.5 米宽。
- 双人自行车的上管和其他任何额外的用于加强强度的架管可以倾斜以适应骑手的形态尺寸。

d）跑步比赛管理

（1） 每名运动员必须用绳索和其引导员连接在一起。连接绳需用非弹性材料支撑且不能蓄能，亦不能提升运动员的表现。

（2） 跑步时，运动员可以使用肘部作为引领。引导员在比赛中的任何阶段都不得推、拉或以其他方式推动运动员以获利。引导员可以帮助绊倒或跌倒的运动员重新站立获得平衡，但不得在该辅助过程中为其在前进方向上提供任何有利帮助。

(iii) As the athlete crosses the finish line, the guide must be beside or behind the paratriathlete but not further apart than the required 0.5 meters maximum separation distance.

(iv) Free Leading zones: for safety reasons, contact is allowed 10 meters before and after an aid station, a sharp turn, penalty box, transition area swim exit, pre-transition area or any other section of the run course determined by the Technical Delegate and indicated at the athlete's briefing;

17.18. Hygiene:

a.) It is mandatory for all paratriathletes, who use catheters or other urinary diversion devices, to prevent spillage by using a catheter bag at all times. This includes during training, competition and classification.

17.19. Approval panels:

a.) Decisions on bike adaptations or brace approval will be made by a panel composed of:

(i) An ITU Technical Committee member;

(ii) A representative of the ITU Sport Department;

(iii) A member of the ITU Paratriathlon Committee;

b.) The decisions of the Approval Panel can be appealed to the ITU Arbitration Tribunal. This appeal does not suspend the decision of the Approval Panel, but rather the decision will stay in place during the time the ITU Arbitration Tribunal takes to make a decision on the appeal.

（3） 运动员穿越终点线时，引导员必须在伤残铁三运动员身侧或身后，但最大间隔不能超过 0.5 米。

（4） 自由领跑区：出于安全考虑，急救站、急转弯、罚时区、转换区上水区、预备转换区和技术代表决定的并在运动员技术会上指出的其他任何跑道相关区域 10 米范围内允许身体接触。

17.18 卫 生

a）使用导尿管或其他尿液分流设备的伤残铁三运动员在训练、比赛和分级期间须一直使用尿袋以防止尿液溢出。

17.19 审批小组

a）关于自行车适应性改造或膝关节支架的审批，将由以下人员构成的审批委小组进行：

（1） 1 名国际铁联技术委员会委员。

（2） 1 名国际铁联体育部代表。

（3） 1 名国际铁联伤残铁人三项委员会委员。

b）审批小组的决定可被申诉至国际铁联仲裁法庭。这一申诉不会延缓审批小组的决定，且在国际铁联仲裁庭就申诉做出裁决期间保持有效。

18. WINTER TRIATHLON

18.1. Definition:

a.) Winter Triathlon may take place in two different formats:

(i) Running, mountain biking and cross country skiing, named as Winter Triathlon;

(ii) Running, skating and cross country skiing, named S3 Winter Triathlon.

b.) All segments of the competition will be preferably on snow or ice. The run and bike segment can also take place on a different surface.

18.2. Official Training and Course Familiarisation:

a.) Official training and familiarisation sessions will be conducted by the Technical Delegate and the Local Organising Committee. Athletes and coaches may attend these official training and familiarisation sessions;

b.) Conduct on competition days: Athletes are not allowed to warm up or do any familiarisation on the course while a competition is in progress.

18.3. Run Segment:

a.) Running shoes are mandatory on the running segment. This rule is not applicable to Age Group athletes;

b.) Running shoes with spikes are allowed.

18.4. Mountain Bike Segment:

a.) The minimum tyre dimension is 26x1.5 inches which means the smallest part of the tyre should not be less than 40mm;

b.) Front and rear wheels may have different diameters;

c.) The bike segment of winter triathlon competitions is laid out as a cross-country course over snow and may follow normal roads or paths;

d.) Athletes are allowed to push or carry the bike over the course;

e.) Drafting is allowed. For safety reasons there may be no passing zones on the course. Lapped athletes will not be removed from the competition;

f.) Athletes must bring their own tools and parts and must carry out their own repairs;

g.) Bike shoes are mandatory in the bike segment. This rule is not applicable to Age Group athletes;

h.) Spiked tyres are allowed provided that the spikes are shorter than 5 mm. measured from the tyre surface.

i.) Traditional MTB bar ends are authorised. Ends must be plugged.

18.5. Ski Segment:

a.) Testing of equipment (skis) is allowed prior to the competition on specially marked tracks, or on the competition-course, if announced by the Technical Officials;

b.) Athletes cannot be accompanied by team members, team managers or other pacemakers on the course, during the competition;

18. 冬季铁人三项

18.1 界 定

a）冬季铁人三项两种形式：

（1） 冬季铁人三项由跑步、山地自行车和越野滑雪组成。

（2） S3 冬季铁人三项由跑步、滑冰和越野滑雪组成。

18.2 官方训练和赛道适应

a）官方训练和赛道适应需在技术代表和当地组委会指导下进行。教练员和运动员可参加官方训练和赛道适应。

b）比赛日规定：不允许运动员在比赛期间进行热身或任何形式的赛道适应。

18.3 跑步赛段

a）跑步赛段必须穿跑鞋，此规则不适用于分年龄组运动员。

b）允许使用钉鞋。

18.4 山地自行车赛段

a）自行车轮胎的最小尺寸为 26×1.5 英寸，即轮胎的最小部分应不小于 40 毫米。

b）前轮和后轮直径尺寸可不同。

c）冬季铁人三项中，山地自行车比赛场地可为雪地越野场地也可为常规公路或小径。

d）比赛中运动员可推行或肩扛自行车。

e）比赛中允许尾随。出于安全考虑，赛道上可设禁止超车路段。被套圈的运动员需退出比赛。

f）运动员必须自备工具、零件并自主修理。

g）自行车赛段必须穿自行车鞋。此规则不适用于分年龄组运动员。

h）带钉轮胎可以使用，但从轮胎表面开始测量的钉的长度不得超过 5 毫米。

i）传统山地自行车附加把允许使用，车把末端必须塞住。

18.5 滑雪赛段

a）如果技术官员通知，则赛前可在特殊标识的跑道上或赛道上对滑雪板进行检测。

b）比赛期间，运动员不得由队友、团队领队或其他领跑者在场地内陪同。

c.) Athletes are allowed to change one ski and both poles;
d.) Athletes may ski using their preferred technique;
e.) Specified zones may have restrictions to classic style or double poling;
f.) Wearing the bike helmet during the ski segment is not allowed. However, due to the effect of cold temperatures on mobility, wearing a helmet could be authorised by the Technical Delegate;
g.) Once a request to pass is made by a athlete, the athlete being passed must move to the side as soon as possible;
h.) In the finish chute (30-50m), freestyle skiing may be forbidden. Double poling may be mandatory and prepared tracks for classic technique must be used. This provision will be announced at the athletes' briefing;
i.) Athletes cannot remove their skis until at least 10 meters past the finish line. The last ski check will take place after this line;
j.) Ski shoes are mandatory in the cross country ski segment. This rule is not applicable to Age Group athletes.

18.6. Skating Segment:

a.) All types of skates, including Nordic blades, are allowed;
b.) Athletes are not allowed to change any of the skates;
c.) Once a request to pass is made by a athlete, the athlete being passed must move to the side as soon as possible;
d.) Athletes will wear helmet, as outlined in Competition Rules 5.2 g).

18.7. Transition Area Conduct:

a.) Skiing inside the transition area is forbidden;
b.) Athletes must put on and take off their running shoes and skates within the transition area, in the athletes' own space. If a "Nordic blades changing zone" is provided, athletes may choose to put the Nordic baldes on there;
c.) In the transition area, Technical Officials may assist athletes by receiving and placing their bikes and handing out their equipment. This service must be equal for all athletes;
d.) All athletes must have their helmet securely fastened from the time they remove their bike from the rack at the start of the bike leg or when they put the skates on, until after they have placed their bike on the rack at the finish of the bike leg or when they takes the skates off;

c）运动员可更换一支雪板和两根手杖。

d）运动员可采用擅长的滑雪技术。

e）特定区域对传统式滑行或双杖推撑滑行设有限制。

f）滑雪比赛中不允许戴自行车头盔。但如果技术代表允许，运动员可戴头盔御寒。

g）一旦运动员提出超越的要求，被超越的运动员必须靠边行进。

h）在冲刺滑道上（30~50 米），自由式可能被禁止。运动员须使用双杖推撑滑行，并采用预备好的传统式滑雪雪道。此规定在运动员赛前技术会上进行宣布。

i）运动员必须越过终点线 10 米以上才可以去除雪板。通过终点线后进行最后一次雪板检测。

j）在越野滑雪比赛中必须使用滑雪鞋。此规定不适用于分年龄组比赛。

18.6 滑冰赛段

a）允许使用任何样式的冰刀，包括北欧式冰刀。

b）运动员不允许更换冰刀。

c）一旦运动员提出超越要求，被超越的运动员必须立即靠边行进。

d）如比赛规则 5.2g 所列，运动员须戴头盔。

18.7 转换区管理

a）转换区内禁止滑行。

b）运动员只准在转换区中自己的区域内穿、脱跑鞋和冰刀。如果设有“北欧式冰刀更换区”，运动员则需要在此处更换北欧冰刀。

c）转换区内，技术官员可以协助运动员接收、放置自行车并分发装备。此举应对所有运动员一视同仁。

d）运动员自比赛开始从车架上取下自行车到比赛结束将自行车放回车架上以及从比赛开始穿上冰刀到比赛结束脱下冰刀的整个过程都必须佩戴好安全帽或头盔。

e.) A "Nordic blades changing area" may be created by the side of the edge of the ice;

f.) A littering zone will be placed after the "ski placing line" where the athletes can discard the shoe covers.

18.8. Coaches' Station:

a.) Coaches will have a designated space available on the bike segment in order to supply athletes with their own food and beverages.

18.9. Special Needs Station:

a.) Additional stations on the bike and or run may be provided for special needs;

b.) Any items given out at these stations will be the handed out by volunteers supplied by the Local Organising Committee;

c.) If these stations are not provided no items may be provided by any other person, otherwise this will be considered outside assistance.

d.) A Repair Zone may be provided on the bike section where athletes will have the opportunity to leave special tools and spares provided they are correctly packed and labelled. The athlete is responsible to carry out their own repairs.

18.10. Finish Definition:

a.) An athlete will be judged as "finished," the moment the tip of the front ski boot crosses a vertical line extending from the leading edge of the finish line.

18.11. Weather conditions:

a.) The competition will be cancelled when the air temperature is lower than -18 ºC.

19. CROSS TRIATHLON AND DUATHLON

19.1. General:

a.) Cross Triathlon consists of swimming, mountain biking (MTB) and cross-country running;

b.) Cross Duathlon consists of cross-country running, mountain biking (MTB) and cross-country running.

19.2. Distances:

a.) The distance of Cross Triathlon is outlined in Appendix A;

b.) The distance of Cross Duathlon is outlined in Appendix A;

c.) The course should have demanding hills and challenging technical aspects. A 5% tolerance margin will be accepted for the distance of the bike course, provided it has been approved by the Technical Delegate.

e）“北欧式冰刀更换区”可安置于冰面的边缘处。

f）垃圾丢弃点设置于“冰刀放置线”之后，方便运动员丢弃鞋的封套。

18.8 教练员指导区

a）自行车赛道上设置教练员指导区，教练员们可以在这些区域为运动员提供自备的食品和饮料。

18.9 特别补给区

a）骑行或跑步时可在特别区进行补给。

b）在补给区分发的任何物品都应由本地组织委员会的志愿者完成。

c）如果这些区域不提供物品，那么其他人也不可以提供，否则视作外部帮助。

d）自行车赛段上可提供修理区，运动员可在此区域放置其打包并标记好的修理工具和备用品。运动员应自行修复自己的车辆。

18.10 完成比赛

a）当滑雪鞋的前端穿过终点线前沿的垂直线时，即被认为到达终点。

18.11 天气条件

a）空气温度低于零下 18℃时，比赛将被取消。

19. 越野铁人三项和越野骑跑两项

19.1 总 则

a）越野铁人三项由游泳、山地自行车（MTB）和越野跑组成。

b）越野骑跑两项由越野跑和山地自行车（MTB）组成。

19.2 距 离

a）越野铁人三项距离参见附件 A。

b）越野骑跑两项距离参见附件 A。

c）比赛路线应包含高难度的坡道和技术难度。经技术代表同意，自行车路线的距离允许有 5% 的偏差。

19.3. Official Training and Familiarisation:

a.) Official training and familiarisation sessions will be conducted by the Technical Delegate and the Local Organising Committee. Athletes and coaches may attend these official training and familiarisation sessions;

b.) Conduct on competition days: Athletes are not allowed to warm up or do any course familiarisation while a competition is in progress.

19.4. Mountain Biking Conduct:

a.) The maximum tyre diameter for the MTB is 29 inches. The minimum cross section is 1.5 inch;

b.) Front and rear wheels may have different diameter;

c.) Studded and/or slick tyres are allowed;

d.) Athletes are allowed to push or carry the bike over the course;

e.) Drafting is allowed. For safety reasons there may be no passing zones on the course. Lapped athletes will not be removed from the competition;

f.) Clip-ons are not allowed;

g.) Traditional road handlebars are forbidden;

h.) Traditional MTB bar ends are authorised. Ends must be plugged.

19.5. Transition Area Conduct:

a.) See all reference in Competition Rules, section 7;

19.6. Running Conduct:

a.) Spike shoes are allowed.

19.7. Coaches Stations:

a.) Coaches will have a designated space available on the bike and run segments in order to supply athletes with their own food and beverages.

19.8. Special needs

a.) Additional stations on the bike and or run may be provided for special needs;

b.) Any items given out at these stations will be the handed out by volunteers supplied by the Local Organising Committee;

c.) If these stations are not provided no items may be provided by any other person, otherwise this will be considered outside assistance.

d.) A Repair Zone may be provided on the bike section where athletes will have the opportunity to leave special tools and spares provided they are correctly packed and labelled. The athlete is responsible to carry out their own repairs.

19.3 官方训练和赛道适应

a） 官方训练和赛道适应需在技术代表和当地组委会指导下进行。教练和运动员可参加官方训练和赛道适应。

b）比赛日规定：不允许运动员在比赛期间进行热身或任何形式的赛道适应。

19.4 山地自行车

a）山地自行车的车轮最大直径为 29 英寸。最小的横截面为 1.5 英寸。

b）前后轮直径可不同。

c）允许使用带有防滑钉轮胎或光面的轮胎或混用。

d）允许运动员在场地中推行或肩扛自行车。

e） 允许尾随。出于安全考虑，赛道上可设禁止超车路段，被套圈的运动员须退出比赛。

f） 不允许使用附加把。

g）禁止使用传统公路车把。

h）允许使用传统山地自行车副把，车把端口必须塞住。

19.5 转换区

a） 详情查看第 7 章的竞赛规则。

19.6 跑 步

a） 允许使用钉鞋。

19.7 教练员指导区

a） 自行车和跑步赛道上将分别设置教练员指导区，教练员们可以在这些区域为运动员提供自备的食品和饮料。

19.8 特别补给区

a） 骑行或跑步时可在特别补给区进行补给。

b） 在补给区分发的任何物品都应由本地组织委员会的志愿者完成。

c） 如果这些区域不提供物品，那么其他人也不可以提供，否则视作外部帮助。

d） 自行车赛段上可提供修理区，运动员可在此区域放置其打包并标记好的修理工具和备用品。运动员应自行修复自己的车辆。

20. COMPETITION IN QUALIFYING ROUND FORMAT

20.1. General:

a.) An event in Qualifying Round Format consists of several rounds with a number of heats each qualifying athletes to the next round and eventually finishing with a final to determine a winner.

20.2. Rounds:

a.) The rounds will be called semi-finals and final;

b.) An event will have two rounds;

c.) Semi-finals and final will have 30 athletes as a maximum. The number of semi-finals will be as follows:

Athletes entered	Semi-finals
Less than 30	No semi-finals, direct final
31 to 60	2 semi-finals (15 to 30 athletes each)
61 to 90	3 semi-finals (20 to 30 athletes each)
91 to 120	4 semi-finals (22 to 30 athletes each)
121 to 150	5 semi-finals (24 to 30 athletes each)

20.3. Qualification to final:

a.) Every semi-final will qualify a fixed number of athletes for the final. Additionally, a number of athletes will qualify from semi-final heats, based on fastest times:

Athletes entered	Semi-finals	By position in the semi-final	By time
31 to 60	2	14	2
61 to 90	3	9	3
91 to 120	4	7	2
More than 121	5	5	5

b.) Athletes from different heats and with the same time (in seconds), which are tied in the last qualifying position, will all qualify, increasing the number of athletes qualified for the next round;

c.) Athletes who have not qualified for the final will be sorted by time. In case of athletes withdrawing from the final, replacement will be made by the first athlete who has not qualified. The replacement will happen if the number of athletes in the final drops down to 30 athletes. (a random selection will be made from those athletes who have the same time). The deadline for the replacements will be when registration opens.

d.) In case where an event has a B final, the best 30 athletes from the semi-finals who have not qualified for the A final, will be sorted according to their times and will qualify to the B final.

20.4. Distribution of athletes in the semi-finals:

a.) The Technical Delegate will compose the heats as follows:

(i) If there are not any applicable rankings, the athletes will be distributed among the heats in order to have the same number of athletes per semi-final (some semi-finals can have one more athlete than others). The athletes from the same National Federation will be distributed among the heats following the same principle;

20. 资格赛比赛模式

20.1 总 则

a）资格赛比赛模式是由符合资格的运动员通过若干轮分组预选赛，最后通过决赛角逐出冠军的比赛形式。

20.2 轮 次

a）轮次分为半决赛和决赛。

b）比赛分为两轮。

c）半决赛和决赛的最多参赛人数为 30 人。半决赛的次数如下：

运动员人数	半决赛
少于 30 人	无半决赛，直接决赛
31~ 60 人	两组半决赛（每组 15~30 名运动员）
61~90 人	三组半决赛（每组 20~30 名运动员）
91~120 人	四组半决赛（每组 22~30 名运动员）
121~150 人	五组半决赛（每组 24~30 名运动员）

20.3 决赛资格

a）每一组半决赛筛选出一定数量的运动员，获得决赛资格。此外，各组半决赛中用时最短的部分运动员也获得决赛资格：

运动员人数	半决赛次数	按半决赛名次取	按比赛成绩取
31~60 人	2	14	2
61~90 人	3	9	3
91~120 人	4	7	2
超过 121 人	5	5	5

b）不同分组赛中，晋级成绩相同（精确到秒）的运动员，全部获得晋级资格，下一轮预赛的人数将增加。

c）根据用时对没有获得决赛资格的运动员进行排位。如果有运动员退出决赛，则由未获得资格的排名第一的运动员进行替换。当参加决赛人数低于 30 人时替换启动（如待选者成绩相同则随机挑选）。检录开始时，替换程序关闭。

d）如果赛事中安排有 B 组决赛，则未获得 A 组决赛资格但在半决赛中按成绩排名前 30 名的运动员获得 B 组决赛资格。

20.4 半决赛中运动员分组方法

a）技术代表分组方法如下：

（1） 没有可用的排名情况下，运动员可按人数平均分配到各个预赛组（一些半决赛组可比其他组多一人）。根据相同的原则，同一会员协会的运动员分配到不同组。

(ii) If a ranking is applicable, the ranked athletes will be distributed according to the chart below and the non-ranked athletes will fill the remaining spots by applying the principle of assigning a similar number of athletes from the same National Federation to every heat, and keeping all the heats of equal size.

Chart: Distribution of ranked athletes among the semi-finals:

Semi-final 1	Semi-final 2	Last Semi-final (-1)	Last Semi-final
1			
	2		
		3	
			4
			5
		6	
	7		
8			
9			
	10		
		11	
			12
			13
		14	
	15		
16			
17			
etc...			

Note: The number reflects the ranking order

20.5. Numbering:

a.) The numbers in the final will be assigned as first criteria according to the positions in the semi-finals. The second criteria will be the time in the semi-final, the third, the ITU Points List position, and the fourth a random apportionment.

20.6. Results:

a.) The overall results for the event will be the results of the final round;

b.) If the event is included in any ranking which is allocating points to more positions than finishers in the final, the remaining points will be awarded as follows:

(i) To the DNF athletes in the final, according to their times in the semi-finals;

(ii) To the DNS athletes in the final according to their times in the semi-final;

(iii) If the event does not have a B final: The athletes who did not qualify for the final, will have points allocated according to their times in the semi-finals. If the event has B final: The results from the B final will determine their points.

(iv) DSQ athletes will not earn any points.

20.7. Prize money:

a.) Prize money distribution will follow the general rules (Appendix I) and the preceding paragraph if necessary.

（2） 如有可用排名，运动员根据下表进行分组，没有排名的运动员填补入空格处。同一会员协会的运动员分配到不同组。每组运动员数量相等。

表格：半决赛运动员按排名分组办法：

半决赛第一组	半决赛第二组	半决赛倒数第二组	半决赛最后一组
1			
	2		
		3	
			4
			5
		6	
	7		
8			
9			
	10		
		11	
			12
			13
		14	
	15		
16			
17			
等等……			

注释：数字代表排名顺序

20.5 号码分配

a）决赛中号码分配依据：第一是依据半决赛中的排位；第二是依据半决赛中的用时；第三是依据国际铁联积分排名；第四是随机分配。

20.6 比赛成绩

a）最后一轮成绩为赛事最终成绩。

b）如赛事需向未完成者分配排名积分，分配方案如下：

（1） 未完成决赛赛程者，根据其半决赛成绩获得积分。

（2） 决赛中未出发的运动员，根据其半决赛成绩获得积分。

（3） 如赛事未设置 B 组决赛，没有获得决赛资格的运动员根据半决赛成绩获得积分；如赛事设置 B 组决赛，B 组决赛的成绩决定积分。

（4） 被取消比赛资格的运动员不获得积分。

20.7 奖 金

a）奖金按一般规则（详见附件 I）及前项说明发放。

21. EVENT IN TIME TRIAL QUALIFYING ROUND FORMAT

21.1. General:

a.) An event in Time Trial Qualifying Round Format consists of two competitions, the first one (qualifier) conducted as a time trial with athletes starting individually one by one, and the second one (final) conducted as a mass start event, in which the participants are the best ranked in the time trial competition;

b.) The result of the event is the result of the final.

21.2. Rounds:

a.) An event will have two rounds;

b.) The rounds will be called qualifier and final;

c.) The qualifier will be time trial with draft-illegal bike segment, and the final will be mass start with a draft legal bike segment. In both qualifier and final competitions, athletes must use draft legal bikes and bike equipment.

d.) The Technical Delegate will determine the time interval between the start of each athlete in the time trial qualifier, which can be between 15 seconds and 3 minutes.

e.) The final will have 30 athletes. The Head Referee will decide, according to the available technological resources, if a tie will be declared for two or more of the athletes. In this case, the final may have more than 30 athletes.

21.3. Qualification to final:

a.) The athletes with the best 30 times in the qualifiers will qualify for the final.

b.) Athletes who have not qualified for the final will be placed according to their time in the qualifiers. In case of athletes withdrawing from the final, replacement will be made by the next fastest athlete who has not qualified. The replacement will only happen if the number of athletes in the final drops down below 30 athletes. The deadline for the replacements will be when registration opens.

c.) In case where an event has a B final, the athletes with the best 30 times from the qualifier, who have not qualified for the A final, will be sorted according to their times and will qualify to compete in the B final.

21.4. Numbering and distribution of athletes in the qualifier:

a.) Race numbers will be allocated to the athletes as regulated in the Competition Rules 2.10.

b.) Athletes will start one by one starting by the highest number in decreasing order.

c.) In case of athletes not showing up to the start or if any race number is not assigned, the start sequence will follow as if there was an athlete competing in the time allotted to this unused number.

21. 计时赛时资格赛比赛模式

21.1 总 则

a）计时资格赛有两种比赛形式：第一种（资格赛）为运动员依次出发进行个人计时。第二种（决赛）为运动员集体出发，参赛者为资格赛中成绩优异者。

b）比赛成绩为最终成绩。

21.2 轮 次

a）比赛分为两轮。

b）两轮比赛分别为资格赛和决赛。

c）资格赛自行车赛段采用不允许尾随的计时赛形式，决赛采用集体出发形式且自行车赛段允许尾随。资格赛和决赛中的运动员必须使用允许尾随规则所规定的自行车及自行车装备。

d）技术代表决定计时资格赛中运动员出发时间间隔，一般为 15 秒到 3 分钟。

e）决赛参赛者为 30 名。在可用的技术资源下，如出现 2 个或多个成绩相同者，由裁判决定参赛人数。决赛人数可超过 30 人。

21.3 决赛资格

a）资格赛前 30 名有资格进入决赛。

b）没有进入决赛的运动员将根据资格赛中的成绩进行排名。退出比赛的运动员，将由候补名单上排名最靠前的运动员替换。由于运动员的退出而致使参加决赛的人数不足 30 人时，替换机制才可启动。检录开始时，替换程序关闭。

c）如赛事设置 B 组决赛，未进入 A 组决赛的成绩最好的前 30 名进入 B 组决赛。

21.4 资格赛的比赛号码分配及运动员分组

a）运动员比赛号码分配规则详见比赛规则 2.10。

b）运动员按比赛号码的降序顺序逐一出发。

c）如有运动员未出现在出发点或有号码未被分配出去，出发仍按号码顺序正常执行。

d.) The start list will be created following this model:

Race number	First Name	Last Name	NF	Start Time
102	Grzegorz	Zgliczynski	POL	09:00:00
101	Andrew	Farrell	USA	09:00:30
100	Todd	Martin	AUS	09:01:00
99	Gervasio	Da Silva	BRA	09:01:30

21.5. Qualifier start system:

a.) Principles set in ITU Competition Rules 4.7 will apply:

(i) Athletes are responsible for being at the start line on time;

(ii) A video camera shall be used to record the entire start;

(iii) The Start Technical Officials are responsible for synchronizing their own and the Timekeepers' watches;

(iv) Start Technical Officials must provide all athletes with the opportunity to start at their correct times. An assistant responsible for recording the details for any violations at the start must be placed near the starter. The athletes' actual start time must be noted with both electric and hand timing; in case the Competition Jury decides his/her late start was due to force majeure;

(v) Athletes will line up according to the start order. Athletes will need to report at the pre-start area at least 2 minutes before their start time;

(vi) Athletes will be informed by the starter about the remaining time to the start, 15 and 5 seconds before the start time;

(vii) The Start Technical Official will announce the start time by using an electronic/manual horn;

(viii) Athletes starting the competition before the start time will be recalled to the start line. Any athlete failing to do this will be disqualified. Athletes starting after their start time, must get the approval of the Start Technical Official to proceed. The start time of those athletes will be the start time originally assigned.

21.6. Race number allocation in the final:

a.) The race numbers in the final will be assigned as first criteria according to the time in the qualifier. The lowest time in the qualifier will receive number 1 in the final. Tied athletes will be numbered randomly.

21.7. Results:

a.) The overall results for the event will be the results of the final round. Awards, and prize money will be distributed accordingly;

b.) If the event is included in any ranking which is allocating points to more positions than finishers in the final, the remaining points will be awarded as follows:

(i) To the DNF athletes in the final, according to their times in the qualifier;

d）出发名单按如下模式制定：

比赛号码	名	姓	国籍	出发时间
102	Grzegorz	Zgliczynski	POL	09:00:00
101	Andrew	Farrell	USA	09:00:30
100	Todd	Martin	AUS	09:01:00
99	Gervasio	Da Silva	BRA	09:01:30

21.5 资格赛出发程序

a）基本原则参见《国际铁联竞赛规则》4.7：

（1） 运动员有责任按时到达出发线。

（2） 应使用摄像机全程录制出发过程。

（3） 出发技术官员有责任保证出发时间与计时人员的时间同步。

（4） 出发技术官员必须保证所有运动员在正确的时间出发。发令员须配备出发助理以记录出发过程中的任何犯规行为。为了便于仲裁委员会确定运动员晚出发是否是由于不可抗力造成的，运动员的确定出发时间必须由手计时和电计时同时记录。

（5） 根据出发顺序，运动员在出发线就位。运动员需在出发前 2 分钟到准备区报到。

（6） 发令员需在出发前 15 秒和 5 秒提醒运动员。

（7） 发令员使用电子或手按喇叭发出出发指令。

（8） 抢跑者会被重新召回至出发线。如果运动员在出发程序开始前出发或未在指定的时段出发，将被取消比赛资格。运动员晚于其被指定的时段出发必须得到出发技术官员的允许。其出发时间即是原来的指定时间。

21.6 决赛号码分配

a）决赛号码分配第一依据为资格赛成绩。资格赛中用时最短者将获得决赛 1 号号码，成绩并列的运动员将随机编号。

21.7 成 绩

a）决赛成绩为最终比赛成绩。根据实际情况分配奖牌和奖金。

b）如赛事需向未完成者分配排名积分，分配方案如下：

（1） 未完成决赛赛程者，根据其资格赛成绩获得积分。

(ii) To the DNS athletes in the final according to their times in the qualifier;

(iii) If the event does not have a B final: The athletes who did not qualify for the final, will have points allocated according to their times in the qualifier. If the event has B final: The results from the B final will determine their points;

(iv) DSQ athletes will not earn any points.

22. AQUABIKE

22.1. General

a.) Aquabike consists of Swimming, Transition area 1, biking and Transition area 2.

b.) Aquabike events will be organised only-for Age Group categories, and included in the program of an event with same swim and bike distances.

22.2. Distance

a.) 1500m swim followed by 40km bike, mirroring the distance of the Standard Distance Triathlon events in which the aquabike is included;

b.) From 1900 meter swim and longer followed by 80 km bike or longer, mirroring the distance of the Long Distance Triathlon event in which the aquabike is included.

22.3. Specific Rules

a.) Aquabike is ruled by the same rules that the Long Distance Triathlon event in which is included.

22.4. Finish

a.) Athletes will finish the competition at the finish line located at the end of the bike course.-The finish occurs at the instant that the tyre of the front wheel meets the vertical plane rising from the starting edge of the finishing line. The time registered in this point is the final time.

（2） 决赛中未出发的运动员，根据其资格赛成绩获得积分。

（3） 如赛事未设置 B 组决赛，没有获得决赛资格的运动员根据半决赛成绩获得积分；如赛事设置 B 组决赛，B 组决赛的成绩决定积分。

（4） 被取消比赛资格的运动员不获得积分。

22. 游骑两项

22.1 总 则

a） 游骑两项由游泳、第一换项、自行车组成。

b） 游骑两项只针对分龄组，游泳和自行车距离应与相关赛事铁人三项一致。

22.2 距 离

a） 纳入标准距离铁人三项比赛的游骑两项与标准距离铁人三项相关段落距离一致：先游泳 1500 米，再骑自行车 40 公里。

b） 纳入长距离铁人三项比赛的游骑两项与长距离铁人三项相关段落距离一致：先游泳大于等于 1900 米，再骑自行车大于等于 80 公里。

22.3 特殊规则

a） 游骑两项的比赛规则与长距离铁人三项规则一致。

22.4 终 点

a） 游骑两项的终点坐落在自行车赛道的末端。自行车前轮轮胎触碰到终点线垂直线后沿的一瞬间为到达终点。此时记录的成绩为运动员最终成绩。

APPENDICES

23. APPENDIX A COMPETITION DISTANCES AND AGE REQUIREMENTS

Triathlon:

	Swim	Bike	Run	Minimum age required
Team relay	250m to 300m	5km to 8km	1.5km to 2km	15
Super Sprint Distance	250m to 500m	6.5km to 13km	1.7km to 3.5km	15
Sprint Distance	Up to 750m	Up to 20km	Up to 5km	16
Standard Distance	1500m	40km	10km	18
Middle Distance	1900m to 3000m	80km to 90km	20km to 21km	18
Long Distance	1000m to 4000m	100km to 200km	10km to 42.2km	18

Duathlon:

	Run	Bike	Run	Minimum age required
Team Relay	1.5km to 2km	5km to 8km	0.75km to 1km	15
Sprint Distance	5km	20km	2.5km	16
Standard Distance	5km to 10km	30km to 40km	5km	18
Middle Distance	10km to 20km	60km to 90km	10km	18
Long Distance	10km to 20km	120km to 150km	20km to 30km	18

Aquathlon:

	Run	Swim	Run	Minimum age required
Standard Distance	2.5km	1000m	2.5km	16
Standard Distance (cold waters)		1000m	5km	16
Long Distance	5km	2000m	5km	18
Long Distance (cold waters)		2000m	10km	18

附 件

23 附件 A 竞赛距离和年龄要求

铁人三项

	游泳	自行车	跑步	最小年龄要求
团体接力	250~300 米	5~8 千米	1.5~2 千米	15
超短距离	250~500 米	6.5~13 千米	1.7~3.5 千米	15
短距离	最长 750 米	最长 20 千米	最长 5 千米	16
标准距离	1500 米	40 千米	10 千米	18
中等距离	1900~3000 米	80~90 千米	20~21 千米	18
长距离	1000~4000 米	100~200 千米	10~42.2 千米	18

骑跑两项

	跑步	自行车	跑步	最小年龄要求
团体接力	1.5~2 千米	5~8 千米	0.75~1 千米	15
短距离	5 千米	20 千米	2.5 千米	16
标准距离	5~10 千米	30~40 千米	5 千米	18
中距离	10~20 千米	60~90 千米	10 千米	18
长距离	10~20 千米	120~150 千米	20~30 千米	18

游跑两项

	跑步	游泳	跑步	最小年龄要求
标准距离	2.5 千米	1000 米	2.5 千米	16
标准距离(低水温)		1000 米	5 千米	16
长距离	5 千米	2000 米	5 千米	18
长距离（低水温）		2000 米	10 千米	18

Winter Triathlon:

Winter Triathlon	Cross-Country Run	Mountain Bike	Cross-Country Ski	Minimum age required
Team Relay	2 to 3 km	4 to 5 km	3 to 4 km	15
Sprint Distance	3 to 4 km	5 to 6 km	5 to 6 km	16
Standard Distance	7 to 9 km	12 to 14 km	10 to 12 km	18

S3 Winter Triathlon	Run	Skating	Cross-Country Ski	Minimum age required
Standard Distance	4 to 6 km	10 to 14 km	7 to 9 km	16

Cross Triathlon:

	Swim	Mountain Bike	Cross Country Run	Minimum age required
Team Relay	200m to 250m	4km to 5km	1.2km to 1.6km	15
Sprint Distance	500m	10km to 12km	3km to 4km	16
Standard Distance	1000m to 1500m	20km to 30km	6km to 10km	18

Cross Duathlon:

	Cross Country Run	Mountain Bike	Cross Country Run	Minimum age required
Team Relay	1.2km to 1.6km	4km to 5km	0.6km to 0.8km	15
Sprint Distance	3km to 4km	10km to 12km	1.5km to 2km	16
Standard Distance	6km to 8km	20km to 25km	3km to 4km	18

Aquabike:

	Swim	Bike	Minimum age required
Standard Distance	1500m	40km	18
Long Distance	1000 to 4000 m	100 to 200 km	18

冬季铁人三项

	越野跑	山地自行车	越野滑雪	最小年龄要求
团体接力	2~3 千米	4~5 千米	3~4 千米	15
短距离	3~4 千米	5~6 千米	5~6 千米	16
标准距离	7~9 千米	12~14 千米	10~12 千米	18

S3 冬季铁人三项	跑步	滑冰	越野滑雪	最小年龄要求
标准距离	4~6 千米	10~14 千米	7~9 千米	16

越野铁人三项

	游泳	山地自行车	越野跑	最小年龄要求
团体接力	200~250 米	4~5 千米	1.2~1.6 千米	15
短距离	500 米	10~12 千米	3~4 千米	16
标准距离	1000~1500 米	20~30 千米	6~10 千米	18

越野骑跑两项

	越野跑	山地自行车	越野跑	最小年龄要求
团体接力	1.2~1.6 千米	4~5 千米	0.6~0.8 千米	15
短距离	3~4 千米	10~12 千米	1.5~2 千米	16
标准距离	6~8 千米	20~25 千米	3~4 千米	18

游骑两项

	游泳	自行车	最小年龄要求
标准距离	1500 米	40 千米	18
长距离	1000~4000 米	100~200 千米	18

24. APPENDIX B COMPETITION PROTEST FORM

INTERNATIONAL TRIATHLON UNION

ITU

PROTEST FORM

Part 1: To be completed by the protester.
Protest must be filed and signed by the protester under the conditions outlined in the ITU Competition Rules and submitted to the Head Referee.

Event Name: ________________ Event Date:________________

Event Location:________________ Time Protest Submitted:__________

Name of Protester:______________ Race Number:________________

Country of Protester:______________ Email: ________________

Address of Protester:______________ ____________________________

(street address) (City and Postal Code)

Telephone (home):____________ Telephone (mobile):____________________

Name of Protestee:___________ Race Number:________________

Country of Protestee:___________

A protest is a formal complaint against the conduct of a fellow athlete or race official, or against conditions of the competition. You must have substantial evidence, including witnesses, and you must be willing to take part in an interview. Any protest must be accompanied with a cheque or cash for $50 USD or equivalent amount.
What type of Protest is involved? (Check one box only.)

- ❒ Protest Concerning the Course
- ❒ Protest Against Another Athlete or a Technical Official
- ❒ Protest Concerning Eligibility
- ❒ Protest Concerning Timekeeping
- ❒ Protest Concerning Equipment

Witness Details (2):

Name of Witness 1: ____

Name of Witness 2: ____

Rule(s) Violated: ______________________ **Time of Incident:** ______________________

24. 附件 B　比赛抗议书

国际铁人三项联盟（ITU）

ITU

抗议书

第一部分　由抗议人填写

抗议应按照《国际铁联规则》说明的要求，由抗议人本人签字，提交给裁判长。

比赛名称：________________　　比赛日期：________________

比赛地点：________________　　抗议提交的时间：__________

抗议人姓名：______________　　比赛号码：________________

抗议人国籍：______________　　电子邮件：________________

抗议人地址：______________　　__________________________

（街道）　　　　　　（城市和邮政编码）

电话（宅电）：____________　　手机：____________________

抗议对象的姓名：__________　　比赛号码：________________

抗议对象的国籍：__________

抗议是指对其他参赛运动员或技术官员的行为或比赛环境条件不满而提出的正式控告。你必须有实质性的证据，包括证人。你必须愿意接受问讯。抗议的同时必须交纳抗议费 50 美元的支票、现金或其他等额币种。

抗议是属于什么类型的？请选择其中一项。

- ❐　关于比赛路线的抗议
- ❐　对另一名参赛运动员或技术官员的抗议
- ❐　关于参赛资格的抗议
- ❐　关于计时的抗议
- ❐　关于比赛装备的抗议

证人（2 名）：

证人 1 姓名：__________________________________

证人 2 姓名：__________________________________

违反的规则：______________　　**事件发生时间：**______________

Where did the Violation occur. (Define location. If required use additional paper and draw a diagram.)			
Who was involved in the Violation?			
How did the Violation occur (brief statement explaining alleged violation)?			
Signature of Protester:		Date:	

Part 2　Official use only

Protest Fee $50 USD attached	Yes ❑　No ❑
Competition Jury / Appeal Panel Members (Names) and tick box to indicate if it was a 3 person jury or 5 person. ❒ **3 person jury** ❒ **5 person jury**	1. 2. 3. 4. 5.
Competition Jury / Appeal Panel action:	
Competition Jury / Appeal Panel Chair's Name:	
Signature:	
Time, Date Protes received:	
Time, Date Protest processed:	
Amount of fee withheld/refunded:	

犯规行为发生的地点（描述位置，如需要可图示）：____________________________

____

与犯规有关的人员：____

____

犯规行为是如何发生的（对于犯规行为的简单描述）：__________________________

____

____

____

抗议人签字：__________ 日期：__________

第二部分 官方使用

是否已交纳 50 美元抗议费	是□ 否□
比赛仲裁委员会 / 申诉小组成员姓名，并在方框内标注是 3 人还是 5 人 **□3 人** **□5 人**	1. 2. 3. 4. 5.
仲裁委员会 / 申诉小组决定	
仲裁委员会 / 申诉小组主席姓名	
签字	
收到抗议的日期 / 时间	
处理抗议的日期 / 时间	
保留 / 退回的金额	

25.APPENDIX C COMPETITION APPEAL FORM

INTERNATIONAL TRIATHLON UNION

ITU

APPEAL FORM

Part 1: To be completed by the appellant:

Appeals must be filed and signed by the appellant under the conditions outlined in the ITU Competition Rules, and submitted to the Technical Delegate. An appeal is a request for a review of a decision made by the Head Referee. This is the first level of appeal and will be heard by the Competition Jury. All appeals must be accompanied with a cheque or cash for $50 USD or equivalent amount.

Event Name:	______	Event Date:	______
Event Location:	______	Time Appeal Submitted	______
Name of Appellant:	______	Race Number:	______
Country of Appellant:	______	Email:	______
Address of Appellant:	______ (street address)		______ (City and Postal Code)
Telephone (home):	______	Telephone (mobile):	______
Reason for penalty received:	______	Type of penalty received (DQ, Suspension):	______
Was the penalty confirmed by the Head Referee?	**Yes** ❑ **No** ❑		

Type of Appeal: (Check one box only.)

❑ Appeal against the Head Referee's ruling on a Violation Report

❑ Appeal against the Head Referee's ruling on a Protest:

Specific Location on the Course:

______

Name and Number of Race Official(s) / Athlete(s)/ Spectator(s) if Known: ______

Description of the Incident (Use additional paper if required) : ______

25. 附件 C　比赛申诉书

国际铁人三项联盟（ITU）

ITU

申诉书

第一部分　由抗议人填写

申诉应按照国际铁联规则说明的要求，由申诉人签字，提交给技术代表。申诉是指对裁判长的判决提出审查的请求。这是一级申诉，将由仲裁委员会受理。所有申诉必须同时交纳申诉费 50 美元的支票、现金或其他等额币种。

比赛名称：______________________　比赛日期：______________________

比赛地点：______________________　提交申诉的时间：________________

申诉人姓名：____________________　比赛号码：______________________

申诉人国籍：____________________　电子邮件：______________________

申诉人地址：____________________　______________________________

（街道）　（城市和邮政编码）

电话（宅电）：__________________　电话（手机）：__________________

处罚原因：__________　处罚类型：（取消比赛资格，停赛）

判罚是否已由裁判长确认：　是 □　否 □

申诉是属于什么类型的？请选择其中一项。

- ❐ 申诉针对裁判长对于某犯规行为的判罚
- ❐ 申诉针对裁判长对于某抗议的裁决：

比赛路线上的具体位置：______________________________________

____

技术官员 / 运动员 / 观众的姓名和号码（如果知道）：______________________

____

对于事件的描述（如需要可使用附加纸张）：______________________________

____

Witness Details (2):

Name of Witness 1: ________________________________

Name of Witness 2: ________________________________

Signature of Appellant: ______________________ Date: ____________

Part 2 Official use only

Appeal Fee $50 USD attached	Yes ❑ No ❑
Is this Appeal to reverse a Competition Jury / Appeal Panel decision?	Yes ❑ No ❑
If 'Yes', attach Competition Jury / Appeal Panel Decision and action(s) and Head Referee's decision and action(s).	
Competition Jury / Appeal Panel Members (Names) and tick box to indicate if it was a 3 person jury or 5 person. ❑ 3 person jury ❑ 5 person jury	1. 2. 3. 4. 5.
Competition Jury / Appeal Panel Action:	
Competition Jury / Appeal Panel Chair's Name:	
Signature:	
Time, Date Appeal Received:	
Time, Date Appeal processed:	
Amount of fee withheld/refunded:	

证人（2 名）：

证人 1 姓名：________________________________
证人 2 姓名：________________________________

申诉人签字：______________日期：__________

第二部分　官方使用

是否已缴纳 50 美元申诉费	是☐　否☐
此申诉是否请求改变仲裁委员会 / 申诉小组的决定？	是☐　否☐
如果“是”，附上仲裁委员会 / 申诉小组的决定，以及裁判长的决定。	
比赛仲裁委员会 / 申诉小组姓名，并在方框内标注是 3 人还是 5 人 ☐ **3 人** ☐ **5 人**	1.
	2.
	3.
	4.
	5.
仲裁委员会 / 申诉小组的决定	
仲裁委员会 / 申诉小组主席姓名	
签字	
收到申诉的日期 / 时间	
处理申诉的日期 / 时间	
保留 / 退回的金额	

26. APPENDIX D DEFINITIONS

Age	The age of the athlete on the 31st of December of the year of the competition.
Age group Team Managers Briefing	Meeting with the Age group team manager and coaches in which they are informed by the Technical Delegate about all the specifications of the event.
Aid/Outside Assistance	Any kind of material support or personal assistance received by the athlete. Depending on its nature, it may be allowed or forbidden.
Ambush Marketing	Deliberately using the opportunity of live television and media photographers to expose the sponsor logos larger than the approved sizes, and/or equipment or objects not provided by Local Organising Committee or ITU.
Appeal	A request to the Competition Jury of an event or the ITU Arbitration Tribunal for a review of the decision of the Head Referee/Competition Jury. (Note: This cannot include an appeal against the finding of a doping violation or against the penalty imposed for the finding of a doping violation. These appeals must be directed to ITU Arbitration Tribunal independently.)
Appeal Panel	The Appeal Panel consist of a member of the ITU Technical Committee, the ITU Sport Department and the Technical Delegate of the event or if such not available the representative of the LOC for appeals to be dealt with after the medal ceremonies, but before 48 hours after the end of the competition. It is held responsible to determine the eligibility of the protest or appeal, to hear and to rule on all appeals against decisions handed down through the Head Referee, including decisions on protests.
Appellant	An athlete submitting an appeal.
Aquabike	Multisport which combines swim and cycle in two segments: the first segment is swimming and finishing with cycling.
Aquathlon	Multisport which combines swim and run in three segments: the first segment is run, followed by swimming and finishing with running.
Assistance	Any attempt by an unauthorised or unofficial source to help or to stabilise an athlete.
Assistant Chief Technical Official	Responsible to the Chief Technical Official for coordinating the employment of the Technical Officials assigned to his/her competition course segment or area.
Athletes	Individuals who register for and compete in events.
Athletes' Briefing	Meeting with the athletes in which they are informed by the Technical Delegate about all the specifications of the event.
Bag Drop System	Conducting transitions by: 1. Taking a pre-prepared bag containing all equipment to be used in the next segment; 2. Changing the equipment in the designated area; 3. Putting all the used equipment into the same bag and drop it at the designated spot.
Bicycle	The bicycle is a human powered vehicle with two wheels of equal diameter. The front wheel shall be steerable; the rear wheel shal be driven through a system comprising pedals and a chain. Bicycles are also referred as bikes.
Bike catchers	Local Organising Committee personnel located after the dismount line, who take the bikes from the athletes and delivering them to the location from where the athletes can collect them after the competition.
Blocking	The deliberate impeding or obstructing of progress of one athlete by another. An athlete on the bike course, who is not keeping to the appropriate side of the road.

26. 附件 D 概念界定

年龄	运动员在比赛年 12 月 31 日时的年龄。
分龄组领队技术会	技术代表与分龄组领队和教练会面并通报赛事细则。
协助 / 外界援助	运动员接收到的所有物质或者个人援助。取决于援助性质，援助或被允许或禁止。
隐性营销	蓄意在电视直播和媒体照片上展示比规定尺寸大的赞助商的标志，或使用非当地组委会和国际铁联所提供的装备和物品。
申诉	对裁判长或仲裁委员会的决定向赛事仲裁委员会或国际铁联仲裁法庭提出重新审查的请求。（备注：不包含对使用违禁药物的申诉和对使用违禁药物而受到惩罚的申诉。此类申诉应直接向国际铁联仲裁法庭单独提出。）
国际铁联 申诉小组	国际铁联申诉小组由国际铁联技术委员会成员 1 名、国际铁联体育部和技术代表组成，若无法邀请到技术代表，则由当地组委会指派相应的代表加入申诉小组。该专家组主要是处理比赛颁奖仪式后 48 小时内出现的申诉行为。其主要职责是断定抗议和申述的合理性，听证和决定针对裁判长的决定的所有抗议或申诉，包括裁判长对抗议的裁决。
申诉人	提交申诉的运动员。
游骑两项	由游泳和自行车两个赛段组成的运动：起始赛段为游泳，终点赛段为自行车。
游跑两项	由跑步－游泳－跑步三个赛段组成的运动：第一赛段为跑步，第二赛段为游泳，第三赛段为跑步。
帮助	任何非授权或非官方的援助或支持运动员的举动。
首席技术官员助理	向首席技术官员负责，协调技术官员的使用及其所辖赛段区域的分配。
运动员	报名并在国际铁联赛事中竞技的个人。
运动员技术会	技术代表与运动员会面并通报赛事技术细节。
备包放置系统	组织转换过程的一种方式： 1. 赛前准备一个可装下个赛段需用物品的袋子。 2. 在指定区更换装备。 3. 把所有使用过的装备装进这个袋子并放到指定地点。
自行车	由相同直径的两个轮子组成且由人力驱动的车辆。前轮须可转向，后轮则由通过脚蹬和车链组成的系统驱动。
自行车协放员	在下车线后的当地组织委员会人员，他们把运动员的车辆送到指定地点，赛后运动员可前去领取。
阻挡	运动员对其他运动员的行进所造成的故意阻拦或妨碍。自行车赛段的运动员行进位置不当。

Blue card	Card, which is used to inform athletes when being penalised for drafting infringement during cycling segment.
Charge	The contacting of one athlete by another from the front, rear or side, and hindering that athlete's progress.
Check in	Control established at the entrance of the athletes lounge and at the entrance of the transisition area, before the competition. In both places a time of admission is set by the Technical Delegate.
Chief Technical Official	Appointed by the Technical Delegate and is responsible for the control and co-ordination of the deployment of Technical Officials.
Clean Start	All the athletes start after the horn. The competition continues.
Coaches meeting	Meeting with the coaches in which they are informed by the Technical Delegate about all the specifications of the event.
Competition	Single and continuous sport action from start to finish. Most cases it fits within the definition of Race, except the semi-final/final or the time trial qualifying format.
Competition Jury	The Competition Jury appointed and chaired by the Technical Delegate. It is held responsible to determine the eligibility of the protest or appeal, to hear and to rule on all appeals against decisions handed down through the Head Referee, including decisions on protests.
Conflict of interest	A set of circumstances that creates a risk that professional judgement or actions regarding a primary interest will be unduly influenced by a secondary interest.
Continent	Each of the five geographical divisions established in ITU. They are: Africa, The Americas, Asia, Europe and Oceania
Continental Technical Officials (CTOs)	The Level 2 Technical Officials certified by ITU.
Course	A forward line of progress from start to finish, which must be clearly marked and measured to prescribed specifications.
Crawling	The action by an athlete of bringing three or more limbs in contact with the ground, either together or in any sequence, to enable forward propulsion.
Cycling Segment	Part of the competition course over which it has been defined in the Athletes' Briefing the bike is to be ridden, walked or carried within distinctive lane boundaries. The bike course commences from the Mount Line and concludes at the Dismount Line.
Development Event	Event sanctioned by ITU or any of the Continental Confederations, where ITU may allow the participation of athletes only from certain pre-defined National Federations.
Dismount Before The Dismount Line	An athlete's foot must contact the ground before the dismount line after the athlete dismounts the bike.. If this contact doesn't occur, it is considered an infringement of the rules.
Dismount Line	A designated line at the entrance of the transition area from the bike course before which athletes are to dismount their bikes fully and proceed to the bike racks. The Dismount Line will normally extend for the width of the entrance to the transition area and be identified by flags/line/Technical Official, or combinations thereof.
Disqualification	A penalty assigned as appropriate for the rule violation, which has been reported, or for which a protest has been upheld. As a result of this penalty, the athlete will not be given finish or split times for the event, no account will be taken of the athlete when placings are assessed for any category or for the competition as a whole, and the athlete's results will appear as DSQ.
Draft Zone Bicycle	Zone defined by an athlete during the cycling segment which is extended to the whole width of the road and 10 meters long in the standard and shorter events and 12 meters long in middle and long distance events.

蓝牌	在自行车赛段，示意运动员因尾随犯规而被处罚的蓝色卡片。
冲撞	被另一运动员从前方、后方或旁边接触并妨碍其行进。
检录	赛前，在准备区和转换区入口处对运动员进行的检查验证。技术代表须确定运动员进入此区域的时间。
首席技术官员	由技术代表任命，负责控制、协调技术官员的调度部署。
有效出发	所有运动员在喇叭声后出发。比赛继续进行。
教练员会议	技术代表与教练见面并通告赛事技术细节。
竞赛	有始有终的单独和持续性体育活动。除了半决赛、决赛或计时资格赛的具体概念之外，在多数情况下它符合比赛的概念。
仲裁委员会	仲裁委员会由技术代表任命并由技术代表任主席。负责对一切抗议和申诉的资格做出裁决，对裁判长决定提出的上诉进行听证并做出裁决，包括对抗议的裁决。
利益冲突	危害专业判断和行为的一组状况，使得主要利益过度被次要利益影响。
大洲	国际铁联建立的五个地理区划，分别为非洲、美洲、 亚洲、欧洲和大洋洲。
洲际技术官员（CTOs）	国际铁联认证的 2 级技术官员。
比赛路线	从出发点到终点的行进路线。路线必须根据规定清楚标示并仔细测量。
爬行	运动员三个或更多的肢体与地面接触，或同时着地或轮流着地以向前移动。
自行车赛段	运动员技术会上明确告知的比赛路线的一部分。在明显可辨识的路线范围内，自行车或被骑、或被推、或被扛。自行车赛段路线始于上车线，止于下车线。
发展性赛事	由国际铁联或洲际联合会管理的赛事，国际铁联仅允许从预先确定的某些国家联合会的运动员参加。
下车线之前下车	运动员下车后，在下车线之前必须脚触地。如没有触地则被视为犯规。
下车线	结束自行车赛段后的转换区入口处标明的线，在此线之前运动员应完全从自行车上下车并继续前进到放置自行车的架子处。下车线一般应与转换区的宽度一样，并且由旗帜、线条或技术官员明确标明。
取消比赛资格	对于已上报或被抗议的犯规行为的一种处罚。作为处罚，运动员将不会获得全程比赛或分段赛的成绩和排名。运动员的成绩被标明为 DSQ（被取消比赛资格运动员）。
自行车尾随区	自行车赛段中根据运动员设定的区域。该区域宽为路面宽度，在标准距离和短距离比赛中长度为 10 米，在中、长距离比赛中长度为 12 米。

Draft Zone Motorbike	Zone defined by a motorbike during the cycling segment which is extended to the whole width of the road and 12 meters long.
Draft Zone Vehicle	Zone defined by a vehicle during the cycling segment which is extended to the whole width of the road and 35 meters long.
Drafting	To enter in a drafting zone and not completing the overtake in 20 seconds in standard and shorter events or 25 seconds in middle and long distance events.
Duathlon	Multisport which combines cycle and run in three segments: the first segment is running, followed by cycling and finishing with running.
Early start	When an athlete's foot crossed the vertical plane of the start line, before the start signal.
Elite	Elite athletes are those competing in elite competitions.
Event	Group of Races of the same category usually happening in the same day or on the following days (i.e.: World Championship, Continental Cup).
Event Organisers Manual (EOM)	A document which has been developed to ensure the implementation of consistently high global event management and marketing standards.
Event-weekend	The days when an event is taking place, which may include days other than Saturday and Sunday.
Expulsion	An athlete penalised by expulsion will not be permitted, during his or her lifetime, to take part in any ITU sanctioned event, or any event sanctioned by one of its member associations (National Federation) affiliated with the ITU.
Festival	Group of different multisport events happening in a short period of time (up to ten days) at the same location.
Field of Play (FOP)	The course on which the competition portions of the ITU event will take place.
Field of Play Decision	The application and interpretation of the ITU Competition Rules by Technical Officials and/or Competition Jury.
Final	Last round of an event in qualifying round format. The final decides the winner and the medallist of the event.
Finisher	An athlete who completes the entire competition course within the rules and crosses the finish line, or a vertical extension of the forward edge of the finish line, with any part of the torso (i.e. as distinct from the head, neck, arms, legs, hands or feet).
Force Majeure	Action of the elements, strike, lockout or other industrial disturbance, unlawful act against public order or authority, war blockade, public riot, lightning, fire or explosion, storm, flood, blacklisting, boycott or sanctions however incurred, freight embargo, transportation delay or any other, event which is not reasonably within the control of the party affected.
Incapable Athlete	An athlete deemed by race medical staff as not being able to continue the event without the likelihood of causing injury to him/herself or another athlete.
Indecent Exposure	The willful uncovering of either or both buttocks, or of the pubic area or of the genital area. In addition, in the case of a female athlete, the willful complete uncovering of one or both nipples.
Inland Water	Lakes, lochs, canals and rivers up to the point the tide affects them in terms of changes to their level.
Interference	A deliberate block, charge or abrupt motion, which impedes another athlete.
International Technical Officials (ITOs)	The Level 3 Technical Officials certified by ITU.
International Triathlon Union (ITU)	The world governing body of triathlon, duathlon, aquathlon, winter triathlon and all other related multisport, a non-profit corporation domiciled and residing at Maison du Sport International, Av de Rhodanie 54, CH-1007 Lausanne, Switzerland.

摩托车尾随区	自行车赛段根据摩托车设定的区域。该区域宽为路面宽度，长度为 12 米。
机动车尾随区	自行车赛段根据机动车设定的区域。该区域宽为路面宽度，长度为 35 米。
尾随	进入尾随区，在标准距离和短距离比赛中未能在 20 秒内完成超越，在中、长距离比赛中未能在 25 秒内完成超越。
骑跑两项	由自行车和跑步以三赛段形式组成的运动：第一赛段为跑步，第二赛段为自行车，第三赛段为跑步。
抢跑（跳）	开始信号给出前，运动员的脚越过出发线的垂直平面。
优秀组	参加优秀组赛事的运动员。
赛事	在同一天或连续几天内组织的同类型的一系列竞赛（如世锦赛、洲际杯）
赛事操作手册（EOM）	确保全球赛事持续高水准管理和营销标准实施的文件。
非周末比赛	举办多日且不占用双休日的赛事。
终身禁赛	被终身禁赛的运动员终身不得参加国际铁联比赛或者国际铁联会员协会批准的比赛。
赛事节	在同一地点短期内（最多十天内）举办不同多项全能的赛事群。
赛场（FOP）	国际铁联赛事进行比赛的场地。
赛场决定	由技术官员或仲裁委员会对国际铁联规则所做出的应用与解释。
决赛	资格赛最后一轮，角逐出赛事优胜者和奖牌获得者。
完成者	未犯规情况下，完成整个比赛赛程并越过终点线或躯干（即明显区别于头、脖子、胳膊、腿、手或脚的部分）的任何部分穿过终点线前沿垂直线的运动员。
不可抗力	因罢工、闭厂或其他工厂骚乱，违反公共秩序或权威的非法行为，战争封锁，公共暴动，闪电，火灾或爆炸，风暴，洪水，列入黑名单，抵制或制裁等因素而招致货物禁运、运输延误或其他的事件，此类事件具有不可克服性。
无参赛能力运动员	被赛事医务人员认定可能对自己和其他运动员造成伤害不能继续比赛的运动员。
不雅暴露身体行为	有意暴露一侧或两侧臀部或阴部或生殖部位。女性运动员有意暴露一个或两个乳头。
内陆水	不会受潮汐影响的湖泊、运河和河流等。
干扰	有意阻挡、指控或粗鲁妨碍其他运动员的行为。
国际技术官员（ITOs）	国际铁联认证的 3 级技术官员。
国际铁联（ITU）	铁人三项、骑跑两项、游跑两项、冬季铁人三项以及其他相关分项的非营利管理机构，位于瑞士洛桑 CH-1007， Rhodanie 大街 54 号。

ITU Competition Rules	The document that contains all the rules and regulations that governs fair and safe competitions.
ITU Members	The National Federations and Continental Confederations affiliated to ITU.
ITU Rules	The ITU Event Organisers' Manual (latest edition), ITU Competition Rules, ITU Constitution and By-Laws, ITU Guidelines Regarding Authorised Identification, ITU Anti-Doping Rules and WADA Code, ITU Athletes' Agreement, ITU Qualification Criteria, ITU Ranking Criteria and any other rules adopted and amended by ITU from time to time and available for consultation via the download section of the ITU's official website www.triathlon.org.
Invalid Start	Some athletes start clearly before the horn and some others stay behind the start line. The start is not clean and is declared invalid.
Last Biker – First Runner Scenario	This occurs when the bike and run courses are partly common, and the first runner reaches the point where both courses merge and there are still bikers on the course before this point.
Local Organising Committee (LOC)	The organising entity of an ITU event.
Medal Events (Paratriathlon)	A competition, which may include athletes from one or more sport classes competing for the same medals.
Mount After The Mount Line	An athlete's foot must contact the ground past the mount line, before the athlete mounts the bike. If this contact doesn't occur, it is considered an infringement of the rules.
Mount Line	A designated line at the exit from the transition area onto the bike course or after which athletes are to mount their bicycles and proceed. The Mount Line will normally extend for the width of the exit of the transition area and be identified by flags/line/Technical Official, or combinations thereof.
National Federation (NF)	National triathlon governing body affiliated with ITU.
National Federation Quota	The maximum quota allocated to a National Federation in a specific competition.
National Technical Officials (NTOs)	The Level 1 Technical Officials certified by the National Federation.
Overtake	On the bike course, when the leading edge of the front wheel of the overtaking bike moves in front of the leading edge of the front wheel of the bike being overtaken. An athlete can pass another athlete only on the appropriate side.
Pack	Two or more athletes with overlapping draft zones.
Panel	A temporary or permanent body composed by minimum three (3) people representing pre-defined stakeholders, which takes decisions or make proposals in specific tasks.
Pass	When one athlete's bike draft zone overlaps another athlete's bike draft zone, makes continual forward progress through that zone and overtakes within a maximum period of 20 seconds. An athlete can pass another athlete only on the appropriate side.
Penalty	The consequence on an athlete, who is assessed by an ITU Technical Official to have unintentionally committed a rule infringement/violation. A penalty may take the form of a time delay, disqualification, suspension or expulsion.
Penalty Box	An area on the bike course or the run course, set aside for the implementation of a time penalty for a rule infringement/violation.
Prosthesis	An artificial device used to replace a missing body part.
Protest	A formal complaint against the conduct of another athlete or a race official, or against the conditions of the competition.

国际铁联竞赛规则	保证公平、安全比赛的所有规章制度。
国际铁联成员	国际铁联下属的国家会员协会和洲际联合会。
ITU 规则	《国际铁联比赛操作手册》（最新版本）、《国际铁联竞赛规则》、《国际铁联及章程》及其附则、《国际铁联（比赛服）授权认证指南》、《国际铁联反兴奋剂规则》和《世界反兴奋剂条例》、《国际铁联运动员协议》、国际铁联参赛资格标准、国际铁联比赛积分排名办法和其他由国际铁联采纳并不时修正，可在国际铁联官方网站（www.triathlon.org.）下载区查询的规则。
无效出发	部分运动员在喇叭声响起前出发而其他运动员仍在出发线之后。此出发被宣布为无效。
最后的自行车运动员——第一个跑步运动员情境	当自行车路线与跑步路线部分重叠时，领先跑步运动员到达两条路线合并处而仍有自行车运动员落后于此点的情况。
当地组委会（LOC）	国际铁联赛事的组织实体。
奖牌赛事（伤残铁人三项）	来自一个或多个伤残分级的运动员共同争夺奖牌的比赛。
上车线后上车	运动员上车前，其脚必须与上车线后地面接触。如没有触地，则被视为犯规。
上车线	由转换区出口进入自行车路线或运动员通过后上车并前行的指示线。上车线的延展一般应与转换区出口的宽度一样并且由旗帜、线、技术官员或它们的结合体明确标明。
国家会员协会（NF）	隶属于国际铁联的国家铁人三项管理实体。
国家会员协会参赛名额	在一特别比赛中分配给国家会员协会的最大参赛名额。
国家技术官员（NTOs）	由国家会员协会认证的 1 级技术官员。
超车	在自行车路线上，当追超车的前轮前沿超过被超越车前轮前沿时即为超车。运动员只能在恰当一侧超越。
集团	两个或两个以上运动员尾随区交叠。
专门小组	由至少三名预先确定的利益相关人员组成的临时或永久团体，针对特殊任务决策或提议。
超越	当一名运动员的尾随区与另一名重叠，并通过持续向前，在 20 秒内穿越其尾随区并超过另一名运动员。必须从许可的一侧完成超越。
处罚	保留对国际铁联技术官员判定的非故意犯规运动员所做的惩戒。处罚形式有时间处罚、取消比赛资格、停赛或终身禁赛。
处罚区	为实施时间处罚而在自行车路线旁或跑步路线旁设置的区域。
假体	代替人体所失去部分的人工装置。
抗议	针对其他运动员、技术官员行为或比赛的环境和条件进行的正式投诉。

Race	A competition or group of competitions, which determine a winner, the medals and a result list. In the case of Paratriathlon, this is named as "Medal Event" (i.e.: elite men's race, 50-54 women).
Head Referee	A Technical Official, who is responsible to the Technical Delegate to hear and make final decisions on all rules violations reported by Technical Officials. Technical Delegate appoints the Head Referee.
Red card	Card, which is used to inform athletes about disqualification.
Region	Group of National Federations, from the same or different continents, linked by geographical or cultural reasons.
Registration	Point of control established at the entrance of athletes briefing and coaches meeting. Attenders to these meetings will sign the attendance list.
Results	The timed finish positions of all athletes after violation reports have been ruled on, protests and appeals have been heard, and penalties have been awarded.
Right of Way	When an athlete has established a lead position and pursues a desired course within the limits of the ITU Competition Rules.
Round	Each of the stages of an event with qualifying format. One event in qualifying round format has two rounds: semi-finals and final.
Run Course	Part of the competition course, which has been defined at the Athletes' Briefing where the athlete is to run or walk within distinctive lane boundaries. In triathlons and aquathlons, the run course commences at the exit from the transition area and concludes at the Finish Line. In duathlons, the first run course commences at the start line and finishes at the entry to the transition area; the second run course commences at the exit from the transition area and concludes at the Finish Line.
Sanction	A permit issued by the National Federation for the conduct of an event. The issue of such a permit is a declaration by the sanctioning authority that plans for the event have been thoroughly inspected and have been found to comply fully with the requirements of National Federation operating requirements to provide the greatest potential for the conduct of a safe and fair event.
Sea and Transition Water	Ocean, seas and the part of the river affected by the tides, including river mouths, deltas, estuaries and rias.
Semi-final	Preliminary round of an event in qualifying round format. The semi-finals determine the athletes qualified to the final.
Smart Helmet	Bike helmet with a built in sound system covering or not covering the ears.
Sorted Waiting List	A list of athletes not yet included in the start list, ordered according to the specific qualification criteria.
Sport Class	Paratriathlon sport class is a category defined by ITU in which athletes are categorised in reference to an activity limitation resulting from impairment.
Sportsmanship	The behavior of an athlete during competition. Sportsmanship is interpreted as fair, rational and courteous behavior, while bad sports conduct is any behavior judged to be unfair, unethical or dishonest, a violent act, intentional misconduct, abusive language, intimidating behavior, or persistent infringement of the rules.
Standard Bridge Piece	A rigid piece, of plastic or metal, which joins both sides of the handlebar clip-on at the ends and is commercially available.
Start List	A list of athletes approved to compete on a competition.
Start Wave	A group of athletes starting together at the same time. A start wave can include different races (i.e.: different Paratriathlon Sport Classes, or different Age Groups), but also a race can be split in different Start Waves (i.e.: Age Group 20-24A and Age Group 20-24B).
Stop and Go	Penalty consisting on stop, correct the fault and continue the competition.

比赛	一场或多场决出胜者、奖牌和最终结果排名的竞赛。在伤残人铁人三项中，叫作“奖牌赛事”（比如男子优秀组比赛、50~54 岁女子组比赛）。
裁判长	向技术代表负责的技术官员。负责并对技术官员上报的所有犯规行为进行审理并做最终裁决。裁判长由技术代表指定。
红牌	告知运动员比赛资格被取消的红色卡片。
地区	根据地理或文化划分的来自相同或不同大洲的会员协会团体。
报到处	设置在运动员技术会和教练员会议入口处的管制点，参会者需在此处签到。
成绩	犯规报告已被裁决，抗议和申诉已被受理，处罚已被执行的情况下全部运动员的计时排名。
路权	运动员已取得领先位置并在《国际铁联竞赛规则》的规定范围内继续前行的路线。
轮次	资格赛的一个阶段。赛事中的资格赛分为两轮：半决赛和决赛。
跑步路线	在运动员技术会上被指定的赛事的部分路线。运动员在明显标识的路线范围内或跑或走。在铁人三项和游跑两项中，跑步路线始于转换区出口止于终点线。在骑跑两项中，第一段跑步路线始于起跑线止于转换区入口处，第二段跑步路线始于转换区出口处止于终点线。
授权	国家会员协会公布的赛事行为的许可。 此许可是筹备赛事的授权机构的声明即已通过全面检验，符合会员协会要求，能够全力组织安全、公平的赛事。
海水和过渡水	大洋、海和受海潮影响的河流，包括江口、三角洲、河口和溺湾。
半决赛	资格赛比赛模式的首轮。半决赛决定运动员进入决赛的资格。
智能头盔	装有声音系统包耳 / 不包耳的自行车头盔。
候补排名名单	在出发名单之外，根据特定的资格标准进行排序的运动员名单。
运动分级	国际铁联对伤残运动员比赛进行的分级。分级参数为伤残对运动员活动所造成的受限程度。
运动员精神	运动员在比赛中的行为。运动员精神指公平、理性、礼貌的行为，而坏的体育行为指不公平、不道德、不诚实、运用暴力、故意违规、语言辱骂、恐吓、或持续违反规则的行为。
标准桥接件	市售的连接副把端口的或塑料或金属的硬件。
出发名单	经批准参赛的运动员名单。
出发批次	同时出发的一批运动员。一个批次可以包括参加不同比赛的运动员（比如不同的伤残分级或不同分龄的各组），也可以是同一项目的不同出发批次（比如 20-24A 组和 20-24B 组）
停一走	一种处罚形状，包括：叫停、纠正错误、继续比赛。

Suspension	An athlete awarded this penalty will not be permitted during the stated suspension period, to take part in any event sanctioned by ITU or its member associations (where determined) affiliated with ITU. For any suspension because of a doping violation, the athlete will not be able to compete in any IOC affiliated sport at any local, regional, state, national or international level. The suspension period may vary in length, depending on the severity of the violation. In the case of a suspension imposed by ITU, the length of the suspension will be determined by the ITU Arbitration Tribunal.
Swim Course	Part of the competition course over which it has been defined in the Athletes' Briefing that the athlete is to swim within distinctive lane boundaries. In triathlons and aquathlons, the swim course commences at the start line and concludes at the water's edge/exit prior to entry to the transition area.
Technical Delegate	A Technical Official, who is qualified by ITU, and responsible for ensuring all aspects of the ITU Competition Rules and ITU Event Organisers' Manual are fulfilled in preparation for, during, and after the event. Where appeals are lodged, the Technical Delegate will be the Chair of the Competition Jury. The Technical Delegate will normally be responsible for conducting or overseeing the conduct of event sanctioning.
Technical Official	A member of the joint team of International Technical Officials (ITOs), Continental Technical Officials (CTOs) and National Technical Officials (NTOs) at an ITU event.
Time Penalty	Penalty consisting on stop at the penalty box for a certain time. Early start time penalty is served in T1 instead the at the penalty box.
Torso	The human body excluding the neck, the head and the limbs.
Transition Area	A location within a defined boundary, which is not a part of the swim course, the bike course or the run course and within which each athlete is allocated an area for the storage of individual items of clothing and equipment.
Triathlon	A sport of individual or team character and motivation, which combines swimming, cycling and running skills in continuum.
Valid Start with Early Starters	Start in which few athletes started before the signal. Early starters will receive a time penalty in Transition 1.
Venue	All warm-up and competition areas, the air space above such areas, official hotel, broadcasters, press and media areas, sport expo area, contiguous areas, including without limitation spectators' area, VIP areas, transition area, finish area and all other areas under control of Local Organising Committee.
Violation	A rule infringement which results in a penalty.
Waiting List	A list of athletes not yet included in the start list before the creation of the start list.
Warning	A caution issued by a Technical Official to an athlete during the course of a competition. The purpose of a warning is to alert the athlete of the potential for a rule violation to occur and to promote a pro-active attitude.
Winter Triathlon	Multisport which combines different winter sports. It may have two different formats, either starting with running on snow, followed by cycling on snow and finishing with cross country skiing, or starting with snow shoeing followed by skating on ice and finishing with cross country skiing.
Yellow card	Card, which is used to inform athletes about infringements which may result in warning, time penalty or stop and go.

停赛	在停赛期间，运动员不得参加任何国际铁联比赛或其下属会员组织所管辖的赛事。如停赛是因为使用违禁药物，运动员不能参加国际奥委会附属的任何级别的比赛 [地方、区域、州（省）、国家或国际级别]。停赛期时长根据犯规行为的严重程度不等。如停赛由国际铁联施加则由国际铁联仲裁法庭裁决停赛期时长。
游泳路线	在运动员技术会上被指定的赛事的部分路线。运动员在明显标识的路线范围内游泳。在铁人三项或游跑两项比赛中游泳路线始于入水线止于水域边缘或进入转换区之前的出口。
技术代表	由国际铁联认证的技术官员，负责确保《国际铁联竞赛规则》及《国际铁联比赛操作手册》中的各项内容在赛前、赛中、赛后都得到实施。当有申诉提出时，技术代表为仲裁委员会主席。技术代表负责实施或监督赛事授权。
技术官员	国际铁联赛事中的国际技术官员 （ITOs）、洲际技术官员（CTOs）或国家技术官员 （NTOs）的一员。
时间处罚	在处罚区停留一定时间的惩罚。抢跑或抢跳在第一换项时而非处罚区实施时间处罚。
躯干	除脖子、头和四肢之外的人体。
转换区	指定区域内的地点，独立于游泳路线、自行车路线和跑步路线。转换区内每一运动员在指定区域内放置个人衣物和装备等物品。
铁人三项	具有个人或团体特色和动机的体育项目之一，游泳、自行车和跑步不间断进行。
有抢跑的有效出发	出发信号发出前个别运动员抢跑（跳）。抢跑（跳）的运动员将在第一换项时接受时间处罚。
场地	所有热身和竞赛的区域及其上空，包括官方酒店、广播、新闻和媒体区，体育博览区，毗邻地区。包括但不限于观众区、VIP 区、转换区、终点区和其他所有处于当地组委会控制下的区域。
犯规	导致处罚的违反规则的行为。
候补名单	在出发名单产生前，还未确定能否进入出发名单的运动员名单。
警告	在比赛路线上由技术官员向运动员发出的警告。警告的目的是为了提醒运动员可能会出现犯规行为，敦促运动员养成前瞻性的态度。
冬季铁人三项	由不同冬季运动组成的运动。一般有两种比赛模式：第一种以雪地跑、雪地自行车、越野滑雪依次进行比赛；第二种以跑、滑冰、越野滑雪依次进行。
黄牌	示意运动员犯规并可能给予警告、时间处罚的黄色卡片。

27. APPENDIX E QUALIFICATION AND RANKING CRITERIA

1. General:

1.1. The specific Qualification Criteria for all ITU and Continental Events are outlined in the ITU website under the following link: https://www.triathlon.org/about/downloads/category/qualification_criteria;

1.2. The specific Ranking Criteria for ITU and Continental Confederations are outlined in the ITU website under the following link: https://www.triathlon.org/about/downloads/category/ranking_criteria;

1.3. The general procedures and rules of qualification is outlined below.

2. Start Lists and Waiting Lists management procedures:

2.1. This section affects all ITU events, except those specificly excluded. Such exclusion is indicated in the qualification criteria. The Qualification Criteria also sets:

a.) The National Federations' quota (*);
b.) The Host National Federation's quota (*);
c.) The extended National Federations' quota (*);
d.) The extended Host National Federation's quota (*);
e.) The quota excess at the discretion of the invitation panel;
f.) The day of the start list's creation;
g.) The number of substitutions allowed per National Federaion;
h.) The last day the National Federation can request substitutions;
i.) The last day the National Federation can comunícate withdrawals without penalty;
j.) The maximum number of invitations to be allocated;
k.) The day of the invitation panel meeting.

(*) These quotas may be reduced as the result of the application of penalties.

2.2. Athletes are entered to the Waiting List 33 days before the first day of a given event by the National Federations. Athletes are sorted according to the following priority criteria:

a.) ITU World Ranking, or the priority indicated in the Qualification Criteria;
b.) Athletes without ITU World Ranking points are sorted as one per National Federation in alphabetical order of the IOC code of the country, starting with the host National Federation;
c.) Once one athlete of every National Federation is on the Waiting List, a second one is included to the Waiting List, with the same principles as above. Then a third athlete, and so on;
d.) Athletes – entered to the Waiting List after this sorting process – are allocated the last positions according to the time of entry.

27. 附件 E　参赛资格标准及积分排名办法

1. 概 述

1.1 国际铁联和洲际联盟所有比赛的参赛资格标准已在国际铁联官方网站公布，请查询：https://www.triathlon.org/about/downloads/category/qualification_criteria。

1.2 国际铁联和洲际联盟比赛的积分排名办法已在国际铁联官方网站公布，请查询：https://www.triathlon.org/about/downloads/category/ranking_criteria。

1.3 参赛资格规定及分配办法如下。

2. 出发名单及候补名单管理办法

2.1 除特殊规定的比赛外，该管理办法适用于国际铁联的所有比赛。参赛资格标准已对特殊规定的比赛进行说明，并且规定了：

a）国家会员协会的员额（*）。

b）东道国国家会员协会的员额（*）。

c）国家会员协会的扩展员额（*）。

d）东道国国家会员协会的扩展员额（*）。

e）超出员额部分由外卡申请委员会裁决。

f）出发名单的产生日期。

g）每个国家会员协会所允许的替补人数。

h）国家会员协会要求替补的最终期限。

i）国家会员协会提请退赛而免受处罚的最终期限。

j）最多外卡员额。

k）外卡申请委员会开会日期。

（）处罚结果可能会造成员额减少。*

2.2 国家会员协会需在第一比赛日前 33 天确认候补运动员名单。候补运动员选拔应遵循下列标准：

a）国际铁联世界排名，或遵循参赛标准择优进入候补名单。

b）每个国家会员协会允许选拔一名无国际铁联世界排名积分的运动员进入候补名单。国家会员协会将从东道国开始，按国际奥组委国家编码在字母表中的顺序轮次。

c）各国家会员协会每轮可挑选一位运动员进入候补名单，第一轮完成后，方可进行下一轮。选拔原则同上。

d）经过选拔进入候补名单的运动员，将根据报名时间指定最终的排位。

2.3. Start list will be created 32 days before the first competition day, unless indicated differently in the specific Qualification Criteria;

2.4. Athletes are approved from this sorted Waiting List to the Start List according to the order in it, provided that the inclusión of the specific athlete does not result the exceeding of the National Federation quota or the Host National Federation quota;

2.5. Those athletes exceeding the quota are tagged with the indication of "Exceeds the National Federation quota";

2.6. The maximum number of athletes approved to the Start List are indicated in the specific Qualification Criteria, minus the number of invitations to be allocated. No more athletes are moved to the start list until 28 days before the event, when the invitation panel decission happens;

2.7. Till 30 days before the first day of competition of a given event:

a.) National Federations may request substitutions;

b.) National Federations may request withdrawals without penalty;

c.) National Federations may request invitations.

2.8. 28 days before the first day of competition of a given event invitations are awarded as outlined below in section 7 of this Appendix;

2.9. The start positions not filled by the invitation panel are filled by the next elegible athlete on the sorted Waiting List;

2.10. Following to the procedure above, when one National Federation withdraws an athlete not tagged with "Exceeds the NF quota", the tag on the first athlete from the same National Federation will be automatically removed;

2.11. Vacancies in the Start List are filled by the next eligible athlete in the sorted Waiting List. A vacancy in the Start List may happen as consequence of a withdrawal or because the low number of entries;

2.12. When all the athletes in the Waiting List are tagged with "Exceeds the NF quota" and there is a vacancy in the Start List, the first athlete will be approved. The acceptance of athletes exceeding the National Federaton or Host National Federation quota follows the order of one athlete per National Federation, according to their positions in the sorted Waiting List. Once all affected National Federations have one exceeding athlete in the Start List, a second one is moved to the start list, etc.;

2.13. No athletes will be admited in the wait list from 48 hours before the Athletes' Briefing;

2.14. Vacancies from 24 hours before the Athletes' Briefing will be filled with athletes present at the briefing.

3. Actions taken:

3.1. Actions taken applicable to the athletes:

a.) Athletes withdrawing from a competition after 13.00 GMT on Monday before the event, are removed from all the start and waiting lists of the events in the next 30 days counted from the day of the withdrawal;

2.3 出发名单需在第一比赛日前 32 天制定，参赛资格标准细则中有不同规定者除外。

2.4 若运动员在其东道国或其他国际会员协会员名额内，则该运动员可按照候补名单顺序进入出发名单。

2.5 超出员额的运动员将被标为“超额人员”。

2.6 可进入出发名单的最大人数是指参赛资格标准细则规定的人数减去外卡人数。比赛前28天，出发名单不再进行补录，外卡申请委员会裁决生效后方可继续补录。

2.7 需至少在第一比赛日前 30 天进行：

a）国家会员协会要求替换运动员。

b）国家协会要求免罚退赛。

c）国家协会申请外卡。

2.8 第一比赛日前 28 天，将对受邀人员发出外卡，详见本章第 7 部分。

2.9 加上外卡申请委员会仍有空位的出发名单将补入候补名单中符合条件的运动员。

2.10 根据上述分配办法，如果一个国家会员协会将一位非“超额人员”除名，则该国家会员协会中的第一位“超额人员”身份自动消失。

2.11 出发名单中的空位应由符合条件的候补人员补入。出发名单出现空位可能是由于有人退出或报名人数较少。

2.12 如果候补名单中所有运动员都被标为“超额人员”且出发名单中存在空位，排在第一位的运动员将进入出发名单。接纳超额人员，每个国家会员协会每轮只可选派一名超额人员进入出发名单，选派顺序按照候补名单顺序进行，第一轮完成后，方可进行下一轮，以此类推。

2.13 运动员赛前技术会前 48 小时，不再接受运动员进入候补名单。

2.14 运动员赛前技术会前 24 小时的空位将由参加技术会的运动员补入。

3. 处罚措施

3.1 对运动员的处罚措施：

a）如果运动员于赛前周一 13:00（国际标准时间）后退出比赛，则该运动员不得出现在自退赛之日起 30 天内所有比赛的出发名单及候补名单中。

b.) The athlete is not approved to compete in any competition on the same event-weekend of the competition he/she withdraws and on the following one;

c.) The penalty of the second weekend may be avoided by the use of a "joker" as described below.

3.2. Actions taken applicable to the National Federations:

a.) National Federations withdrawing athletes from the start list during the period between 30 days before the first day of competition and the athletes' briefing, will receive a penalty consisting in a reduction of the National Federation quota in future ITU events as outlined in the following tables:

WTS, World Cups and Continental Championships	
Withdrawals(per gender)	Quota reduction(per gender)
1	0
2-3	1
4-5	2
6 or more	3

Continental Cups and Junior Continental Cups	
Withdrawals(per gender)	Quota reduction(per gender)
1	0
2-3	1
4-6	2
7-10	3
11-15	4
16 or more	5

Paratriathlon events	
Withdrawals (both genders, all classes)	Quota reduction (applicable to all classes and both genders)
1-3	0
4-6	1
7 or more	2

b.) Athletes missing the briefing, without previous notice, are added to those withdrawn from the competition by the National Federation.

c.) Also athletes missing the briefing and missing the competition will be added to determine the total numbers of athletes witdrawing from a competition.

d.) Monday after the event, the number of withdrawals per National Federaiton per gender are calculated and the reduction of the quotas are announced to the National Federations affected. The events affected by this reduction will be as the following:

(i) World Triathlon Series: The next two WTS events which Start List are to be produced;

b）退赛运动员不允许参加任何一场与该比赛同一周末及下一周末举行的比赛。

c）如果使用下文提到的“王牌”，则可免去第二周末的禁赛处罚。

3.2 对国家会员协会的处罚措施：

a）如果国家协会在第一比赛日前30天至运动员赛前技术会期间有运动员退赛，国家会员协会在国际铁联未来的比赛中均需减少员额，处罚如下：

世界铁人三项系列赛、世界杯及洲际锦标赛	
退赛人数（男女各）	减员（男女各）
1 人	0 人
2~3 人	1 人
4~5 人	2 人
6 人或以上	3 人

铁人三项洲际杯赛及洲际杯青年组比赛	
退赛人数（男女各）	减员（男女各）
1 人	0 人
2~3 人	1 人
4~6 人	2 人
7~10 人	3 人
11~15 人	4 人
16 人或以上	5 人

铁人三项伤残组比赛	
退赛人数 （不分男女，所有组别）	减员 （适用于所有组别，不分男女）
1~3 人	0 人
4~6 人	1 人
7 人或以上	2 人

b）无故缺席赛前技术会的运动员将计入国家会员协会退赛人数。

c）缺席赛前技术会和未参赛的运动员计入退赛总数。

d）比赛结束后的周一将分别计算每个国家会员协会的男女退赛人数，届时将会向相关国家协会通报减员人数。需减少员额的比赛如下：

（1）世界铁人三项系列赛：尚未确定出发名单的下两届世界铁人三项系列赛。

(ii) World Cups / Continental Championships: The next two events which Start List are to be produced;
(iii) Paratriathlon events: The next two paratriathlon events which Start List are to be produced;
(iv) Continental Cups: The events of which Start List are to be produced in the next 30 days;
(v) Junior Continental Cups: The next two Junior Continental Cups which Start List are to be produced.

b.) A number of unexpected withdrawals without being penalized because last minutes issues are considered by the "jokers";

c.) The number of "jokers" per National Federation depends on the number of participations of each National Federation over the previous year as follows:

Number of "Jokers" in 2018	National Federation
10	JPN, USA
8	AUS, CAN, ESP, FRA, GBR, HUN, ITA, MEX
6	ARG, AUT, BEL, BRA, GER, KOR, NED, NZL, POR, RSA, RUS, SUI
4	CHI, CHN, COL, CRC, CRO, CZE, DEN, ECU, EST, HKG, IRL, ISR, MAS, NOR, PHI, POL, ROU, SLO, TPE, TUR, UKR
2	AZE, BLR, BUL, EGY, FIN, GUA, KAZ, LAT, LTU, LUX, MAC, SGP, SRB, SVK, SWE, TUN, URU, VEN
1	All other National Federation

4. "Jokers":

4.1. The use of one joker means:
a.) To reduce by one the reduction of the quotas;
b.) To give to the penalised athletes the posibility to compete in the second weekend after the withdrawal.

4.2. The quota reductions are cumulative, if generated in different events on the same weekend or in events which their penalty times overlap;

4.3. National Federations have to announce the use of the joker within 48 hours of the annoucement of the reduction of the quota;

4.4. All National Federation will have a minimum quota of one (1), even if the accumulated penalties would eliminate all athletes of the National Federation from an event.

5. Numbering:

5.1. Events will be numbered on the previous Monday by 13:00 GMT according to the criteria indicated in ITU Competition Rules, section 2.10. Athletes admited in the start list after the numbers are assigned, will receive the next highest number.

（2）世界杯 / 洲际锦标赛：尚未确定出发名单的下两届比赛。

（3）铁人三项伤残组比赛：尚未确定出发名单的下两届伤残组比赛。

（4）洲际杯赛：未来 30 天需确定出发名单的比赛。

（5）洲际杯青年组比赛：尚未确定出发名单的下两届青年组比赛。

e）由于紧急事件可使用“王牌”，一些意外退赛可免受处罚。

f）各国家会员协会的“王牌”数量取决于该国家会员协会往年的参赛人数，如下：

2018 年“王牌”数量	国家会员协会
10	日本、美国
8	澳大利亚、加拿大、西班牙、法国、英国、匈牙利、意大利、墨西哥
6	阿根廷、奥地利、比利时、巴西、德国、韩国、荷兰、新西兰、葡萄牙、南非、俄罗斯、瑞士
4	智利、中国、哥伦比亚、哥斯达黎加、克罗地亚、捷克、丹麦、厄瓜多尔、爱沙尼亚、中国香港、爱尔兰、以色列、马拉西亚、挪威、菲律宾、波兰、罗马尼亚、斯洛文尼亚、中华台北、土耳其、乌克兰
2	阿塞拜疆、白俄罗斯、保加利亚、埃及、芬兰、危地马拉、哈萨克斯坦、拉脱维亚、立陶宛、卢森堡、中国澳门、新加坡、塞尔维亚、斯洛伐克、瑞典、突尼斯、乌拉圭、委内瑞拉
1	其他国家

4. “王牌”

4.1 使用一张王牌可以：

a）抵消一个减少的参赛名额。

b）允许受处罚的运动员参加退赛后第二周末的比赛。

4.2 如果同一周末举行不同比赛或处罚时间重合，则减员人数累计计算。

4.3 国家会员协会需在减员人数公布 48 小时内宣布使用王牌。

4.4 即使累计处罚导致国家协会的运动员都不能参加一场比赛，但每个国家协会仍有一个参赛名额。

5. 比赛号码分配

5.1 比赛号码分配需在比赛前的周一 13:00（国际标准时间）以前根据积分排名进行完毕，具体规定参见 2.10。运动员进入出发名单并分配比赛号码后，下一个积分最高的运动员将进入出发名单。

6. Exceptional conditions:

6.1. Non-Asian athletes will not be admitted in the elite competitions of the Asian Triathlon Continental Championships. For other Asian Championships, non-Asian athletes will be admited if the competition is not full, with the same quota limitations than the Asian National Federations. These admissions will be approved 10 days before the event;

6.2. Non-European athletes will not be admitted in the elite competitions of the European Sprint Triathlon Continental Championships. For other European Championships, non-European athletes will be admited if the competition is not full, with the same quota limitations than the European National Federations. These admissions will be approved 10 days before the event;

6.3. African-, American- and Oceania Continental Championships will be open to athletes from any continent if the race is not full, with the same quota limitations than the National Federations of the host continent. These admissions will be approved 10 days before the event.

7. Invitations:

7.1. 28 days (unless outlined differently in the specific Qulaificaiton Criteria) before the first competition day Invitation Panel will award 5 (unless outlined differently in the specific Qualification Criteria) invitations based on the requests, but not limited to it;

7.2. Invitation request must be emailed by the respective National Federation to entries@triathlon.org;

7.3. The Invitation Panel can not extend the National Federation quotas indicated in specific Qualification Criteria;

7.4. The Invitation Panel is composed of following members for ITU events:

a.) The ITU Secretary General or designate;

b.) A representative of the ITU Sport Department;

c.) A representative of ITU Development.

7.5. The Invitation Panel is composed of following members for Continental events:

a.) The Secretary General of the Continental Confederation or designate;

b.) A representative of the ITU Sport Department;

c.) A representative of ITU Development.

8. Substitutions:

8.1. National Federations are allowed to substitute athlete(s) in any event;

8.2. The names of both athletes involved in the substitution must be emailed to entries@triathlon.org;

8.3. Substitutions are only allowed up to 30 days prior to the first competition day;

8.4. The replacer athlete will take the position of the replaced athlete. The replaced athlete will be removed from the competition;

8.5. The number of subsitutions per gender per event are as the following:

a.) One (1) substitution – World Triathlon Series, U23 World Championships;

6. 例外情况

6.1 非亚洲运动员不得参加亚洲铁人三项锦标赛优秀组比赛。若其他亚洲锦标赛未满员，允许非亚洲选手参加，其参赛名额与亚洲国家会员协会相同。参赛申请将于比赛前 10 天获准。

6.2 非欧洲运动员不得参加欧洲铁人三项短距离锦标赛优秀组比赛。若其他欧洲锦标赛未满员，允许非欧洲选手参加，其参赛名额与欧洲国家会员协会相同。参赛申请将于比赛前 10 天获准。

6.3 若铁人三项非洲、美洲、大洋洲锦标赛参赛者未满员，将向所有大洲的运动员开放。其参赛名额与东道主大洲的国家会员协会相同。参赛申请将于比赛前 10 天获准。

7. 外 卡

7.1 在第一比赛日前 28 天（除非参赛资格标准细则有不同规定），外卡申请委员会将基于但不限于申请，将发出 5 组外卡（除非参赛资格标准细则有不同规定）。

7.2 各国家会员协会须将外卡申请以电子邮件形式发送至邮箱 entries@triathlon.org。

7.3 外卡申请委员会不得增加细则中规定的各国际会员协会员额。

7.4 国际铁联比赛外卡申请委员会由下列人员组成：

a） 国际铁联秘书长或指定人选。

b） 国际铁联体育部代表。

c） 国际铁联发展部代表。

7.5 洲际比赛的外卡申请委员会由下列人员组成：

a） 洲际比赛秘书长或指定人选。

b） 国际铁联体育部代表。

c） 国际铁联发展部代表。

8. 替 补

8.1 允许各国家会员协会在任一比赛中进行替补。

8.2 替补及被替补运动员的姓名必须以邮件形式发送至邮箱 entries@triathlon.org。

8.3 第一比赛日前 30 天起可受理替补。

8.4 替补运动员替补之前运动员的位置。被替补的运动员退出比赛。

8.5 不同比赛男女分别替补机会：

a） 世界铁人三项系列赛，U23 世界锦标赛：1 次替补。

b.) Two (2) substitutions – Triathlon World Cup, Multisport Events, Continental Championships;

c.) Three (3) substitutions – Triathlon Continental Cups, Junior Continental Cups, Development Event.

d.) One (1) subsitution per medal event on all Paratriathlon Events.

9. Late withdrawal:

9.1. Athletes present at the Athletes' Briefing, but are forced to withdraw from the competition due to a last minute illness or injury, as proven by a certificate from a medical doctor with the approval of the Medical Delegate, will not be penalized;

9.2. They will be marked as DNS and the next eligible athlete will be added to the start list;

9.3. In the event of lack of Medical Delegate, the Technical Delegate may consult with the Event Medical Director.

b）铁人三项世界杯赛、分项比赛、洲际锦标赛：2 次替补。

c） 铁人三项洲际杯赛、洲际杯青年组比赛、发展赛：3 次替补。

d）所有的铁人三项残疾人比赛中，每个奖牌项目均可有一次替补机会。

9. 未按时退赛

9.1 已参加运动员赛前技术会，但由于突发疾病或受伤而被迫退赛者，需资格医师出具证明，经医务代表批准，方可免受处罚。

9.2 运动员将被记为未出发者（DNS），下一位符合要求的运动员将进入出发名单。

9.3 如果比赛没有医务代表，技术代表可向比赛医务主任咨询。

28. APPENDIX F ITU GUIDELINES REGARDING AUTHORISED IDENTIFICATION

1. Overview:

1.1. To compete in ITU Events, athletes must comply with the ITU Guides Regarding Authorised Identification and the reference to the Uniform at 2.8 of the Competition Rules;

1.2. The images on this document are reproducing a typical triathlon uniform. For winter triathlon and, in some cases, in triathlon, duathlon and aquathlon, the long sleeves and lower leg covering are allowed. This appendix applies in the same way for all the cases:

2. Purpose:

2.1. Provide a clean and professional image of our sport to local and global spectators and media;

2.2. Provide sponsors with reasonable space for viable exposure;

2.3. Provide a framework for enabling ITU member National Federations and athletes to have a mutually beneficial relationship with respect to rights and responsibilities, as per Section 12.

3. General Requirements:

3.1. Uniforms will be completely clean of any logos or images other than those described below;

3.2. Logos will be measured on a flat surface when the athlete is not wearing the uniform. The "ITU Logo Measurement Template" will be used to measure the logo sizes;

3.3. There is no restriction on the type of logo used in the sponsor spaces other than those representing tobacco, spirits and products containing any substance on the WADA Prohibited List;

3.4. There must be a minimum clearance space of 1.5cm around all marks including:

a) The ITU logo;

b) The family name;

c) The country code;

d) All sponsor logos.

4. Uniform Colour and Design:

4.1. Uniforms must be in the colours chosen by the National Federation as the following:

a) Elite: ITU World Triathlon Series Grand Final, ITU World Triathlon Series, Continental Championships and ITU Multisport World Championships events;

b) Junior, U23: ITU World Championhips and Continental Championships;

c) Paratriathlon: ITU World Championhips, ITU World Paratriathlon Series and Continental Championships;

d) Youth: Continental Championships.

28. 附件 F　国际铁联（比赛服）授权认证指南

1. 概 述

1.1 所有参加国际铁联比赛的运动员必须遵守《国际铁联（比赛服）授权认证指南》和比赛规则 2.8 服装要求。

1.2 本细则中的图片说明的是常规的铁人三项比赛服。冬季铁人三项以及某些铁人三项、骑跑两项、游跑两项比赛，允许穿长袖和覆盖小腿的长裤。此细则均同样适用。

2. 目的

2.1 使铁人三项运动以整洁、专业的形象展现给当地和国际观众和媒体。

2.2 为赞助商提供适当的展示空间。

2.3 为国际铁联会员协会和运动员提供一个框架，使得双方就各自的权利和义务达成一个互利的关系（见本章 12 节）。

3. 总体要求

3.1 运动员比赛服上除本细则所述之外，不得有任何其他标志或图案。

3.2 在非着装状态下，比赛服上的所有标志应在同一个平面上，使用“国际铁联标志测量模板”进行测量。

3.3 比赛服赞助商标志不可以是烟草、烈酒或世界反兴奋剂组织（WADA）禁用清单上所列物质的产品。

3.4 在以下标志的周围必须至少留有 1.5 厘米的空间：

a）国际铁联标志。

b）运动员姓氏。

c）国家代码。

d）所有的赞助商标志。

4. 比赛服颜色和样式

4.1 比赛服必须使用国家会员协会选定的颜色：

a）优秀组：世界铁人三项系列赛总决赛，世界铁人三项系列赛，洲际锦标赛，多项运动锦标赛。

b）青年组，23 岁以下组：世界锦标赛，洲际锦标赛。

c）伤残组：世界锦标赛，世界伤残系列和洲际锦标赛。

d）少年组：洲际锦标赛。

4.2. For all other ITU Events the uniform colors have no restrictions;

4.3. The colour and design of the uniform and podium apparel must be distinct to that country and must be approved by ITU in advance;

4.4. Country uniforms must have a distinct look, however the design requirements should not impact on technical requirements athletes might have due to body shape or size;

4.5. The approval process for the uniform colour and design is outlined in Appendix F7. The goal of the approval process is to ensure countries do not have the same uniform colour and design;

4.6. For Elite athletes, ITU reserves the right to establish a specific rule till 30th of January of the given calendar year, regarding the color of the uniform of the actual leader of ITU World Triathlon Series has to wear:

Diagram 1: Location of sponsor spaces	
Uniform Front	Uniform Back

5. Family Name and Country Code:

5.1. The family name (not applicable for Age Group athletes) and the IOC country code must be placed on the upper front of the uniform and also on the buttocks. The initial of the first name may be added before the family name: athletes with the same family name are encouraged to add the initial of the first name. The representation of both the family name and country code must meet the following criteria:

a) Font Type:

i. The font type must be "Arial";

ii. Letters for the family name and country code must be in upper case, unless the name is more than 9 letters, in which case lower case letters should be used following the first capital letter. Symbols such as ' - ' and space are considered as characters (See Diagram 2: Family Name Layout).

4.2 其他国际铁联赛事对比赛服颜色没有限制。

4.3 各国家比赛服的颜色和样式、包括领奖服饰，必须是国家特有的，并且须经国际铁联批准。

4.4 不同国家运动员的比赛服应具有不同的外观。但对于“样式”的定义不应影响运动员由于体型特征导致的需求。

4.5 关于比赛服颜色和样式的“审批程序”已在附件 F7 中说明。此审批程序的目的是确保各个国家所使用的比赛服颜色和样式各不相同。

4.6 对于优秀组运动员，国际铁联保留在比赛当年 1 月 30 日前就世界铁人三项系列赛领先运动员的比赛服颜色制定特殊规则的权利。

图 1：赞助商标志位置	
正面	背面

5. 姓氏和国家代码

5.1 运动员的姓氏（不适用于分龄组运动员）和国际奥委会国家代码须印制在体前上方和臀部。运动员名字的首字母可添加在姓氏之前，鼓励姓氏相同的运动员添加名字的首字母。运动员的姓氏和国家（地区）代码或名称必须符合以下要求：

a）字 体

（1） 必须使用“Arial”字体。

（2） 姓氏和国家代码应使用大写字母，除字母数超过 9 个的情况下可以出于空间因素考虑使用小写字母，但首字母仍应大写。类似于“–”的符号和空格视作字符（见图 2：姓氏布局）。

b) Colour:
   i. If the uniform is a dark colour, the letters must be white. If the uniform is a light colour, the letters must be black.

c) Position:
   ii. Front: The position on the front is below the ITU logo and Sponsor Spaces B and F. The athlete's family name is above the country code and Sponsor Space A;
   iii. Back: The position on the back is below the waistline so that it is clearly visible when the athlete is on the bike. The athlete's family name is above the country code;
   iv. Height: The family name and the country code must be 5cm in height, regardless of the number of letters in the name;
   v. Width: The length for the family name is a minimum of 12cm and a maximum of 15cm. A family name with few letters must still be a minimum length of 12 cm. (See Diagram 2: Family Name Layout) The width for the country code must be 6cm to 10 cm;

Diagram 2. Family Name Layout
MAY
For family names such as "MAY" above, the height is 5cm and the width is 12cm. For longer names such as "Polikarpenko" below, the height is still a minimum 5cm but the name should take up the full 15cm.
Polikarpenko

6. ITU Logo:

6.1. The official ITU logo will appear on the upper right shoulder;
6.2. It will conform to the official ITU rings with the letters ITU on the bottom right;
6.3. The horizontal dimension will be 4cm;
6.4. The white/orange version should be applied to dark coloured uniforms, the blue/orange version should be applied to light coloured uniforms (see this appendix 6.5, 6.6, Diagram 3);

b）颜 色

（1） 深色比赛服必须使用白色，浅色比赛服必须使用黑色。

c）位 置

（1） 体前：在国际铁联标志和赞助商 B 和 F 的位置下方、国家代码和赞助商 A 的位置上方。

（2） 背部：背部的位置在腰线下方，以便运动员在自行车比赛过程中清晰可见。运动员的姓氏在国家代码上方。

（3） 高度：姓氏和国家代码在垂直方向上的高度必须为 5 厘米，不论包含多少字母。

（4） 宽度：姓氏的宽度至少 12 厘米，至多 15 厘米。即使是字母很少的姓也必须至少达到 12 厘米（见图 2）。国家代码的宽度必须为 6~10 厘米。

图 2：运动员姓名的布局

MAY

——与“MAY”类似的较短的姓氏，高 5 厘米，宽 12 厘米。
——对于比较长的姓，如“Polikarpenko”，高度仍然是 5 厘米，但宽度应占满整个 15 厘米。

Polikarpenko

6. 国际铁联标志

6.1 国际铁联标志必须印制在右肩部。

6.2 应使用官方的国际铁联标志。

6.3 宽度为 4 厘米。

6.4 深色比赛服应使用“白橙”版本，浅色比赛服应使用“蓝橙”版本（见 6.5、6.6 及图 3）。

6.5. Click here for the print version of the ITU logo:

Diagram 3. ITU Logo Layout

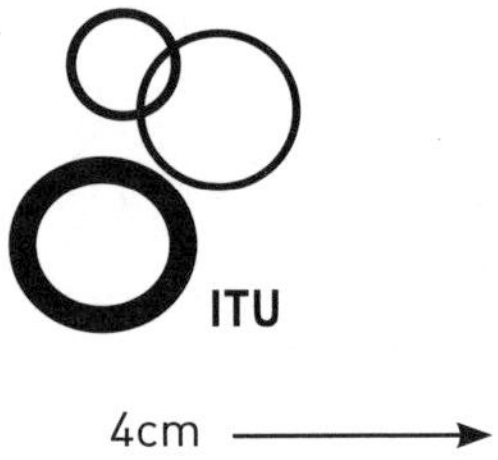

6.6. Diagram 3 above shows the correct layout for the ITU Logo:
- a) ITU Orange:
  - i. Pantone 144C (Coated papers);
  - ii. CMYK conversion (4 colour process) - C:0%, M:49%, Y:100%, K:0%.
- b) ITU Blue:
  - i. Pantone 2955C (Coated papers);
  - ii. CMYK conversion (4 colour process) - C:100%, M:45%, Y:0%, K:37%.

6.7. The Elite individual World Champions are allowed to add below the ITU Logo the design element of the WTS recognizing this honor. Graphic details will be published separately.

7. Sponsor Spaces:

7.1. Sponsor Space A:
- a) This space is directly below the country code (See Diagram 1. Sponsor Logos: size and space);
- b) The maximum height is 20cm;
- c) The maximum length is 15cm;
- d) Up to 3 sponsor logos may be positioned in this space;
- e) The athlete may have 1, 2 or 3 logos in this space. Each of the logos must represent a different sponsor.

7.2. Sponsor Space B: upper left front:
- a) This space is for the manufacturer of the uniform or for another sponsor;
- b) The maximum height is 4cm;
- c) The maximum length is 5cm;
- d) The space must be on the left hand shoulder of the uniform – not the middle.

7.3. Sponsor Spaces C: side panels:
- a) Sponsor logos may appear on the side panel;
- b) The maximum width is 5cm;
- c) The maximum length is 15cm;

6.5 国际铁联标志的印刷版本可从国际铁联官方网站上下载：

图 3 国际铁联标志布局

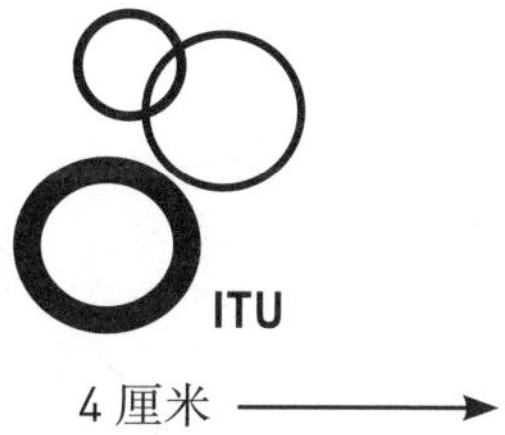

6.6 图 3 说明了国际铁联标志的正确布局：

a）国际铁联标志的橙色：

（1）潘通色卡 144C（铜版纸）。

（2）颜色模式：青：0%，品红：49%，黄：100%，黑：0%。

b）国际铁联标志的蓝色：

（1）潘通色卡 2955C（铜版纸）。

（2）颜色模式：青：100%，品红：45%，黄：0%，黑 37%。

6.7 允许优秀人个项目世界冠军运动员在比赛服的国际铁联标志下面加上 WTS 的设计元素以示荣誉。详细图解另外发布。

7. 赞助商位置

7.1 赞助商位置 A

a） 位于国家（地区）代码正下方（见图 1）。

b） 最高 20 厘米。

c） 最宽 15 厘米。

d） 这个位置最多可以印制 3 个赞助商标志。

e） 可以选择放置 1、2 或 3 个赞助商标志，但各个标志必须代表不同的赞助商。

7.2 赞助商位置 B：体前左上方

a） 此位置是比赛服的制造商或者其他赞助商。

b） 最高 4 厘米。

c） 最宽 5 厘米。

d） 赞助商位置 B 应位于比赛服左肩部，不可以是中间。

7.3 赞助商位置 C：两侧

a） 赞助商标志可以出现在侧面。

b） 最宽不超过 5 厘米。

c） 最高不超过 15 厘米。

d) Only one sponsor logo is allowed on each side and it must be the same sponsor logo;

e) This space must be visible from the side of the body. If, due to the athlete body, this space is partly visible from the front, it has to be visible also from the back;

7.4. Sponsor Space D: lower front:

a) The maximum height is 4cm;

b) The maximum length is 5cm;

c) This space can be on the lower left or right side of the uniform but not both.

7.5. Sponsor Space E: upper back:

a) One logo of any sponsor may appear above the family name on the back;

b) The maximum height is 10cm;

c) The maximum length is 15cm;

7.6. Sponsor Space F: upper front:

a) One logo of any sponsor may appear above the family name on the front;

b) The maximum height is 5cm;

c) The maximum length is 15cm.

8. Wetsuits:

8.1. Only the wetsuit manufacturer's logo may appear on the wetsuits;

8.2. The maximum size is $80cm^2$ on the front and back. This space is allowed both on the inside and outside of the wetsuit;

8.3. If the manufacturer wishes to have two or more logos on the front or back, the combined total must not exceed $80cm^2$;

8.4. Logos on the side panel must be included within either the $80cm^2$ for the back or the $80cm^2$ for the front.

9. Temporary Tattoos:

9.1. Athletes are not allowed to place any temporary tattoo, other than the race numbers and logos provided by ITU, on their body during ITU Events.

10. Podium apparel:

10.1. All the sponsor spaces and design colors indicted in this document applies as well to the podium apparel.

11. Specific rules for PTVI Sport Class:

11.1. The uniform of the Guide must comply with the rules above and use the same sponsors' logos and spaces as on the Paratriathlete's uniform;

11.2. The uniform of the Guide must display the word "GUIDE" in the Family Name space;

11.3. The font type must be "Arial", the height 5cm and the width 12 cm.

d） 每侧各允许有一个赞助商标志，并且必须相同。

e） 此位置必须从体侧可见。如果因运动员体型原因，从体前可见一部分，则必须从体后也可见。

7.4 赞助商位置 D：体前下方

a） 最高 4 厘米。

b） 最宽 5 厘米。

c） 赞助商位置 D 可以位于左下侧或者右下侧，但不可以两侧都有。

7.5 赞助商位置 E：体后上方

a） 任何一个赞助商标志都可以出现在背部上方。

b） 最高 10 厘米。

c） 最宽 15 厘米。

7.6 赞助商位置 F：体前上方

a） 任何一个赞助商标志都可以出现在体前运动员姓名上方。

b） 最高 5 厘米。

c） 最宽 15 厘米。

8. 防寒泳衣

8.1 防寒泳衣上只能出现防寒泳衣制造商的标志。

8.2 泳衣制造商的标志最大面积为前后各 80 平方厘米，内外均可。

8.3 如果制造商想在防寒泳衣的正面或背面放置两个或两个以上的标志，则总面积不能超过 80 平方厘米。

8.4 两侧的标志面积计入正面或背面的 80 平方厘米之内。

9. 临时纹身贴

9.1 运动员在参加国际铁联比赛期间不可以使用任何其他除比赛号码和标志之外的临时纹身贴。

10. 领奖服

10.1 本文说明的赞助商位置、样式和颜色均适用于领奖服。

11. PTVI 级别特殊规则

11.1 引导员的比赛服须与以上规则一致，赞助商标志和位置适用于伤残运动员的比赛服。

11.2 引导员的比赛服须在其姓氏处展示“GUIDE”（“引导员”）字样。

11.3 必须用 Arial 字体，高度 5 厘米宽度 12 厘米。

12. Rights and responsibilities:

	World Triathlon Series (Elite) World Triathlon Grand Final (Elite) Triathlon World Championships Triathlon Continental Championships Multisport World Championships Multisport Continental Championships World Paratriathlon Series	All ITU and Continental events not specified in this table
Uniform Colour and Design	As per the catalogue	To be agreed in good faith between Athlete and National Federation
Family Name	Optional for Age Group athletes Mandatory for all other categories	
Country Code	Mandatory as per ITU Competition Rules	
ITU Logo	Mandatory as per ITU Competition Rules	
Sponsor Spaces A to F	To be agreed in good faith between Athlete and National Federation	

ITU COMPETITION UNIFORM APPROVAL PROCESS

1. **Overview:**
   1.1. This process is part of the ITU Guides Regarding Authorised Identification and is a specific addition to the ITU Competition Rules.

2. **Purpose:**
   2.1. The process was created to regulate the ITU's approval of the design of each National Federaton's competition uniform to be used by their athletes in all ITU competitions according with the ITU Guides Regarding Authorised Identification.

3. **General Requirements:**
   3.1. Every National Federation uniform has to be different from any other National Federation uniform, according to the ITU Guides Regarding Authorised Identification. The difference will be significant to avoid confusion between two different National Federations;
   3.2. Artistic or creative elements are acceptable provided that the ITU Competition Rules are followed. Specifically, if the design contains recognisable commercial logos or trade marks which exceed the surface limits, it will not be approved;
   3.3. The same design applies to all types of uniforms: men, women, triathlon style, duathlon style, summer, winter, etc.
   3.4. Every National Federation can request the approval of one different uniform design for every different multisport. Two uniform options can be requested for the Age Group athletes, indicating which is the 1st option and which is the 2nd option. However, all athletes from the same National Federation, competing in the same event, will wear the National Federation's same distinctive design.

12. 权利与义务

	世界铁人三项系列赛和总决赛（优秀组）/ 世界锦标赛 / 洲际锦标赛 / 多项运动世界锦标赛 / 多项运动洲际锦标赛 / 世界伤残人系列赛	未列入本表的所有国际铁联和洲际比赛项目
比赛服颜色和样式	依据目录	由运动员与会员协会友好协商
运动员姓氏	分龄组非强制，所有其他组别强制执行	
国家代码	根据《国际铁联竞赛规则》强制执行	
国际铁联标志	根据《国际铁联竞赛规则》强制执行	
赞助商 A 至 F	由运动员与会员协会友好协商	

国际铁联比赛服审批程序

1. 概 述

1.1 比赛服审批程序是《国际铁联（比赛服）授权认证指南》的一部分，也是国际铁联竞赛规则新增部分。

2. 目 的

2.1 制定此审批程序是为了根据《国际铁联（比赛服）授权认证指南》规范国际铁联对各会员协会运动员参加所有国际铁联比赛所用比赛服进行审批的过程。

3. 总体要求

3.1 根据《国际铁联（比赛服）授权认证指南》，各会员协会的比赛服应互不相同，以便于区分。

3.2 在遵循《国际铁联竞赛规则》的前提下，可以使用艺术性或创造性的元素。但需要特别说明的是，如果使用超出本文限制的可视的商标或标志，将不予批准。

3.3 所有比赛服使用同样的设计：男子、女子、铁人三项、骑跑两项、夏季、冬季等。

3.4 每个会员协会可为每个分项分别申请一例比赛服设计样式，分龄组运动员可申请两个设计样式，并说明第一选择和第二选择。但同一个会员协会参加同一场比赛的运动员，必须穿着同样的比赛服。

4. Timeline for Approval:

4.1. National Federations will submit a proposed design of their Competition Uniform for the following year, according to these specifications:

a) A pattern provided by ITU will be used;

b) Sponsor spaces and dimensions, as outlined the ITU Guides Regarding Authorised Identification. The athlete's family name and National Federation code positions (front and back) and dimensions of both;

c) The position and dimensions of the ITU logo. The colour(s) used in the design, including the pantone. The proposed design may be submitted in .jpg .gif .bmp or .tif format;

d) Once approved, the Uniform approval is extended till the the National Federation must seek approval for a new design.

5. Approval:

5.1. ITU will inform each National Federation in writing about the approval or disapproval of their National Federations uniform if the design is:

a) Compliant with all the ITU Guides Regarding Authorised Identification;

b) Distinct from other National Federation designs.

5.2. If the request is not approved ITU will:

a) Ask the National Federation for a new design if the submitted one did not comply with the ITU rules, or;

b) Ask the National Federations that submitted similar requests to agree to modifying their proposed designs in order to have different uniforms;

c) If the National Federations do not get an agreement ITU will decide on which National Federation can use the proposed design according with these priorities:

i. The National Federation that used the proposed uniform in the past will be given preference;

ii. If both National Federations are proposing new uniforms, a draw will be conducted to choose which National Federation will use the submitted design and which National Federation(s) will have to submit a new one.

5.3. ITU will produce an electronic catalogue of approved National Federation's competition uniforms. This catalogue will be updated monthly;

5.4. Requests for uniform approval received will be considered on a monthly basis. National Federations requesting approval will choose designs that are different from those already approved.

6. Approval Panel:

6.1. All decisions on uniform approval will be made by a panel composed of:

a) A member of the ITU Technical Committee;

b) A representative of the ITU Sport Department;

c) A representative of the ITU Marketing Department;

6.2. The decisions of the Approval Panel can be appealed to the ITU Arbitration Tribunal. This appeal does not suspend the decision of the Approval Panel, but rather the decision will stay in place during the time the ITU Arbitration Tribunal takes to make a decision on the appeal.

4. 审批时间

4.1 各会员协会根据以下要求将第二年拟使用的比赛服设计方案提交国际铁联审查：

a）按照本细则规定的模版设计（见国际铁联比赛规则图 1）。

b）赞助商标志的位置和尺寸、运动员姓氏和国家（地区）代码的位置和尺寸应符合《国际铁联（比赛服）授权认证指南》。

c）国际铁联标志的位置和尺寸、颜色应符合本细则；设计方案可以 .jpg、.gif、.bmp 或者 .tif 的格式提交。

d）比赛服一旦得到批准，已批准的比赛服设计方案将持续有效，直至会员协会提出新的设计并报批。

5. 审批过程

5.1 国际铁联将书面通知各会员协会其比赛服设计方案是否得到批准：

a）设计方案是否符合《国际铁联（比赛服）授权认证指南》。

b）设计方案是否与其他会员协会的设计方案有明显区别。

5.2 如果比赛服设计方案没有得到批准，国际铁联将：

a）要求会员协会提供新的设计方案。

b）要求提供相似设计方案的会员协会互相协商并修改设计方案。

c）如果有关会员协会未能通过协商达成一致意见，则国际铁联将根据以下原则决定哪个会员协会可优先使用所提交的方案：

（1） 以往曾使用过所提交设计方案的会员协会拥有优先使用该方案的权利。

（2） 如果有关会员协会提交的均为新设计方案，则通过抽签的方式决定哪个会员协会可使用所提交的方案，其他会员协会必须提交新方案。

5.3 国际铁联将以电子版形式公布已经得到批准的比赛服清单。该清单将每月更新。

5.4 比赛服的设计方案申请每月审批一次，且会员协会需提交与已公布的经批准的设计方案不同的方案。

6. 审批小组

6.1 比赛服设计方案审批小组由以下人员组成：

a）1 名国际铁联技术委员会成员。

b）1 名国际铁联体育部代表。

c）1 名国际铁联营销部代表。

6.2 对比赛服审批小组的决定有异议，可上诉至国际铁联仲裁法庭。但该上诉以及国际铁联仲裁法庭对该上诉的仲裁均不会中止审批小组的决定。

29. APPENDIX G PARATRIATHLON CLASSIFICATION RULES

The Paratriathlon Classification Rules can be found in the ITU website under the following link: https://www.triathlon.org/about/downloads/category/competition_rules

30. APPENDIX H PRIZE MONEY BREAKDOWN

1. **Introduction:**
   1.1. The Prize Money Percentages were created to provide a fair and equitable formula to distribute prize money to athletes;
   1.2. If an ITU Event Organiser wants to modify these percentages, they must request a rule exception. If the modification is approved, it must be posted on the ITU event's webpage and on www.triathlon.org;
   1.3. The amount and depth of prize money must be equal for women and men.
2. **Percentages:**
   2.1. The table below shows the five basic prize money percentages and the applicable based on the total amount on an ITU Event;
   2.2. For an easy tool to calculate the prize money percentage based on the event prize money, please visit www.triathlon.org:

	Top 20 (150 001 USD and more overall prize money)	**Top 15** (50 001 – 150 000 USD overall prize money)	**Top 10** (10 001 – 50 000 USD overall prize money)	**Top 5** (3 001 – 10 000 USD overall prize money)	**Top 3** (3 000 USD and less overall prize money)
1.	23.00%	25.00%	25.00%	30.00%	50.00%
2.	18.00%	20.00%	20.00%	25.00%	30.00%
3.	14.00%	15.00%	15.00%	20.00%	20.00%
4.	10.00%	10.00%	10.00%	15.00%	
5.	8.00%	7.00%	8.00%	10.00%	
6.	6.00%	6.00%	7.00%		
7.	4.00%	5.00%	6.00%		
8.	3.00%	3.00%	4.00%		
9.	2.30%	2.25%	3.00%		
10.	1.90%	1.75%	2.00%		
11.	1.60%	1.50%			
12.	1.40%	1.25%			
13.	1.20%	1.00%			
14.	1.10%	0.75%			
15.	1.00%	0.50%			
16.	0.90%				
17.	0.80%				
18.	0.70%				
19.	0.60%				
20.	0.50%				

29. 附件 G 伤残铁人三项比赛分级规则

伤残铁人三项比赛方法规则见国际铁联官方网站 www.triathlon.org.about/downloads/category/competition_rules。

30. 附件 H 奖金分配表

1. 概 述

1.1 国际铁联奖金分配表提供了一个公正公平的奖金分配方式。

1.2 如国际铁联比赛承办方需更改奖金分配比例，则必须申请特许规则。如果修改奖金分配比例的申请得到批准，则必须在国际铁联官方网站 www.triathlon.org 上公布。

1.3 奖金分配的金额和范围必须男、女运动员相同，对此不可更改。

2. 分配比例

2.1 下表说明了 5 种基本的奖金分配比例和基于国际铁联赛事总奖金的应用。

2.2 国际铁联官方网站 www.triathlon.org 上有方便的奖金分配计算工具。

美元	前 20 名（奖金额 150001 及以上）	前 15 名（奖金额 50001 至 150000）	前 10 名（奖金额 10001 至 50000）	前 5 名（奖金额 3001 至 10000）	前 3 名（奖金额 3000 或以下）
1	23.00%	25.00%	25.00%	30.00%	50.00%
2	18.00%	20.00%	20.00%	25.00%	30.00%
3	14.00%	15.00%	15.00%	20.00%	20.00%
4	10.00%	10.00%	10.00%	15.00%	
5	8.00%	7.00%	8.00%	10.00%	
6	6.00%	6.00%	7.00%		
7	4.00%	5.00%	6.00%		
8	3.00%	3.00%	4.00%		
9	2.30%	2.25%	3.00%		
10	1.90%	1.75%	2.00%		
11	1.60%	1.50%			
12	1.40%	1.25%			
13	1.20%	1.00%			
14	1.10%	0.75%			
15	1.00%	0.50%			
16	0.90%				
17	0.80%				
18	0.70%				
19	0.60%				
20	0.50%				

31. APPENDIX I ITU RELATED MULTISPORTS

- Triathlon
- Long Distance Triathlon (including Middle Distance)
- Aquathlon
- Duathlon
- Long Distance Duathlon (including Middle Distance)
- Winter Triathlon
- Cross Triathlon
- Cross Duathlon
- Indoor Triathlon
- Aquabike

31. 附件 I　国际铁联管辖的分项清单

- 铁人三项
- 长距离铁人三项（包括中距离）
- 游跑两项
- 骑跑两项
- 长距离骑跑两项（包括中距离）
- 冬季铁人三项
- 越野铁人三项
- 越野骑跑两项
- 室内铁人三项
- 游骑两项

32. APPENDIX J ITU EVENTS AND ITU EVENT CATEGORIES

ITU Events

- World Championships
- World Triathlon Series
- World Triathlon Series Grand Final
- World Series
- World Cup
- Continental Championships
- Continental Cup
- Continental Cup Premium
- Continental Cup Final
- Development Event
- Regional Championships

ITU Event Categories

- Elite
- U23
- Junior
- Youth
- Paratriathlon
- Age Group
- Team Relay

32. 附件 J　国际铁联赛事和比赛组别

国际铁联赛事

- 世界锦标赛
- 世界铁人三项系列赛
- 世界铁人三项系列赛总决赛
- 世界系列赛
- 世界杯赛
- 洲际锦标赛
- 洲际杯赛
- 高级洲际杯赛
- 洲际杯决赛
- 发展赛事
- 区域锦标赛

国际铁联比赛组别

- 优秀组
- U23 组（23 岁以下组）
- 青年组
- 少年组
- 残疾人组
- 分龄组
- 团体接力组

ITU Events	Categories
World Championships. Triathlon Standard Distance	U23, Age Group
World Championships. Triathlon Sprint Distance	Junior, Age Group, Paratriathlon
World Championships. Triathlon Mixed Team relay	Elite, U23 & Junior (combined)
World Championships. Triathlon Long Distance	Elite, Age Group, Paratriathlon
World Championships. Duathlon Standard Distance	Elite, U23, Age Group
World Championships. Duathlon Sprint Distance	Junior, Age Group, Paratriathlon
World Championships. Duathlon Team relay	Elite, Junior.
World Championships. Duathlon Long Distance	Elite, Age Group, Paratriathlon
World Championships. Duathlon Middle Distance	Elite, Age Group, Paratriathlon
World Championships. Winter Triathlon.	Junior, U23, Elite, Age Group, Mixed Relay, Paratriathlon PTS2, PTS3, PTS4 and PTS5
World Championships. Aquathlon.	Junior, U23, Elite, Age Group, Paratriathlon
World Championships. Cross Triathlon.	Junior, U23, Elite, Age Group, Mixed Relay, Paratriathlon, PTS2, PTS3, PTS4, PTS5
World Championships. Aquabike	Age Group
World Series. Triathlon. (Both Standard or Sprint)	Elite, Paratriathlon
World Series Grand Final. Triathlon.	Elite
World Cup. Triathlon. (Both Standard or Sprint)	Elite, Paratriathlon
World Cup. Winter Triathlon	Elite
World Series. Duathlon (Both Standard or Long)	Elite
World Series. Long Distance Triathlon	Elite
Continental Championships. Triathlon Standard distance	Elite, U23, Age Group
Continental Championships. Triathlon Sprint Distance	Elite, U23, Junior, Age Group, Paratriathlon
Continental Championships. Triathlon Long Distance.	Elite, Age Group, Paratriathlon.
Continental Championships. Triathlon Team Relay	Elite, Junior, Youth.
Continental Championships. Duathlon Standard Distance.	Elite, U23, Age Group
Continental Championships. Duathlon Sprint Distance	Elite, U23, Junior, Age Group, Paratriathlon
Continental Championships. Duathlon Team Relay	Elite, Junior
Continental Championships. Duathlon Long distance.	Elite, Age Group, Paratriathlon.
Continental Championships. Winter Triathlon	Junior, U23, Elite, Age group, Mixed Relay, Paratriathlon PTS2, PTS3, PTS4 and PTS5
Continental Championships. Aquathlon.	Junior, U23, Elite, Age group, Paratriathlon
Continental Championships. Cross Triathlon.	Junior, U23, Elite, Age group, Mixed Relay, Paratriathlon PTS2, PTS3, PTS4 and PTS5
Continental Cup (All distances and all multisports)	Elite
Continental Tour events	Elite
Junior Continental Cup. Triathlon	Junior

国际铁联赛事	组别
世界锦标赛，标准距离铁人三项赛	U23 组，分龄组
世界锦标赛，短距离铁人三项赛	青年组，分龄组，伤残组，
世界锦标赛，团体混合接力铁人三项赛	优秀组， U23 组和青年组（混合）
世界锦标赛，长距离铁人三项赛	优秀组，分龄组，伤残组
世界锦标赛，标准距离骑跑两项赛	优秀组，U23 组，分龄组
世界锦标赛，短距离骑跑两项赛	青年组，分龄组，伤残组
世界锦标赛，团体接力骑跑两项赛	优秀组，青年组
世界锦标赛，长距离骑跑两项赛	优秀组，分龄组，伤残组
世界锦标赛，中距离骑跑两项赛	优秀组，分龄组，伤残组
世界锦标赛，冬季铁人三项赛	青年组，U23 组，优秀组，分龄组，团体接力组，伤残组 PTS2，PTS3，PTS4，PTS5
世界锦标赛，游跑两项赛	青年组， U23 组，优秀组，分龄组，伤残组
世界锦标赛，越野铁人三项赛	青年组， U23 组，优秀组，分龄组，混合接力组，伤残组，PTS2，PTS3，PTS4，PTS5
世界锦标赛，游骑两项	分龄组
世界系列赛，铁人三项赛（包括标准和短距离）	优秀组，伤残组
世界系列赛总决赛，铁人三项赛	优秀组
世界杯赛，铁人三项赛（包括标准和短距离）	优秀组，伤残组
世界杯赛，冬季铁人三项赛	优秀组
世界系列赛，骑跑两项赛（包括标准和短距离）	优秀组
世界系列赛，长距离铁人三项赛	优秀组
洲际锦标赛，标准距离铁人三项赛	优秀组，U23 组，分龄组
洲际锦标赛，短距离铁人三项赛	优秀组， U23 组，青年组，分龄组，伤残组
洲际锦标赛，长距离铁人三项赛	优秀组，分龄组，伤残组
洲际锦标赛，团体接力铁人三项赛	优秀组，青年组，少年组
洲际锦标赛，标准距离骑跑两项赛	优秀组，U23 组，分龄组
洲际锦标赛，短准距离骑跑两项赛	优秀组， U23 组，青年组，分龄组，伤残组
洲际锦标赛，团体接力组骑跑两项赛	优秀组，青年组
洲际锦标赛，长距离骑跑两项赛	优秀组，分龄组，伤残组
洲际锦标赛，冬季铁人三项赛	青年组， U23 组，优秀组，分龄组，混合接力组，伤残组 PTS2，PTS3，PTS4，PTS5
洲际锦标赛，游跑两项赛	青年组， U23 组，优秀组，分龄组，伤残组
洲际锦标赛，越野铁人三项赛	青年组， U23 组，优秀组，分龄组，混合接力组，伤残组 PTS2，PTS3，PTS4，PTS5
洲际杯赛（所有距离和分项）	优秀组
洲际巡回赛	优秀组
青年洲际杯赛，铁人三项赛	青年组

33. APPENDIX K PENALTIES AND VIOLATIONS

This list is a resume of the most common penalties and infringements. In case of different interpretation of the text in this appendix and the main body of the Competition Rules, the main body of the Competition Rules will be applied.
All the refences to Elite in the charts below, include Elite, U23, Junior and Youth athletes.
The procedures and the amount of penalties for all categories and distances are outlline in section 3 of the Competition Rules.

General	
Rules	**Penalties**
1. An athlete who competes in a category different from his/her age, in a distance in which it is not allowed, or before the 36 hour period;	- DSQ from all the events included in this period
2. Failing to follow the prescribed course;	- Warning and re-enter the competition by the same point - If not: DSQ
3. Departing the course for reasons of safety, but failing to re-enter at the point of departure when advantage is gained;	- If advantage is gained: Time penalty
4. Using abusive language or behaviour toward any official;	- DSQ and report to the ITU Arbitration Tribunal for possible suspension
5. Using unsportsmanlike behavior;	- DSQ and report to the ITU Arbitration Tribunal for possible suspension
6. Blocking, charging, obstructing, or interfering the forward progress of another athlete;	- Unintentionally: warning and amend - Intentionally: DSQ
7. Unfair contact. The fact that contact occurs between athletes does not constitute a violation. When several athletes are moving in a limited area, contact may occur. This incidental contact between athletes in equally favourable positions, is not a violation;	- Unintentionally: warning and amend - Intentionally: DSQ
8. Accepting assistance from anyone other than a Technical Official, race official or other athlete;	- Warning and amend if it is possible and return to the original situation - If not: DSQ
9. Refusing to follow the instructions of Technical Officials or race officials;	- DSQ
10. Failure to wear the unaltered race numbers if provided by the Local Organising Committee, in the proper way ordered by the Technical Delegate and announced at the Athletes' Briefing;	- Warning and amend - If not corrected: DSQ
11. Wearing race number during the swim segment when wetsuits are forbidden;	- Warning and amend - If not corrected: DSQ
12. To dispose of rubbish or equipment around the course outside the clearly identified places, such as aid stations or rubbish disposal points;	- Warning and amend - If not corrected: Time penalty
13. Using illegal, dangerous or unauthorised equipment to provide an advantage or which will be dangerous to others.	- Warning and amend - If not corrected: DSQ
14. Violating competition-specific traffic regulations;	- Unintentionally: Warning and amend if possible - If not corrected or intentionally: DSQ
15. Contrived or intentional ties by elite, U23, junior and youth athletes, or Paratriathletes in ITU sanctioned events;	- DSQ

33. 附件 K 犯规行为和处罚

本细则所列为最常见犯规行为和处罚方式。为避免对本附件和比赛规则中主要部分有不同解读，附上比赛规则主要部分。

下表中优秀组包括优秀组、U23 组、青年组和少年组。

所有组别和距离的处罚程序与处罚次数见比赛规则第 3 章。

总 则	
犯规行为	**处罚方式**
1. 运动员参加与其实际年龄不符或不允许参加的组别的比赛，或在 36 小时之内参赛	取消此期间所有赛事比赛资格
2. 不按规定路线比赛	警告并原路返回重新进入比赛路线 否则：取消比赛资格
3. 出于安全原因离开比赛路线未原路返回，并且获利	如果获利：时间处罚
4. 对任何官员使用不文明语言或行为	取消比赛资格并向仲裁法庭报告，决定是否给予停赛
5. 违反体育道德行为	取消比赛资格并向仲裁法庭报告，决定是否给予停赛
6. 阻挡、冲撞或阻碍其他运动员比赛	非故意：警告，纠正 故意：取消比赛资格
7. 不公平的接触 当几名运动员同时进入一个狭小的区域时，接触就可能发生；运动员之间在同等位置条件下的非故意接触不犯规	非故意：警告，纠正 故意：取消比赛资格
8. 接受除技术官员、竞赛管理人员或其他运动员以外的协助	警告，恢复受助前状况 否则：取消比赛资格
9. 不遵从技术官员或竞赛管理人员的指示	取消比赛资格
10. 错误使用比赛号码（比赛号码由当地组委会提供，由技术代表确定使用方式并在运动员技术会上宣布）	警告，纠正 无法纠正：取消比赛资格
11. 不允许穿防寒泳衣时，游泳赛段佩戴号码	警告，纠正 无法纠正：取消比赛资格
12. 在指定地点（如饮水站或垃圾投放点）之外的比赛路线上随意丢弃垃圾和装备	警告，纠正 无法纠正：时间处罚
13. 使用非法危险或未授权比赛装备，并由此获利或对他人构成危险	警告，纠正 无法纠正：取消比赛资格
14. 违反比赛特定的交通规则	非故意：警告，尽可能纠正 故意或无法纠正：取消比赛资格
15. 优秀组、U23、青年组、少年组、伤残组运动员在国际铁联批准的比赛中故意同时冲过终点	取消比赛资格

General	
Rules	**Penalties**
16. Wearing a different uniform than the one presented in the check-in, either in competition or in the award ceremony;	- Warning and amend - If not corrected: DSQ
17. Wearing during the competition or the award ceremony a uniform which doesn't meet the Competition Rules;	- DSQ
18. Not covering the arms during the competition following a request from the Technical Delegate based on the weather conditions;	- Before the competition: Warning and amend - If not corrected: DSQ
19. In Middle and Long Distance events, wearing a uniform with front zipper undone below the point of the end of the breastbone (sternum) during the competition;	- Warning and amend - If not corrected: DSQ
20. In Middle and Long Distance events, wearing a uniform with front zipper undone during the last 200m of the run;	- Warning and amend
21. Displaying any kind of demonstration of political, religious or racial propaganda;	- Warning and amend - If not: DSQ
22. Fraud by entering under an assumed name or age, falsifying an affidavit, or giving false information;	- DSQ and inform ITU Arbitration Tribunal for a possible suspension
23. Participating when not eligible;	- DSQ and inform ITU Arbitration Tribunal for a possible suspension
24. Repeated intentional violations of ITU Rules;	- DSQ and inform ITU Arbitration Tribunal for a possible suspension
25. Drug abuse;	- Penalties will apply according to the WADA rules
26. For an unusual and violent act of unsportsmanlike behaviour;	- DSQ and inform ITU Arbitration Tribunal for a possible suspension
27. Compete with a bare torso.	- Warning and amend - If not corrected: DSQ
28. Indecent exposure or nudity;	- Warning and amend - If not corrected: DSQ
29. Outside assistance: To give another athlete a complete bike, frame, wheel(s), helmet or any other item equipment which results in the donor athlete being unable to continue with their own competition;	- DSQ of both athletes
30. Gain unfair advantage from any vehicle (excluding drafting).;	- DSQ
31. Not stopping in the next penalty box being obliged to do so;	- DSQ
32. Warming up on the course while another competition is in progress;	- Warning and amend - If not corrected: DSQ
33. Competing under suspension;	- DSQ and report to ITU Arbitration Tribunal for extending suspension or expulsion.
34. Carrying out ambush marketing in the award ceremony;	- Forfeit the prize money earned in the event.
35. Intentionally missing a technological fraud test after being selected;	- DSQ and report to ITU Arbitration Tribunal for potential suspension.
36. Using any device, which makes the bike not only human powered and resulting technological fraud;	- DSQ and report to ITU Arbitration Tribunal for potential suspension.
37. Using any device distracting the athlete from paying full attention to their surroundings;	- Warning and amend - If not corrected: DSQ
38. An athlete physically assists the forward progress of another athlete;	- DSQ

续表

总 则	
犯规行为	**处罚方式**
16. 比赛或颁奖过程中穿着与检录时不同的比赛服	警告，纠正 无法纠正：取消比赛资格
17. 比赛或颁奖过程中穿着不符合规则要求的比赛服	取消比赛资格
18. 未执行技术代表根据天气情况做出的比赛时覆盖手臂的要求	赛前：警告，纠正 无法纠正：取消比赛资格
19. 中长距离比赛中，穿着前拉链比赛服时，拉链低于胸骨的末端	警告，纠正 无法纠正：取消比赛资格
20. 中长距离比赛中，穿着前拉链比赛服时，在跑步最后 200 米，前拉链未拉上	警告，纠正
21. 展示任何政治、宗教或种族宣传	警告，纠正 否则：取消比赛资格
22. 提供虚假报名资料或信息	取消比赛资格并向仲裁法庭报告，决定是否给予停赛
23. 在未取得参赛资格的情况下参赛	取消比赛资格并向仲裁法庭报告，决定是否给予停赛
24. 反复故意违反竞赛规则	取消比赛资格并向仲裁法庭报告，决定是否给予停赛
25. 使用兴奋剂	根据世界反兴奋剂组织规则处罚
26. 特别严重的违反体育道德的行为	取消比赛资格并向仲裁法庭报告，决定是否给予停赛
27. 裸露躯干比赛	警告，纠正 无法纠正：取消比赛资格
28. 不雅的暴露身体行为	警告，纠正 无法纠正：取消比赛资格
29. 外力协助：为其他运动员提供整辆自行车、车架、车轮、头盔、骑行鞋、跑鞋或任何其他装备，并导致其自身无法继续比赛	取消两名运动员的比赛资格
30. 试图利用车辆或物体等外部力量的不公平方式获利（尾随除外）	取消比赛资格
31. 未按要求在下一个处罚区接受处罚	取消比赛资格
32. 在其他进行中的赛事场地热身	警告，纠正 无法纠正：取消比赛资格
33. 停赛期间参加比赛	取消比赛资格并向国际铁联仲裁法庭报告，决定延长停赛或终身禁赛
34. 在颁奖仪式上进行隐性营销	没收在比赛中获得的奖金
35. 故意逃避被选中的自行车技术欺诈检测	取消比赛资格并向仲裁法庭报告，决定是否给予停赛
36. 在自行车上使用非人力装置，形成技术欺诈	取消比赛资格并向仲裁法庭报告，决定是否给予停赛
37. 使用让运动员注意力不能专注于赛事环境的装置	警告，纠正 无法纠正：取消比赛资格
38. 运动员身体帮助（助力）另一运动员前进	取消比赛资格

Briefing (Non-applicable for Age Group)	
Rules	**Penalties**
39. Not attending the Athletes' Briefing, without notifying the Technical Delegate;	- Athletes not attending the briefing, without informing the Technical Delegate about their absence, will be removed from the start list of the event and from all start and wait list in the events on the next 30 days
40. Athletes entering the briefing hall after the briefing has started and athletes not attending the briefing but informed the Technical Delegate about their absence;	- Delayed start, which delay will be according to the time penalty applicable for the specific distance
41. Athletes missing 3 or more briefing in Triathlon/Paratriathlon World Cup or World Triathlon/Paratriathlon Series in the same calendar year, no matter if the athlete informed the Technical Delegate or not;	- Remove from the start list from every subsequent competition at which they miss the briefing

Start	
Rules	**Penalties**
42. Starting before the starter's signal.	- Time penalty
43. Starting in a wave earlier than the one the athlete is assigned to;	- DSQ
44. Not moving forward before touching the water;	- Time penalty
45. To change the start position once selected;	- Warning and amend - If not corrected: DSQ
46. To block more than one start positions;	- Warning and amend - If not corrected: DSQ

Swim	
Rules	**Penalties**
47. Wearing clothing covering any part of the arms below the shoulder and/or clothing covering any part of the legs below knee, in a non-wetsuit swim;	- Warning and amend - If not corrected: DSQ
48. Not wearing the official swim cap from the time of the line-up;	- Intentionally: Warning and amend - If not corrected: DSQ
49. Make contact and continue to impede the progress of the other athlete without making an effort to move apart;	- Time penalty
50. Deliberately target another athlete to impede their progress, gain unfair advantage and potentially cause harm;	- DSQ and may report to ITU Arbitration Tribunal for potential suspension or expulsion;
51. Wearing wetsuit not covering the torso, when the wetsuit is mandatory;	- Warning and amend - If not corrected: DSQ
52. Athletes wearing branded second swim cap visible any time from the athletes' line-up till Transition 1;	- Time penalty

技术会（不适用于分龄组）	
犯规行为	处罚方式
39. 未参加技术会且未向技术代表请假	从本次比赛及其后 30 天内所有比赛出发和候补名单中除名
40. 迟到或未出席技术会但向技术代表请假的	延迟出发，延迟时间将根据特定距离的时间处罚规定执行。
41. 参加世界铁人三项 / 伤残铁人三项系列赛和世界杯赛的运动员，如果在同一年内缺席技术会三次或超过三次，无论是否向技术代表请假的	取消缺席后所有赛事的比赛资格

出 发	
犯规行为	处罚方式
42. 在出发信号发出前，抢跑（跳、游）	时间处罚
43. 运动员在其应出发时间前的任何组提前出发	取消比赛资格
44. 出发入水前没有向前移动	时间处罚
45. 改变选定位置	警告，纠正 否则：取消参赛资格
46. 占用两个或两个以上出发位置	警告，纠正 否则：取消参赛资格

游 泳	
犯规行为	处罚方式
47. 在不允许使用防寒泳衣的游泳比赛中，穿着覆盖整个手臂和小腿的比赛服	警告，纠正 否则：取消比赛资格
48. 从运动员集合开始，未佩戴官方提供的泳帽	故意：警告，纠正 否则：取消参赛资格
49. 接触并持续阻碍其他运动员的进程，没有主动移开	时间处罚
50. 故意针对其他运动员阻碍其进程、获得不公平优势、有可能形成伤害	取消比赛资格并报告国际铁联仲裁法庭，处以可能的停赛或禁赛
51. 在要求使用防寒泳衣的比赛中，穿着未覆盖躯干的防寒泳衣	警告，纠正 否则：取消资格
52. 从运动员入场到第一换项整个过程中，运动员佩戴可看到商标的第二顶泳帽	时间处罚

Transition	
Rules	**Penalties**
53. Rack the bike improperly, outside the athletes' own space or blocking the progress of other athletes;	- Before the competition: Warning and amend - During the competition: - Age Group: Warning and amend - Elite Draft-illegal and Elite Paratriathlon: Time penalty - Elite Draft Legal: Time penalty
54. To have the helmet strap fastened in T1 while completing the first segment;	- Age Group: Technical Official will undo the strap. - Elite and Elite Paratriathlon: Technical Official will undo the strap and time penalty.
55. Wearing the helmet unfastened or insecurely fastened, inside transition area while in possession of the bike;	- Age Group: Warning and amend - Elite and Elite Paratriathlon: Time penalty
56. Mount the bike before the mount line;	- Age Group: Warning and amend - Elite and Elite Paratriathlon: Time penalty
57. Dismount the bike after the dismount line;	- Age Group: Warning and amend - Elite and Elite Paratriathlon: Time penalty
58. Discharge or store the athlete equipment outside the designated area;	- Age-Group: Warning and amend - Elite and Elite Paratriathlon: Time penalty
59. Marking of position in transition area;	- Warning and amend - If not corrected, marking and objects used for marking purposes will be removed and athlete will not be notified
60. Failing to deposit all equipment inside the proper bag provided by the Local Organising Committee on the events where bag drop system is in place; (with the exception of bikes shoes that may remain on the pedals at all times);	- Age Group: Warning and amend - Elite and Paratriathlon: Time penalty
61. Interfering with another athlete's equipment in the Transition Area;	- Age Group: Warning and amend - Elite and Elite Paratriathlon: Time penalty

Bike	
Rules	**Penalties**
62. Not wearing helmet during bike familiarisation and/or official bike training sessions;	- To be excluded from the specific session
63. Make forward progress without the bike, during the bike segment;	- Warning and amend - If not: DSQ
64. Drafting in a draft-illegal competition on sprint and standard distance events;	- 1st offence: Drafting time penalty - 2nd offence: DSQ
65. Overtaken athlete not dropping out of the draft zone of the passing athlete by continuously making rearward progress to clear the drafting zone completed in 20 seconds on sprint and standard distance events;	- 1st offence: Drafting time penalty - 2nd offence: DSQ
66. Re-passing by an overtaken athlete prior to dropping out of the draft zone on sprint and standard distance events;	- 1st offence: Drafting time penalty - 2nd offence: DSQ
67. Drafting in a draft-illegal competition on middle or long distance events;	- 1st and 2nd offences: Drafting time penalty - 3rd offence: DSQ

转换区	
犯规行为	**处罚方式**
53. 不恰当停车，未将自行车停放在自己的空间内或阻碍了其他运动员停车	赛前：警告，纠正 赛中：分龄组：警告，纠正；优秀组（无论是否允许尾随）和伤残优秀组：时间处罚
54. 当第一赛段的比赛时，转换区内头盔搭扣处于扣紧状态	分龄组：技术官员解开头盔搭扣 优秀组和伤残优秀组：技术官员解开头盔搭扣，并给予时间处罚
55. 在转换区内持车过程中头盔搭扣未扣或未扣紧	分龄组：警告，纠正 优秀组和伤残优秀组：时间处罚
56. 上车线之前上车	分龄组：警告，纠正 优秀组和伤残优秀组：时间处罚
57. 下车线之后下车	分龄组：警告，纠正 优秀组和伤残优秀组：时间处罚
58. 将比赛装备放置在非指定位置	分龄组：警告，纠正 优秀组和伤残优秀组：时间处罚
59. 在转换区做标记	警告，纠正 无法纠正：移除标记且不通知运动员
60. 在设置了存包系统的赛事中，没有将所有的比赛装备放进当地组委会提供的包里（骑行鞋可以始终置于自行车踏板上）	分龄组：警告，纠正 优秀组和伤残优秀组：时间处罚
61. 在转换区扰乱其他运动员的设备	分龄组：警告，纠正 优秀组和伤残优秀组：时间处罚

自行车	
犯规行为	**处罚方式**
62. 熟悉比赛路线或自行车官方培训时不戴头盔	取消相关活动资格
63. 自行车段不使用自行车	警告，纠正 否则：取消比赛资格
64. 在短距离和标准距离不允许尾随的比赛中尾随	第一次：尾随时间处罚 第二次：取消比赛资格
65. 在短距离和标准距离比赛中，被超越的运动员在 20 秒之内没有通过持续减速方式退出超越运动员的尾随区	第一次：尾随时间处罚 第二次：取消比赛资格
66. 在短距离和标准距离比赛中被超越运动员在从尾随区退出之前再次超越了前一个运动员	第一次：尾随时间处罚 第二次：取消比赛资格
67. 在中、长距离不允许尾随的比赛中尾随	第一次和第二次：尾随时间处罚 第三次：取消比赛资格

Bike	
68. Overtaken athlete not dropping out of the draft zone of the passing athlete by continuously making rearward progress to clear the drafting zone completed in 25 seconds on middle and long distance events;	- 1st and 2nd offences: Drafting time penalty - 3rd offence: DSQ
69. Re-passing by an overtaken athlete prior to dropping out of the draft zone on middle and long distance events;	- 1st and 2nd offences: Drafting time penalty - 3rd offence: DSQ
70. Drafting off a different gender athlete in draft legal events;	- 1st offence: Warning and amend - 2nd offence DSQ
71. Drafting off an athlete being in a different lap;	- Warning and amend - If not: DSQ
72. Drafting off a vehicle or motorbike;	- Warning and amend - If not corrected: Drafting time penalty
73. Blocking in a draft-illegal competition;	- Time penalty - If not: DSQ
74. Wearing the helmet unfastened or insecurely fastened, during the bike segment;	- Warning and amend - If not corrected: DSQ
75. Take off the helmet on the bike course, even if stopped;	- Warning and amend - If not corrected: DSQ
76. Not wearing a helmet during the bike segment;	- DSQ
77. Competing with a different bicycle than the one presented at the check in, or modified after getting the approval at the check-in;	- DSQ
78. While in the bike penalty box, athletes consume food and/or water other that is on the athlete's bike or person;	- Warning and amend - If not corrected: DSQ
79. Athletes using the restroom while serving a penalty in the bike penalty box;	- Penalty paused
80. Making adjustments to equipment or performing any type of bike maintenance while serving a penalty.	- Warning and amend - If not corrected: DSQ

Run and Ski.	
Rules	**Penalties**
81. Crawl during the running segment;	- DSQ
82. Running together and/or take pace from other athlete/s that is/are one or more laps ahead. (Applicable to Elite, U23, Junior, Youth athletes and Paratriathletes);	- Warning and amend - If not corrected: DSQ
83. Being accompanied by any non-competing athletes, team members, team managers or other pacemakers on the course or along the course;	- Warning and amend - If not corrected: DSQ
84. Run or ski wearing a helmet;	- Warning and amend - If not corrected: DSQ
85. To use posts, trees or other fixed elements to assist maneuvering curves;	- Time penalty
86. Being accompanied by any non-competing person in the finish chute.	- DSQ

续表

自行车	
68. 在中距离和长距离比赛中，被超越的运动员在 25 秒之内没有通过持续减速方式退出超越运动员的尾随区	第一次和第二次：尾随时间处罚 第三次：取消比赛资格
69. 在中距离和长距离比赛中被超越运动员在从尾随区退出之前再次超越了前一个运动员	第一次和第二次：尾随时间处罚 第三次：取消比赛资格
70. 在允许尾随的比赛中尾随异性运动员	第一次：警告，纠正 第二次：取消比赛资格
71. 尾随不同圈的运动员	警告，纠正 无法纠正：取消比赛资格
72. 尾随机动车或摩托车	警告，纠正 无法纠正：尾随时间处罚
73. 在不允许尾随的比赛中阻挡	时间处罚 无法纠正：取消比赛资格
74. 在自行车赛段头盔搭扣未扣或未扣紧	警告，纠正 无法纠正：取消比赛资格
75. 自行车赛段摘掉头盔，即使运动员已经停下	警告，纠正 无法纠正：取消比赛资格
76. 自行车赛段不戴头盔	取消比赛资格
77. 使用不同于检录时的自行车或检录后改装了的自行车进行比赛	取消比赛资格
78. 自行车处罚时，运动员吃非自身或自行车携带的食物或 / 和水	警告，纠正 无法纠正：取消比赛资格，
79. 在自行车处罚区期间运动员去卫生间	暂停处罚
80. 处罚期间对自行车设备做调整或保养自行车	警告，纠正 无法纠正：取消比赛资格

跑、滑雪	
犯规行为	**处罚方式**
81. 跑步赛段爬行	取消比赛资格
82. 与领先一圈或一圈以上的运动员一起跑步和 / 或同跑步节奏（适用于优秀组，23 岁以下组，青年组，少年组和伤残组运动员）	警告，纠正 无法纠正：取消比赛资格
83. 在赛道或赛道边上由非参赛运动员、队友、领队、或其他人员伴跑	警告，纠正 无法纠正：取消比赛资格
84. 跑步或滑雪赛段戴头盔	警告，纠正 无法纠正：取消比赛资格
85. 在弯道处借助杆、树等固定物体转弯	时间处罚
86. 在终点冲刺通道由非参赛运动员陪跑	取消比赛资格

Team Relay Specific	
Rules	**Penalties**
87. Team relay exchange completed outside of the exchange zone;	- Time penalty
88. Team relay exchange not completed, or intentionally completed outside the changing zone;	- DSQ

Paratriathlon Specific	
Rules	**Penalties**
89. Paratriathletes , who use catheters or other urinary diversion devices, have spillage during training, competition or classification;	- Warning and amend - If not corrected: DSQ
90. Using adapted cleats and bike shoes with exposed cleats that are mounted on prosthetic legs (which are allowed in the pre-transition area) and the cleats are not covered or not surrounded by anti-slip material.	- Before the competition: Warning and amend - If not corrected: DSQ
91. Paratriathlete without a temporary, review or confirmed class status according to the regulated timelines;	- DSQ
92. Paratriathlete competes wearing or using any prostheses or special adaptive equipment which are not officially approved;	- Before the competition: Warning and amend - If not corrected: DSQ
93. Paratriathletes using unprotected sharp objects, screws, prosthetic liners, or prosthetic devices that can be harmful;	- Before the competition: Warning and amend - If not corrected: DSQ
94. Paratriathlete's classification is considered Not Completed (CNC);	- Remove from the start list
95. Paratriathlete who have been classified as non eligiblequipe for a paratriathlon competition;	- Remove from the start list
96. Paratriathlete fails to attend scheduled classification session;	- Reasonable explanation: Give second chance - If not: DSQ
97. Paratriathlete who is intentionally misrepresenting his/her skills and/or abilities;	- First offence: DSQ - Second offence: DSQ and report to ITU Arbitration Tribunal for potential suspension or expulsion
98. Guides and personal handlers, who have not registered at the athletes' briefing;	- Do not have access to the FOP
99. Personal handler not carrying the special credentials which were given by the LOC/ITU;	- Warning and amend - If not corrected: DSQ the Paratriathlete that he/she is handling
100. Paratriathlete receiving help from more personal handlers that he/she has registered;	- DSQ
101. Any action taken by the personal handler which propels the paratriathlete forward;	- DSQ the Paratriathlete that he/she is handling
102. Personal handler repairing a Paratriathlete's bike in an area other than the athletes' transition spot or the wheel station during the competition;	- DSQ
103. Paratriathletes' equipment in the pre-transition area which haven't been registered;	- Before the competition: Warning and amend - If not corrected: DSQ
104. Personal handlers' present in the pre-transition area from PTS2, PTS3, PTS4 and PTS5;	- Before the competition: Warning and amend - If not corrected: DSQ the athlete that they are handling

团体接力赛	
犯规行为	处罚方式
87. 团体接力赛未在接力区完成接力	时间处罚
88. 团体接力赛未完成接力，或故意在接力区外完成接力	取消比赛资格

伤残铁人三项特殊问题	
犯规行为	处罚方式
89. 使用导尿管或其他尿流改道装置的伤残铁三运动员在训练、比赛或分级过程中尿液溢出	警告，纠正 若不改正：取消比赛资格
90. 运动员假腿上（在预备转换区被允许使用）安装的防滑钉鞋和自行车鞋上含有暴露在外的钉子，钉子未被覆盖或用防滑材料包裹	赛前：警告，纠正 若不改正：取消比赛资格
91. 在规定的时限内伤残铁三运动员没有进行临时审核或等级确认	取消比赛资格
92. 伤残铁三运动员比赛时穿着或使用的假肢或特殊的自适应设备不是官方认可的	赛前：警告，纠正 若不改正：取消比赛资格
93. 伤残铁三运动员使用未保护的尖锐物体、螺丝、假肢衬垫或者会造成伤害的假肢设备	赛前：警告，纠正 若不改正：取消比赛资格
94. 伤残铁三运动员的分级被认为未完成	从出发名单中移除
95. 伤残铁三运动员在分级时被视为无资格参加比赛	从出发名单中移除
96. 伤残铁三运动员未能参加事先安排的分级会议	若原因合理：给予第二次机会 否则：取消比赛资格
97. 伤残铁三运动员有意谎报自己的技能或能力	初犯：取消比赛资格 再犯：取消比赛资格并向国际铁联仲裁法庭报告决定是否给予停赛或禁赛
98. 引导员或个人助理未在运动员技术会上进行登记	不能进入比赛区域
99. 个人助理未携带由当地组委会或国际铁联开具的特殊证明	警告，纠正 若不改正：取消受其助理的运动员的比赛资格
100. 伤残铁三运动员接受已注册的个人助理之外的其他个人助理的帮助	取消比赛资格
101. 个人助理做出任何能够推动伤残铁三运动员向前移动的动作	取消受其助理的运动员的比赛资格
102. 在比赛过程中，个人助理在运动员转换点或车轮站以外的区域为伤残运动员修理自行车	取消比赛资格
103. 伤残铁三运动员的装备未在预备转换区进行登记	赛前：警告，纠正 若不改正：取消比赛资格
104. 个人助理出现在 PTS2、PTS3、PTS4、PTS5 的预备转换区	赛前：警告，纠正 若不改正：取消受其助理的运动员的比赛资格

Paratriathlon Specific	
105. Paratriathletes with an absent lower limb not using a prosthesis or crutches to reach from Pre-Transition area to Transition 1 and hopping on one leg;	- Before the competition: Warning and amend - If not corrected: DSQ
106. PTWC1 and PTWC2 paratriathles doing the transition outside the individual space;	- Time penalty
107. PTWC1 and PTWC2 athletes not stopping completely at the mount and at the dismount lines or continue before the Technical Official say "Go";	- Time penalty
108. PTWC1 and PTWC2 athletes drafting off a vehicle or motorbike during the run;	- Warning and amend - If not corrected: Drafting time penalty
109. Paratriathletes leaving equipment in pre-transition after exiting it;	- Warning and amend - If not corrected: Time penalty
110. PTVI1, PTVI2 and PTVI3 athletes competing with a guide who is not complying with the requirements;	- DSQ
111. PTVI1, PTVI2 and PTVI3 athletes not be tethered during the swim or the run;	- Warning and amend - If not corrected: DSQ
112. PTVI1, PTVI2 and PTVI3 athletes paced, led or being more than 1.5m away from their guide, during the swim;	- First offence: Time penalty - Second offence: DSQ
113. PTVI1, PTVI2 and PTVI3 athletes paced, led or being more than 0.5m away from their guide, during the after the swim exit;	- First offence: Time penalty - Second offence: DSQ
114. PTVI1, PTVI2 and PTVI3 athletes pulled or pushed by the guide;	- DSQ
115. PTVI1, PTVI2 and PTVI3 paratriathlete crosses the finish line and the guide is beside or behind the paratriathlete but further apart than the required 0.5 meters maximum separation distance;	- DSQ
116. Paratriathlete enters the Field of Play with a guide dog;	- Before the competition: Warning and amend - If not corrected: DSQ
117. PTVI1 athletes not wearing blackout googles or glasses during the applicable segments;	- DSQ

伤残铁人三项特殊问题	
105. 伤残铁三运动员缺少下肢并未使用假肢或拐杖支撑，从预备转换区用单腿跳到到转换区 1	赛前：警告，纠正 若不改正：取消比赛资格
106. 使用轮椅的伤残铁三运动员（PTWC1 和 PTWC2）在个人的空间之外进行项目转换	时间处罚
107. 使用轮椅的伤残铁三运动员（PTWC1 和 PTWC2）未在上车和下车线处完全停止或在技术官员发出“出发”指令前未处于完全停止状态	时间处罚
108. 使用轮椅的伤残铁三运动员（PTWC1 和 PTWC2）在跑步过程中尾随机动车或摩托车	警告，纠正 若不改正：尾随时间处罚
109. 伤残铁三运动员在离开预备转换区后把装备留在预备转换区	警告，纠正 若不改正：时间处罚
110. 有视觉缺陷的伤残铁三运动员（PTVI1、PTVI2 和 PTVI3）的引导员在比赛中不遵守要求	取消比赛资格
111. 有视觉缺陷的伤残铁三运动员（PTVI1、PTVI2 和 PTVI3）在游泳和跑步时没有用绳索进行保护	警告，纠正 若不改正：取消比赛资格
112. 有视觉缺陷的伤残铁三运动员（PTVI1、PTVI2 和 PTVI3I）在游泳时领先引导员或与其间距大于 1.5 米	初犯：时间处罚 再犯：取消比赛资格
113. 有视觉缺陷的伤残铁三运动员（PTVI1、PTVI2 和 PTVI3）在游泳赛道出口之后领先引导员或与其间距大于 0.5 米	初犯：加时处罚 再犯：取消比赛资格
114. 引导员拉或推有视觉缺陷的伤残铁三运动员（PTVI1、PTVI2 和 PTVI3）	取消比赛资格
115. 有视觉缺陷的伤残铁三运动员（PTVI1、PTVI2 和 PTVI3）在冲过终点线时，引导者在其身侧或身后的距离大于规定的 0.5 米的最大间距	取消比赛资格
116. 伤残铁三运动员携带导盲犬进入比赛区域	赛前：警告，纠正 若不改正：取消比赛资格
117. 有视觉缺陷的双眼全部失明的伤残铁三运动员（PTVI1）没有在相关赛段佩戴遮光护目镜或遮光镜	取消比赛资格

34. APPENDIX L RESULTS AND START LIST SAMPLES

The Results and Start List samples can be found in the ITU website.

35. APPENDIX M ATHLETE'S AGREEMENT

The Athletes Agreement is outlined in the ITU website under the following link: https://www.triathlon.org/about/downloads/category/athletes_agreement

36. APPENDIX N TECHNOLOGICAL FRAUD

1. **Location and time:**
   - 1.1. For any event, the technological fraud check will take place at the time that the athletes' bicycles are checked (athletes' lounge or transition zone).
   - 1.2. Ideally two tents should be provided by the LOC (one of them can be without walls).
   - 1.3. Prior to the competition, there will be random selections among the athletes. Post-competition, tests can take place on targeted athletes according to their performance.
2. **Personnel involved:**
   - 2.1. One or two ITU accredited bike check officials should be part of the process.
   - 2.2. A qualified bike mechanic should be provided by the LOC. The bike mechanic should be very familiar with the types of bicycles that are being used at the particular competition and be able to disassemble the bike and reassemble the bike within a short period of time.
3. **Process:**
   - 3.1. The selected athlete will be asked to move his/her bicycle to the 1st tent. The ITU accredited bike check official will explain the process to the athlete, perform a visual check and scan the bicycle including the frame and the wheels.
   - 3.2. In case low readings, the athlete and bicycle will be released.
   - 3.3. In case high readings, if available, the second accredited bike check official will be asked to verify the results. If still high reading, the athlete will be asked to move his/her bike to the closed tent. In case of high reading and there is no second accredited bike check official available, the athlete will be asked to move his/her bike to the closed tent.
   - 3.4. ITU may use any available technology to check the athletes' bicycles.

34. 附件 L　比赛成绩及出发名单样单

比赛成绩及出发名单样单可以在国际铁联官网上下载。

35. 附件 M　运动员参赛协议

国际铁联官网上列出了运动员参赛协议：

https://www.triathlon.org/about/downloads/category/athletes_agreement.

36. 附件 N　技术欺诈

1.　地点和时间

1.1　各项比赛中，技术诈骗的检测在检验比赛用车时进行（在运动员准备区或转换区进行）。

1.2　原则上，当地组委会提供两顶帐篷（其中一顶无四围）。

1.3　赛前，对运动员进行抽检；赛后，根据运动员表现进行针对性检验。

2.　人　员

2.1　应有 1 名到 2 名国际铁联委派的检验官员参与检验。

2.2　当地组委会委派 1 名自行车机械师。此自行车机械师必须熟悉各种特定比赛用车并且可在短时内拆卸和重组自行车。

3.　程　序

3.1　被抽检的运动员将自行车移至第一顶帐篷。国际铁联委派的验车技术官员向运动员解释检验程序，进行目测并仔细检验自行车的车架和车轮。

3.2　如读数低则运动员和自行车被放行。

3.3　如读数高，则由第二位被委派的验车技术官员（如有）进行结果核查。如读数仍高，运动员则被要求将其自行车移至密闭的帐篷中。如读数高而又没有第二位被委派的验车技术官员则要求运动员将其自行车移至密闭的帐篷中。

3.4　国际铁联可运用一切技术手段对自行车进行检验。

3.5. In the closed tent, along with the ITU accredited bike check official, the ITU Head Referee has to be present (or any other official assigned by the Head Referee to represent her/him) and the bike mechanic. This tent has to be closed from any public/media view.

3.6. The athlete will be given the tools to remove the seat post and the chain wheel axle. Alternatively, the athletes' representative can remove the above equipment for them. If the athlete or his/her representative is not willing to remove the above equipment, he/she has to sign a waiver for any damages to the bicycle during removal by ITU approved bike mechanic.

3.7. The bike mechanic or the athlete will remove the chain wheel axle. If a motor exists, the athlete will be referred to the Head Referee for a decision. The Head Referee will disqualify the athlete and refer the case to the ITU Arbitration Tribunal for possible further penalties.

3.8. If the athlete refuses to sign a waiver, the case will be considered as a missed test and as such the Head Referee will disqualify the athlete and refer the case to the ITU Arbitration Tribunal for possible further penalties.

3.9. The athlete is not allowed to compete on another bicycle at any ITU event until the case is closed and during the time of a possible suspension.

37. APPENDIX P NON-TRADITIONAL OR UNUSUAL BIKE APPROVAL PROCESS

1. The manufacturer should provide a product description (with illustrative pictures) about the bike frame to be approved.
2. The manufacturer should declare that the frame (in all available/sold frame sizes) fulfils all the criteria of the actual bike safety standards, at the moment the ISO 4210:2015. This declaration should be part of the document package submitted for approval.
3. The manufacturer should demonstrate the compliance with ISO 4210:2015 standard of the frame with a test report issued by an independent third-party laboratory conducting consumer product safety and compliance testing in the field of mechanical testing and accredited to the requirements of EN/ISO/IEC 17025. Test reports should be provided about all available/sold frame sizes (like 48/50/52 etc.) These test reports should be part of the document package submitted for approval.
4. The certification about the compliance with EN/ISO/IEC 17025 of the accredited test laboratory should be part of the document package submitted for approval.
5. The approval panel will study these documents and will take a decision on the acceptance of the request.

3.5 在密闭的帐篷中，国际铁联委派的验车技术官员、国际铁联裁判长（或由裁判长指派的其他官员）和自行车机械师均需在场。此帐篷不对公众或媒体开放。

3.6 提供工具给运动员进行座管和牙盘轴的移除。运动员代理人可代为移除以上装备。如运动员或其代理人不愿移除以上装备则由国际铁联委派的自行车机械师进行移除，运动员必须签订免责书，免除对由此产生的任何对自行车的损伤的追责。

3.7 自行车机械师或运动员移除牙盘轴。如果发现牙盘轴装有马达，运动员将被提交给裁判长裁决。裁判长将取消运动员比赛资格并将该情况向国际铁联仲裁法庭报告，等待进一步可能的惩罚。

3.8 如运动员拒绝签署免责书，将被视为未检验。裁判长取消运动员资格并将该情况提交给国际铁联仲裁法院做进一步可能的惩罚。

3.9 在案件完结之前和停赛期间运动员不允许骑行别的自行车参加任何国际铁联所管辖的比赛。

37. 附件 P　非常规自行车审批流程

1. 制造商需提供待审的自行车车架的产品描述（配说明图纸）。

2. 制造商必须声明车架（包含所有尺寸车架）达到现行自行车安全标准即 ISO4210：2015。这项声明必须包含在所提交的审批文件之中。

3. 制造商必须提供由独立的第三方实验室公布的车架符合 ISO4210：2015 标准的检验报告。此被授权的第三方执行消费者产品安全检验及机械检验领域内的遵从性测试，并且达到 EN/ISO/IEC17025 要求资质。测试报告应提供所有可能的 / 销售的车架尺寸（如 48/50/52 等）。这些测试报告必须包含在所提交的审批文件之中。

4. 被授权的检验实验室所具有的达到 EN/ISO/IEC17025 标准的证书必须作为申报材料一并提交。

5. 审批委员会研究这些文件并就申请批准与否做出决定。

38. APPENDIX Q PPE – PRE PARTICIPATION EVALUATION

1. The PPE should consist of:

1.1. Answer the Medical Questionnaire : this questionnaire is strictly confidential and must given to the responsible team doctor before the medical examination. The medical questionnaire will be available to be downloaded from the ITU website.

1.2. Physical Examination : by the doctor following the IOC recommendations published in the "Lausanne Recommendations" about the Sudden Cardiovascular Death in Sport Consensus.

a.) Cardiac auscultation:

- Rate /rhythm
- Murmur : systolic/diastolic
- Systolic click

b.) Blood Pressure

c.) Radial and Femoral Pulses

d.) Marfan stigmata

1.3. A 12 lead rest electrocardiogramm (ECG). Doctor to look for anomalies in rhythm, conduction or repolarisation.

1.4. Each National Federation must send one letter/certificate at the beginning of each season, signed by the National Federation representative, confirming that all athletes as outlined in 2.4.c have undertaken the PPE, who will enter in an ITU event in the specific calendar year. This letter will have to be submitted manually, otherwise junior athletes from the specific National Federation will not be admitted to any ITU event.

38. 附件 Q　赛前健康评估（PPE）

1. 赛前健康评估内容包括：

1.1 填写医学问卷：问卷是严格保密的且必须在医学检查前交给主管队医。医学问卷可以从国际铁联网站上下载。

1.2 身体检查：医生根据国际奥委会建议执行。国际奥委会建议参见“洛桑建议书”中关于运动中突发性心脏猝死部分。

a）心脏听诊：

- 心率 / 节律。
- 心脏杂音：收缩 / 舒张。
- 收缩期卡塔音。

b）血压。

c）桡动脉、股动脉脉搏 。

d）马凡氏皮肤红斑（症候群）。

1.3 12 导静息心电图（ECG）。医生检查心脏节律、传导和再极化方面的异常。

1.4 各国家会员协会必须在每个赛季开始前向国际铁联发送由国家会员协会代表签名的确认信或证明材料，确认本国 2.4.c 规定的所有运动员已进行过赛前健康评估。确认信必须每年发送一次，否则该国运动员将不能参加国际铁联赛事。

39. 附件 R　中国铁人三项运动协会犯规行为处罚细则（2018 版）

中国铁人三项运动协会犯规行为处罚细则（2018 版）

一、概 述

为进一步明确对于犯规行为的定义，以及犯规处罚的程序与方法，保障比赛公平、公正举行，根据《国际铁人三项联盟竞赛规则》等相关文件，制定此细则。《国际铁人三项联盟竞赛规则》已经说明的部分，在此不再重复。

二、处罚权限及执行人

（1）运动员非故意、非主动或情节轻微的犯规、且犯规行为易辨别、应给予口头警告或警告处罚的情况，可由当执裁判员直接执行处罚；如运动员犯规行为不易辨别，当执裁判员应报告裁判长，由裁判长执行处罚，或指导当执裁判员执行处罚，或追加处罚。

（2）运动员故意、主动、明显获利，第二次或情节严重的犯规，应给予时间处罚或取消比赛资格处罚的情况，由当执裁判员报告裁判长，由裁判长执行处罚，或授权当执裁判员执行处罚，或追加处罚；如运动员的违规行为十分明显或危及他人或其自身安全，当执裁判员可直接执行处罚。

（3）追加处罚：如果运动员违规时条件不允许，裁判员当场无法给予处罚，或者违规行为不易判断，可事后追加处罚；当执裁判员应做好违规行为记录，必要时使用摄像机记录犯规情况，并报告裁判长。

（4）中国铁人三项运动协会比赛运行团队中以下岗位拥有处罚权，可以执行处罚：裁判长、裁判长助理、检录组、游泳组、转换区组、自行车和跑步组、饮水站和备用车轮站组、终点组以及其他由裁判长指定的人员。

三、犯规行为及处罚细则

序号	犯规行为	犯规性质 / 组别(注1)	处罚方法	执行方式(注2)	犯规行为说明或举例（包括但不仅限于以下示例）
（一）总　则					
1	36 小时内参加两场或两场以上的比赛		取消此期间所有赛事比赛资格或成绩	报告	如其中一场是标准距离或更长距离比赛
2	（1）对任何官员使用不文明语言或行为 （2）违反体育道德行为 （3）提供虚假报名资料或信息 （4）在未取得参赛资格的情况下参赛 （5）停赛期间参加比赛 （6）反复故意违反竞赛规则 （7）运动员参加与其实际年龄不符或不允许参加的组别的比赛 （8）故意逃避被选中的自行车技术欺诈检测 （9）在自行车上使用非人力装置，形成技术欺诈		取消比赛资格 **停赛审查**(注3)	报告	（1）不尊重技术官员、观众、拒绝领奖、散布不负责任的言论、严重影响与干扰比赛 （2）特别严重的违反体育道德的行为，可以终身禁赛
3	（1）不遵从技术官员或竞赛管理人员指示 （2）专业组、伤残组运动员在国际铁联批准的比赛中故意同时冲过终点 （3）裸体行为 （4）未按要求在下一个处罚区接受处罚		取消比赛资格	报告	专业组运动员在冲刺阶段应表现出奋勇争先的竞技精神，如运动员均全力冲刺，即便同时冲过终点，也不视为“故意”
4	（1）运动员身体帮助（助力）另一运动员前进 （2）为其他运动员提供整辆自行车、车架、车轮、头盔或任何其他装备，并导致其自身无法继续比赛		取消两名运动员的比赛资格	报告	（1）如某运动员推、拉另一名运动员前进 （2）运动员之间可以互相提供备用器材物品，如：营养品、饮料（在饮水站之后）、气筒、管胎、内胎和补胎设备

续表

序号	犯规行为	犯规性质 / 组别（注1）	处罚方法	执行方式（注2）	犯规行为说明或举例（包括但不仅限于以下示例）
5	（1）不按规定路线比赛 （2）违反特定的交通规则 （3）冲撞、阻碍其他运动员比赛 （4）不公平的接触 （5）使用非法危险或未授权比赛装备，并由此获利或对他人构成危险 （6）裸露躯干或其他不雅的暴露身体行为 （7）在其他进行中的赛事场地热身 （8）错误使用比赛号码 （9）展示任何政治、宗教或种族宣传 （10）比赛或颁奖过程中穿着不符合规则要求的比赛服 （11）比赛或颁奖过程中穿着与检录时不同的比赛服 （12）未执行技术代表根据天气情况做出的比赛时覆盖手臂的要求 （13）中长距离比赛中，穿着前拉链比赛服时，拉链低于胸骨的末端 （14）中长距离比赛中，穿着前拉链比赛服时，在跑步最后200米，前拉链未拉上 （15）使用让运动员注意力不能专注于赛事环境的装置	非故意或可纠正	警告，纠正	直接执行	（1）不按规定游泳路线绕浮漂 （2）不按技术会说明的方式，穿越隔离墩、公路中央隔离线等 （3）游泳赛段中拉、扯、抓、拽、踢、蹬等 （4）自行车和跑步赛段（尤其在弯道处）阻挡、推搡其他运动员 （5）将在饮水站使用过的水瓶丢弃在其他运动员前方或脚下 （6）运动员参加颁奖仪式可穿着长袖长裤（领奖服）
		故意或无法纠正	取消比赛资格	报告	

续表

序号	犯规行为	犯规性质 / 组别[注1]	处罚方法	执行方式[注2]	犯规行为说明或举例（包括但不仅限于以下示例）
6	（1）接受除技术官员、竞赛管理人员或其他运动员以外的协助 （2）试图利用车辆或物体等外部力量的不公平方式获利（尾随除外） （3）出于安全原因离开比赛路线，但未原路返回	可纠正	警告，纠正	直接执行	（1）在非饮水站区域接水 （2）接受非组委会竞赛人员（裁判、志愿者）递水，如：教练员等随队官员 （3）在非备用车轮站区域接受和更换车轮
		无法纠正或已获利	取消比赛资格	报告	
7	在指定地点（如饮水站或垃圾投放点）之外的比赛路线上随意丢弃垃圾和装备	可纠正	警告，纠正	直接执行	
		无法纠正	报告，时间处罚		
8	使用兴奋剂		根据 WADA 规则处罚	报告	
9	在颁奖仪式上进行隐性营销		没收比赛奖金	报告	
（二）技术会					
10	未参加技术会且未向技术代表请假	专业组	从本次比赛及其后 30 天内所有比赛出发和候补名单中除名。	报告	
11	迟到或未参加技术会但向技术代表请假	专业组	延迟出发，延迟时间将根据特定距离的时间处罚规定执行		
12	无论是否向技术代表请假，参加世界铁人三项 / 伤残人铁人三项系列赛和世界杯赛的运动员，如果在同一年内缺席技术会三次或以上	专业组	取消缺席后所有赛事的比赛资格	报告	
（三）出 发					
13	在出发信号发出前，抢跑（跳、游）或听到出发信号没有向前移动入水	非故意或非主动	时间处罚	报告	在出发浮台上，由于浮台倾斜造成运动员未站稳而跌入水中，视为“非故意或非主动”；反之运动员明显抢跳视为“故意”
		故意 / 或第二次	取消比赛资格	报告	

续表

序号	犯规行为	犯规性质 / 组别（注1）	处罚方法	执行方式（注2）	犯规行为说明或举例（包括但不仅限于以下示例）
14	选定出发位置后变更，或 占用两个或两个以上出发位置	非故意	警告，纠正	直接执行	裁判员警告后仍不纠正，视为“故意”
		故意	取消比赛资格	报告	
15	在运动员应出发时间前的任何组提前出发		取消比赛资格	报告	
（四）游 泳					
16	（1）不合规则的裸露与覆盖胳膊 （2）在要求使用防寒泳衣的比赛中，穿着未覆盖躯干的防寒泳衣 （3）从运动员集合开始，未佩戴官方提供的泳帽	可纠正	警告，纠正	直接执行	
		无法纠正	取消比赛资格	报告	
17	（1）接触并持续阻碍其他运动员的进程，没有主动移开 （2）从运动员入场到第一换项整个过程中，运动员佩戴可看到商标的第二顶泳帽		时间处罚	报告	
18	故意针对其他运动员阻碍其进程、获得不公平优势、有可能形成伤害		取消比赛资格，**停赛审查**（注3）	报告	
（五）转换区（伤残优秀组与优秀组处罚方式相同）					
19	（1）未将自行车停放在自己的空间内，或阻碍了其他运动员的跑进 （2）在转换区扰乱其他运动员的设备	业余组	警告，纠正	直接执行	
		专业组	时间处罚	报告	
20	当第一赛段的比赛时，转换区内头盔搭扣处于扣紧状态	业余组	技术官员解头盔搭扣	直接执行	
		专业组	技术官员解开头盔搭扣，时间处罚	报告	

续表

序号	犯规行为	犯规性质 / 组别（注1）	处罚方法	执行方式（注2）	犯规行为说明或举例（包括但不仅限于以下示例）
21	（1）上车线之前上车 （2）下车线之后下车	业余组	警告，纠正	直接执行	
		专业组	时间处罚	报告	
22	（1）将比赛装备放置或丢弃在非指定位置 （2）转换区内持车过程中头盔搭扣未扣或未扣紧 （3）在设置了存包系统的赛事中，没有将所有的比赛装备放进当地组委会提供的包里（骑行鞋可以始终置于自行车踏板上）	业余组	警告，纠正	直接执行	（1）游泳上水后将泳帽、泳镜等随手丢弃在通道上，丢给教练，进入转换区后扔到其他运动员的自行车上或车架位置上 （2）未将自行车放置在自己车架位置上 （3）将自行车水壶等丢弃在赛道上
		专业组	时间处罚	报告	
23	在转换区做标记		警告，纠正；否则移除标记且不通知运动员	直接执行	
（六）自行车					
24	熟悉自行车比赛路线或官方培训不戴头盔		取消相关活动资格	直接执行	
25	（1）不戴头盔 （2）使用不同于检录时的自行车或检录后改装自行车		取消比赛资格	直接执行	
				报告	
26	（1）头盔未扣紧或未扣 （2）摘掉头盔，即使运动员已经停下 （3）不使用自行车 （4）尾随不同圈的运动员 （5）自行车处罚时，运动员吃非自身或自行车携带的食物或 / 和水，或对自行车设备做调整或保养自行车		警告，纠正	直接执行	
			否则取消比赛资格	报告	
27	（1）在短距离和标准不允许尾随的比赛中尾随 （2）在短距离和标准距离比赛中被超越运动员在从尾随区退出之前再次超越了前一个运动员 （3）在短距离和标准距离比赛中，被超越的运动员在20秒之内没有通过持续减速方式退出超越运动员的尾随区		报告，第一次：尾随时间处罚；第二次：取消比赛资格		

续表

<table>
<tr><th>序号</th><th>犯规行为</th><th>犯规性质／组别（注1）</th><th>处罚方法</th><th>执行方式（注2）</th><th>犯规行为说明或举例（包括但不仅限于以下示例）</th></tr>
<tr><td rowspan="5">27</td><td colspan="2">（1）在中、长距离不允许尾随的比赛中尾随
（2）在中距离和长距离比赛中被超越运动员在从尾随区退出之前再次超越了前一个运动员
（3）在中距离和长距离比赛中，被超越的运动员在25秒之内没有通过持续减速方式退出超越运动员的尾随区</td><td colspan="3">报告，第一次和第二次：尾随时间处罚；第三次：取消比赛资格</td></tr>
<tr><td colspan="2">在允许尾随的比赛中尾随异性运动员</td><td colspan="3">第一次：口头警告，纠正；第二次：报告，取消比赛资格</td></tr>
<tr><td colspan="2">尾随机动车或摩托车</td><td colspan="3">警告，纠正；无法纠正：尾随时间处罚</td></tr>
<tr><td colspan="2">在不允许尾随的比赛中阻挡</td><td colspan="3">报告，时间处罚；无法纠正：取消比赛资格</td></tr>
<tr><td colspan="2">在自行车处罚区期间运动员去卫生间</td><td colspan="3">暂停处罚</td></tr>
<tr><td colspan="6">（七）跑 步</td></tr>
<tr><td>28</td><td colspan="2">跑步赛段爬行或
在终点冲刺通道由非参赛人员陪跑</td><td>取消比赛资格</td><td>报告</td><td></td></tr>
<tr><td>29</td><td colspan="2">跑步赛段戴头盔</td><td colspan="3">警告，纠正；否则：报告，取消比赛资格</td></tr>
<tr><td>30</td><td colspan="2">在弯道处借助杆、树等固定物体转弯</td><td>时间处罚</td><td>报告</td><td>在跑步折返点处拉、拽、推硬质栅栏或其他器材设施以借力转弯</td></tr>
<tr><td rowspan="2">31</td><td rowspan="2">（1）专业组：被套圈后领跑或跟随；尾随（跟跑）被套圈运动员；与领先一圈或一圈以上的运动员一起跑步和／或同跑步节奏
（2）消极比赛等影响比赛形象的行为
（3）在赛道或赛道边上由非参赛运动员、队友、领队或其他人员伴跑</td><td>非主动或不明显</td><td>警告，纠正</td><td>直接执行</td><td rowspan="2">裁判员口头警告后仍不纠正，视为“明显或第二次”</td></tr>
<tr><td>明显或第二次</td><td>取消比赛资格</td><td>报告</td></tr>
<tr><td colspan="6">（八）接力比赛</td></tr>
<tr><td>32</td><td colspan="2">接力赛未在接力区完成接力</td><td>时间处罚</td><td>报告</td><td>相关的两名运动员回到“接力区”，重新进行接力，应视为在接力区内完成接力</td></tr>
<tr><td>33</td><td>接力赛未完成接力或故意在接力区外完成接力</td><td></td><td>取消比赛资格</td><td></td><td></td></tr>
</table>

注 1：上表中专业组包括优秀组、U23 组、青年组和少年组。

注 2：犯规性质和组别中未标注专业组和业余组的，则专业组和业余组全部适用。

注 3：执行方式：（1）"直接执行"：当执裁判员直接执行；（2）"报告"：当执裁判员报告裁判长，由裁判长决定如何执行。

注 4：报告中国铁人三项运动协会，视情节决定是否给予停赛处罚；根据情节轻重和后果严重程度，停赛期可从 1 年至 4 年不等，后果特别严重、影响特别恶劣的犯规行为，可给予终身禁赛。

注 5：（1）尾随时间处罚（自行车）：中、长距离比赛 5 分钟；标准距离比赛 2 分钟；短距离比赛 1 分钟。（2）时间处罚（其他犯规行为）：长距离比赛 1 分钟；中距离比赛 30 秒；标准距离比赛 15 秒；短距离比赛 10 秒。

四、竞赛规则部分条款释义

（一）赛前技术会（本条适用于专业组）

1. 被列入候补名单的运动员也需参加技术会，否则将失去候补资格。

2. 运动员未在技术会开始之前在签到表上签字，视为未参加技术会。

3. 向技术代表请假的方式：

（1）技术会开始前 1 小时之前给技术代表发电子邮件。

（2）技术会结束后 5 分钟内给技术代表打电话或当面说明。

（二）出发的定义

运动员的脚通过出发线垂直面视为出发。

（三）自行车套圈规则（本条适用于专业组）

根据竞赛规则，优秀组、U23、青年组和少年组运动员在自行车赛段被套圈，将被取消比赛资格。

如竞赛规程或赛前技术会说明实行特别的竞赛规则，则在自行车赛段被套圈的运动员可继续比赛，但不得尾随或阻挡其他正常比赛的运动员，不得影响其他运动员的比赛，具体方式由技术代表决定并在赛前技术会上说明。

（四）跑步尾随犯规（本条适用于专业组不对等条件下的运动员之间：如被套圈）

1. 处于跟跑位置的运动员，有义务避免跟跑犯规行为的发生。

2. 跑步尾随区定义如下：以运动员躯干最前沿为宽边中点的宽 2 米、长 5 米的长方形区域。

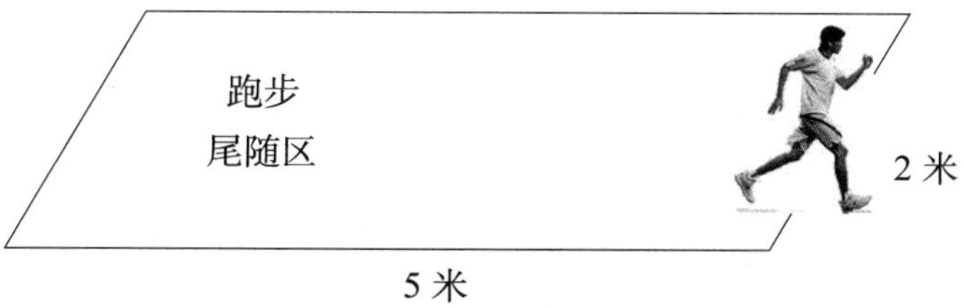

3. 领跑与跟跑的定义：

（1）本人处于其他运动员的跑步尾随区，视为跟跑；

（2）其他运动员处于本人的跑步尾随区，视为领跑；运动员被动地被其他运动员跟跑，不视为领跑犯规。

（3）本人虽位于其他运动员尾随区之外，但有明显、持续地尾随、跟跑行为，视为跟跑。

（4）虽然其他运动员位于本人尾随区之外，但本人有明显、持续的领骑、领跑行为，视为领跑。

（5）运动员在 15 秒内超越其他运动员或被其他运动员超越，不视为领跑或跟跑。

五、附 则

1. 运动员犯规行为包括并不仅限于此细则所列项目，如裁判员认为运动员实施了非公平获利或危险的行为，即使运动员的行为不在此细则所列举项目之内，裁判员也可以给予处罚。

2. 本细则自 2018 年 1 月 1 日起开始执行。

3. 本细则解释权归中国铁人三项运动协会。